NEW X MEN

XAVIER INSTITUTE FOR HIGHER LEARNING

MUTATIS MUTANDIS

ACADEMY X

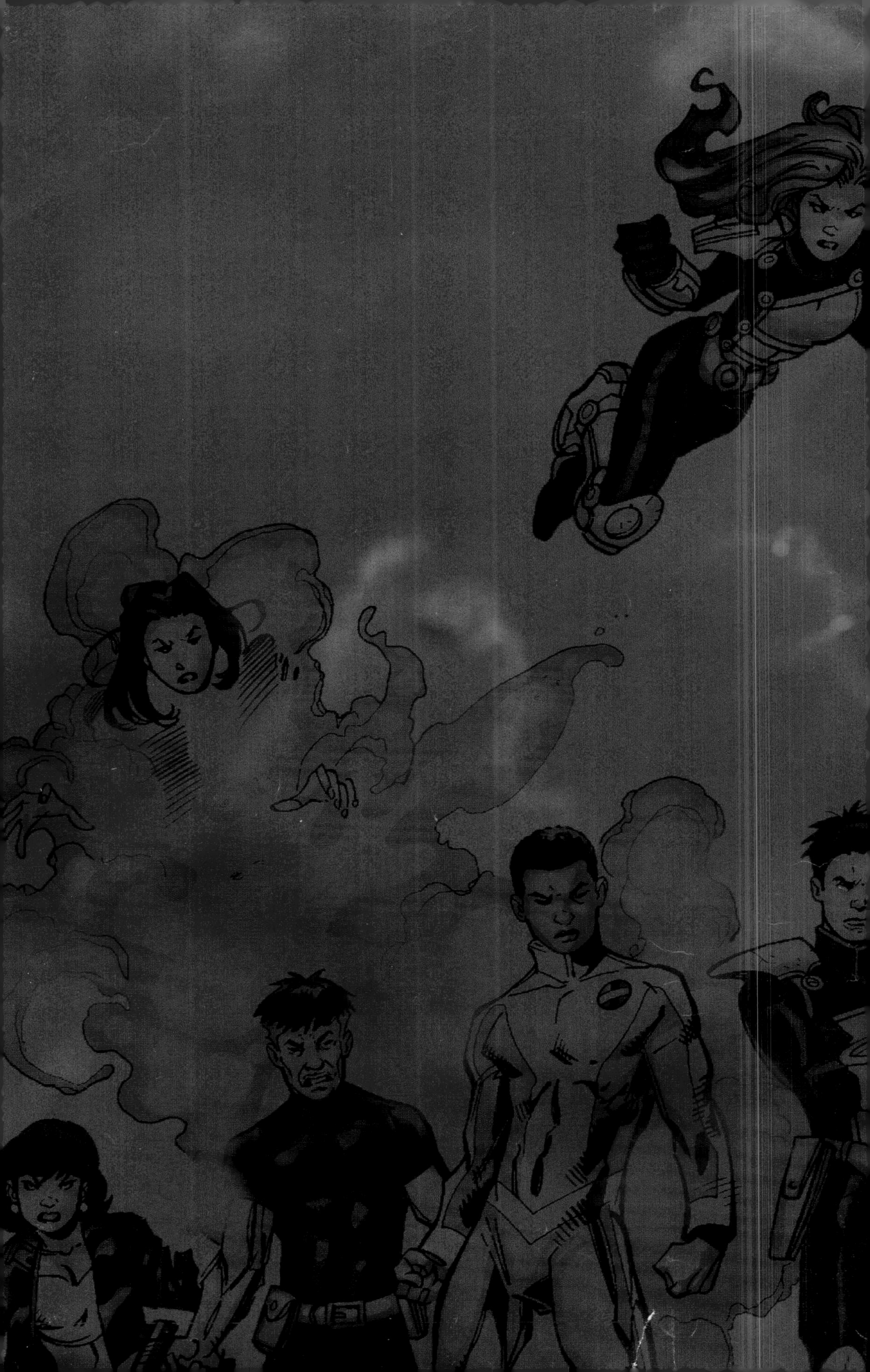

HOUSE OF M

NEW X-MEN ACADEMY X

Writers: NUNZIO DEFILIPPIS & CHRISTINA WEIR
Pencils: AARON LOPRESTI
Inks: BRAD VANCATA
Colors: PETE PANTAZIS & TOM CHU
Letters: DAVE SHARPE
Assistant Editor: SEAN RYAN
Associate Editor: NICK LOWE
Editor: MIKE MARTS

SECRETS OF THE HOUSE OF M PART TWO

Writer: MIKE RAICHT
Inspiration: BRIAN MICHAEL BENDIS
Cover Artist: ESAD RIBIC
Select Coloring: CHRIS SOTOMAYOR
Special thanks to JEFF CHRISTIANSEN, STUART VANDAL, MICHAEL HOSKIN, SEAN MCQUAID, CORY SEDLMEIER, POND SCUM & MELISSA MARVELLI

Collection Editor: JENNIFER GRÜNWALD
Assistant Editor: MICHAEL SHORT
Senior Editor, Special Projects: JEFF YOUNGQUIST
Director of Sales: DAVID GABRIEL
Production: LORETTA KROL
Book Designer: MEGHAN KERNS
Creative Director: TOM MARVELLI

Editor in Chief: JOE QUESADA
Publisher: DAN BUCKLEY

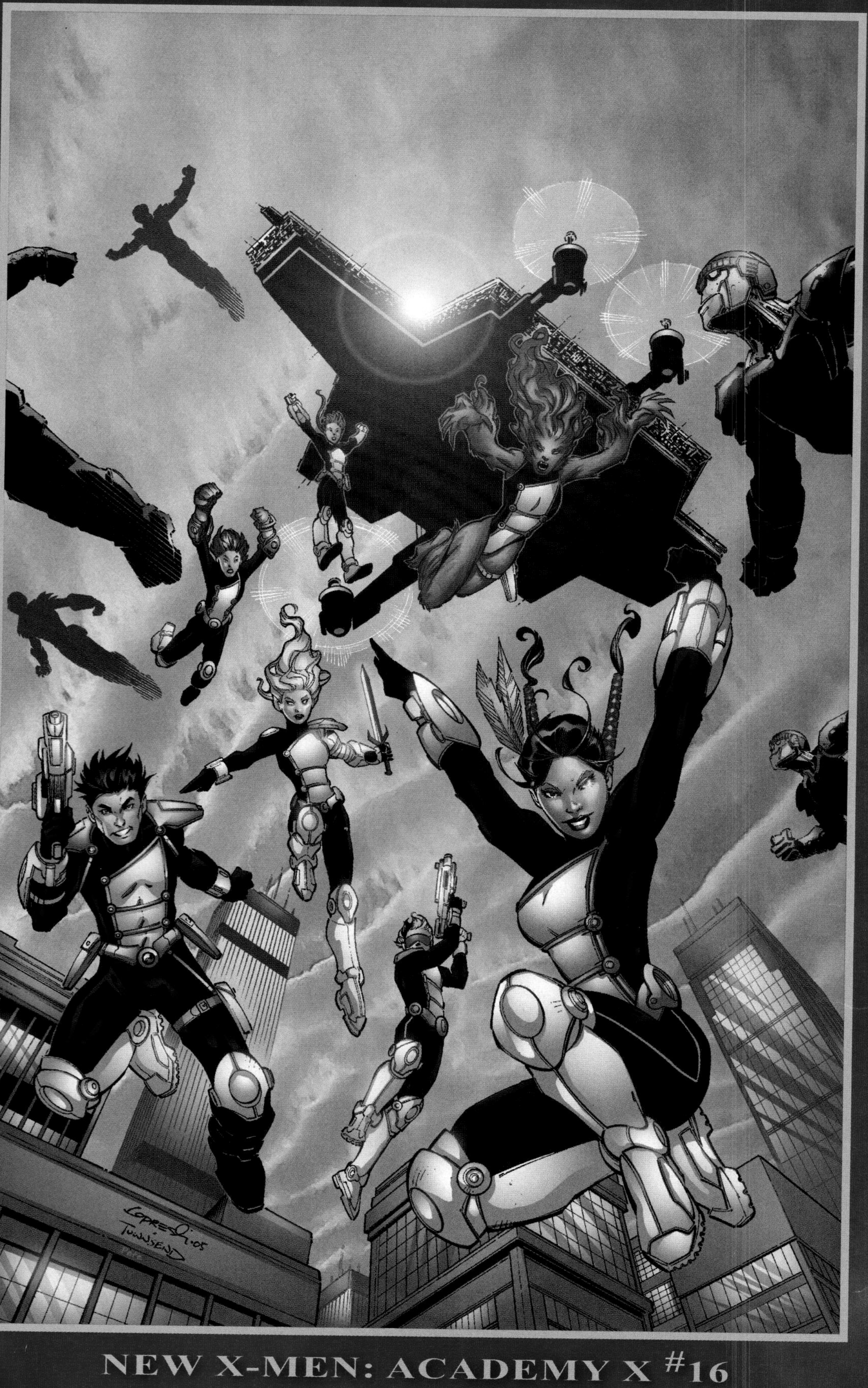

NEW X-MEN: ACADEMY X #16

THE WORLD WE KNEW...

Born with genetic mutations that give them abilities beyond those of normal humans, mutants are the next stage in evolution. As such, they were feared and hated. But a group of mutants known as the X-MEN fought for the safety of mutants and peaceful co-existence between mutant and humankind. Their headquarters also served as a school for the next generation of mutants. These students trained in squads, and two squads, the NEW MUTANTS and the HELLIONS, frequently clashed in training exercises and personal matters. And then the world burned white...

HOUSE OF M

NEW X-MEN

ACADEMY X

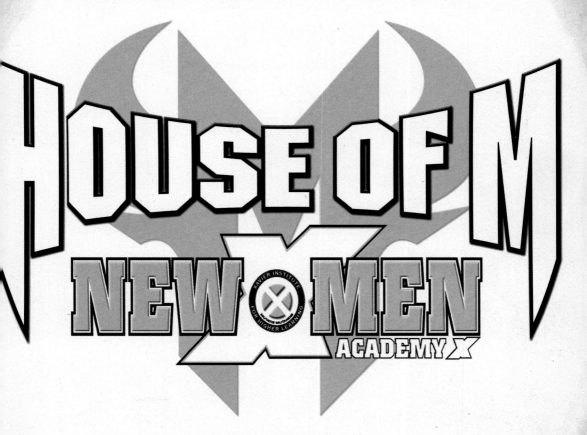

THE WORLD WE NOW LIVE IN...

The world has been remade. In the new world, ERIK MAGNUS, the man known as MAGNETO, won his war in defense of mutant-kind. He has made a better life for all mutants, or Homo Superior, and the world is under his control. Homo Superior live ideal lives and outnumber their genetic predecessors, Homo Sapiens. The remaining Homo Sapiens must live in a world now dominated by mutants.
Welcome to the HOUSE OF M.

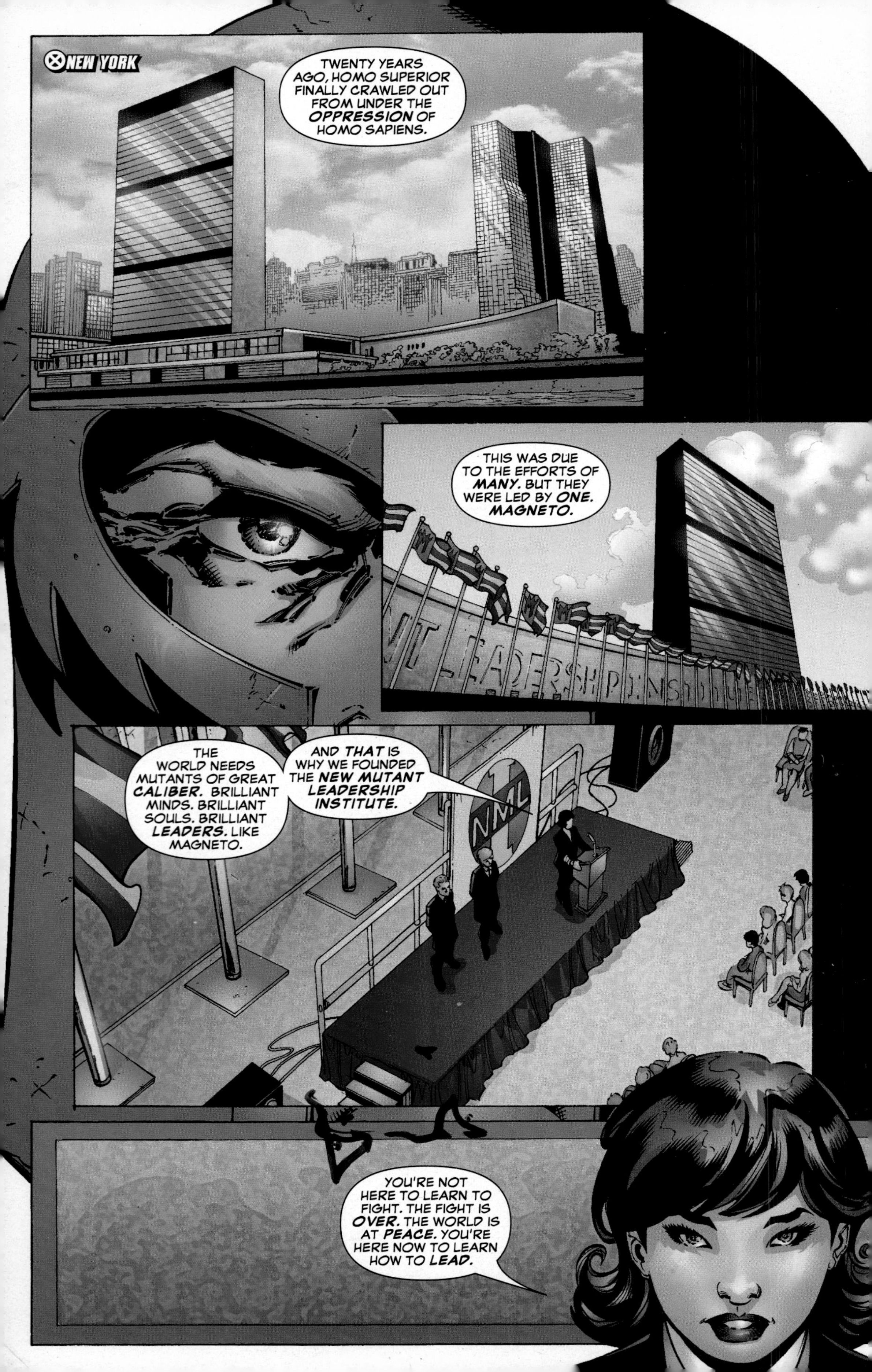
NEW YORK
TWENTY YEARS AGO, HOMO SUPERIOR FINALLY CRAWLED OUT FROM UNDER THE OPPRESSION OF HOMO SAPIENS.
THIS WAS DUE TO THE EFFORTS OF MANY. BUT THEY WERE LED BY ONE. MAGNETO.
THE WORLD NEEDS MUTANTS OF GREAT CALIBER. BRILLIANT MINDS. BRILLIANT SOULS. BRILLIANT LEADERS. LIKE MAGNETO.
AND THAT IS WHY WE FOUNDED THE NEW MUTANT LEADERSHIP INSTITUTE.
NML
YOU'RE NOT HERE TO LEARN TO FIGHT. THE FIGHT IS OVER. THE WORLD IS AT PEACE. YOU'RE HERE NOW TO LEARN HOW TO LEAD.

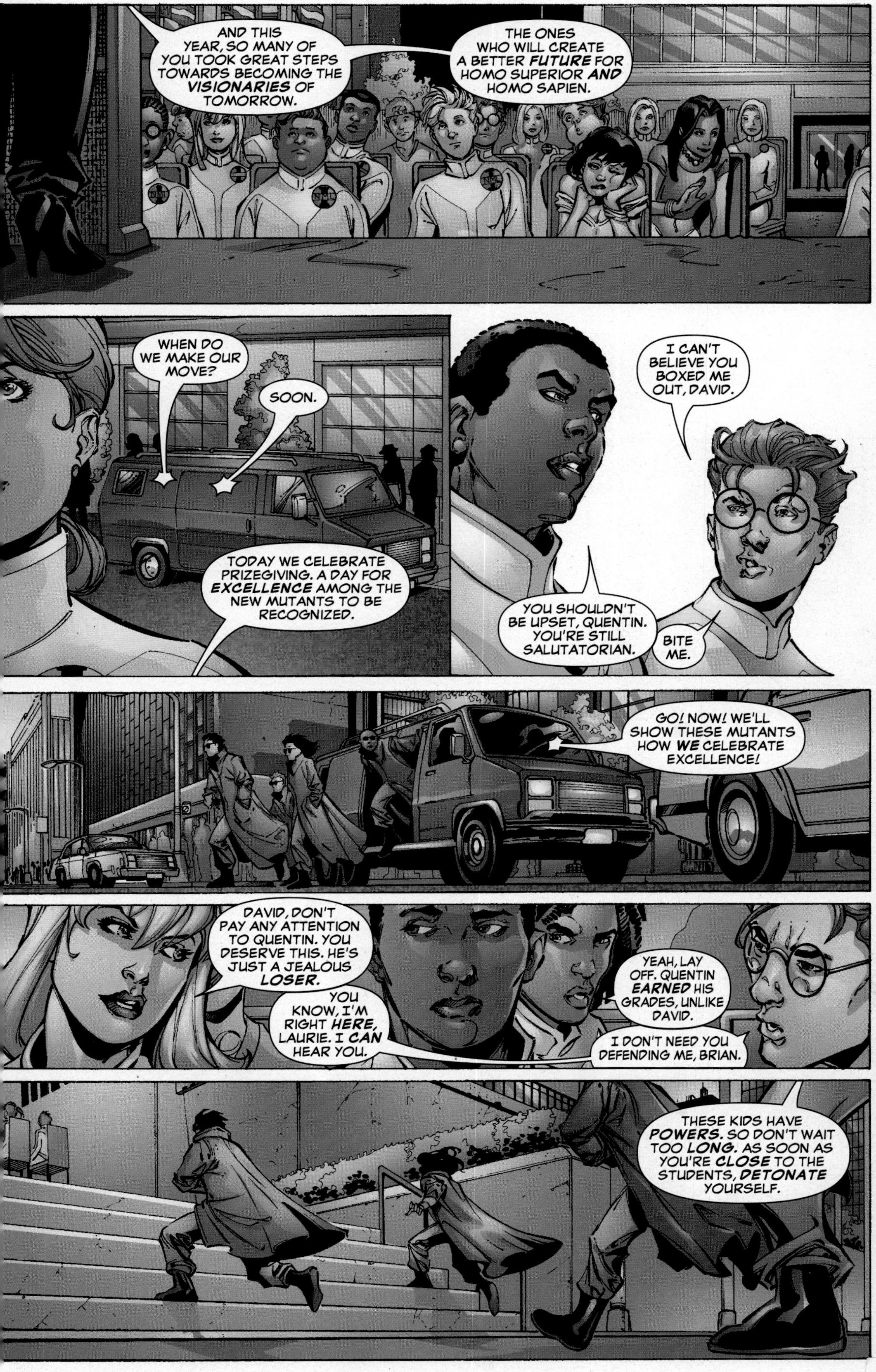
AND THIS YEAR, SO MANY OF YOU TOOK GREAT STEPS TOWARDS BECOMING THE VISIONARIES OF TOMORROW.
THE ONES WHO WILL CREATE A BETTER FUTURE FOR HOMO SUPERIOR AND HOMO SAPIEN.
WHEN DO WE MAKE OUR MOVE?
SOON.
TODAY WE CELEBRATE PRIZEGIVING. A DAY FOR EXCELLENCE AMONG THE NEW MUTANTS TO BE RECOGNIZED.
I CAN'T BELIEVE YOU BOXED ME OUT, DAVID.
YOU SHOULDN'T BE UPSET, QUENTIN. YOU'RE STILL SALUTATORIAN.
BITE ME.
GO! NOW! WE'LL SHOW THESE MUTANTS HOW WE CELEBRATE EXCELLENCE!
DAVID, DON'T PAY ANY ATTENTION TO QUENTIN. YOU DESERVE THIS. HE'S JUST A JEALOUS LOSER.
YOU KNOW, I'M RIGHT HERE, LAURIE. I CAN HEAR YOU.
YEAH, LAY OFF. QUENTIN EARNED HIS GRADES, UNLIKE DAVID.
I DON'T NEED YOU DEFENDING ME, BRIAN.
THESE KIDS HAVE POWERS. SO DON'T WAIT TOO LONG. AS SOON AS YOU'RE CLOSE TO THE STUDENTS, DETONATE YOURSELF.

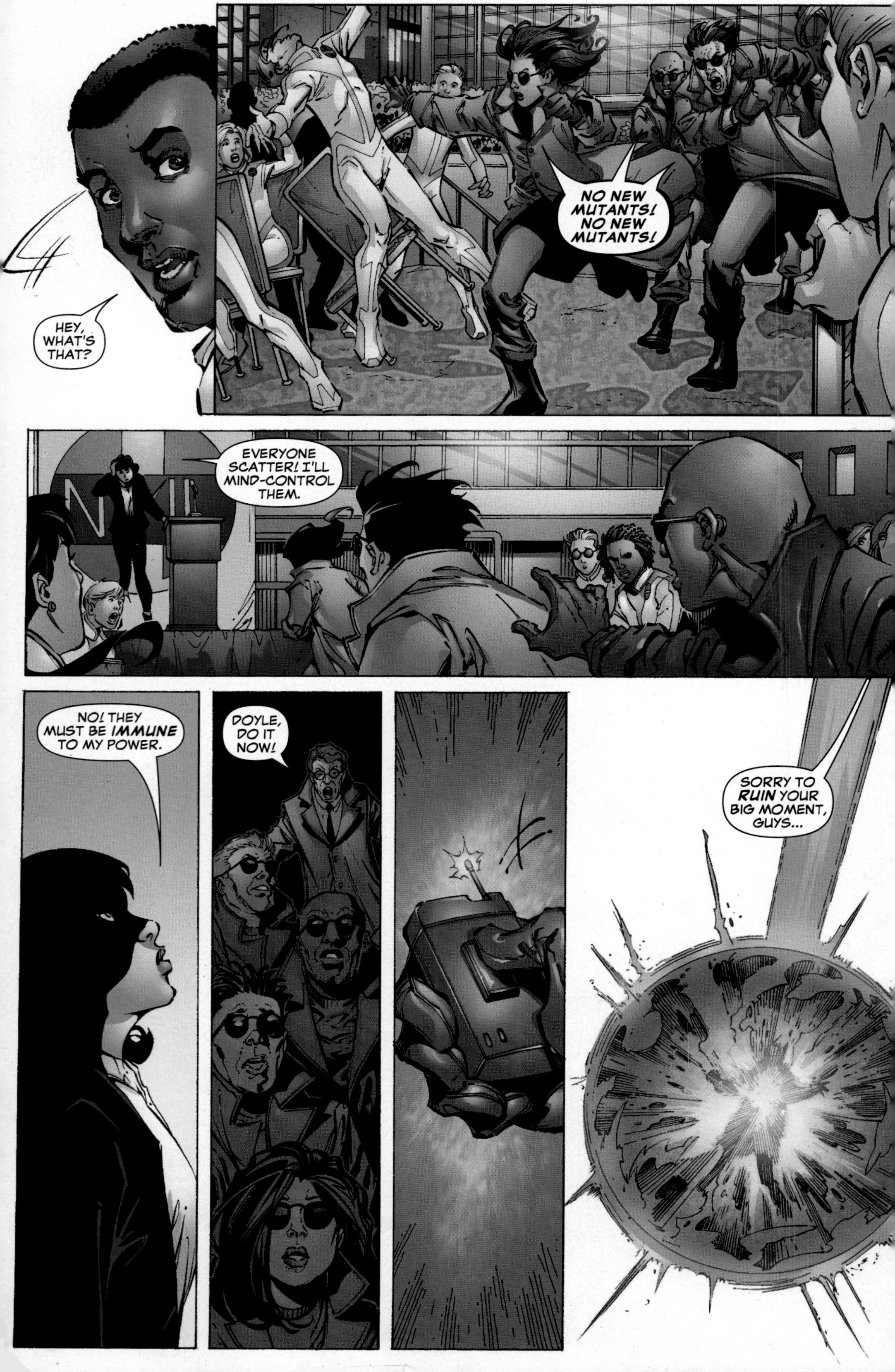
HEY, WHAT'S THAT?
NO NEW MUTANTS! NO NEW MUTANTS!
EVERYONE SCATTER! I'LL MIND-CONTROL THEM.
NO! THEY MUST BE IMMUNE TO MY POWER.
DOYLE, DO IT NOW!
SORRY TO RUIN YOUR BIG MOMENT, GUYS...

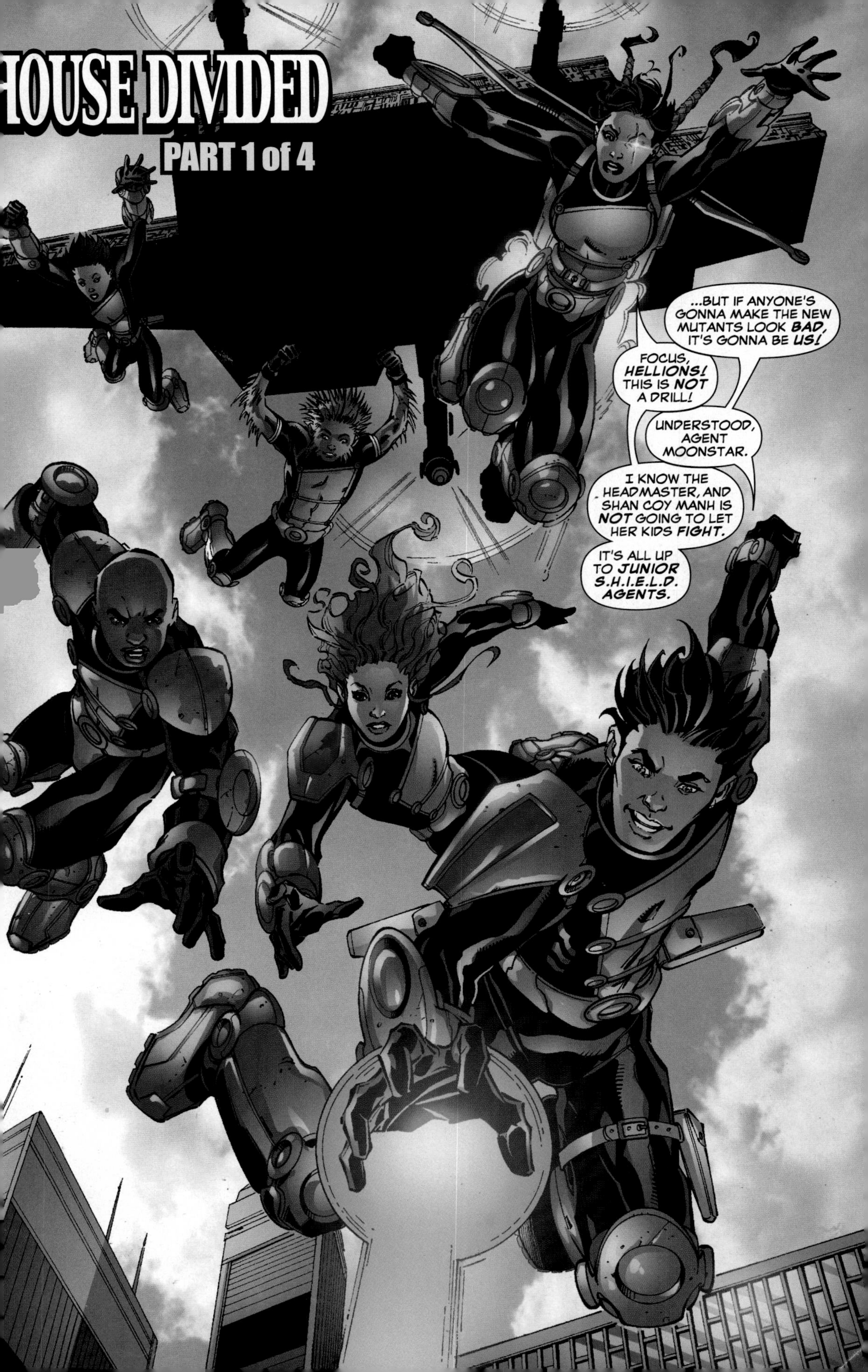
HOUSE DIVIDED
PART 1 of 4
...BUT IF ANYONE'S GONNA MAKE THE NEW MUTANTS LOOK BAD, IT'S GONNA BE US!
FOCUS, HELLIONS! THIS IS NOT A DRILL!
UNDERSTOOD, AGENT MOONSTAR.
I KNOW THE HEADMASTER, AND SHAN COY MANH IS NOT GOING TO LET HER KIDS FIGHT.
IT'S ALL UP TO JUNIOR S.H.I.E.L.D. AGENTS.

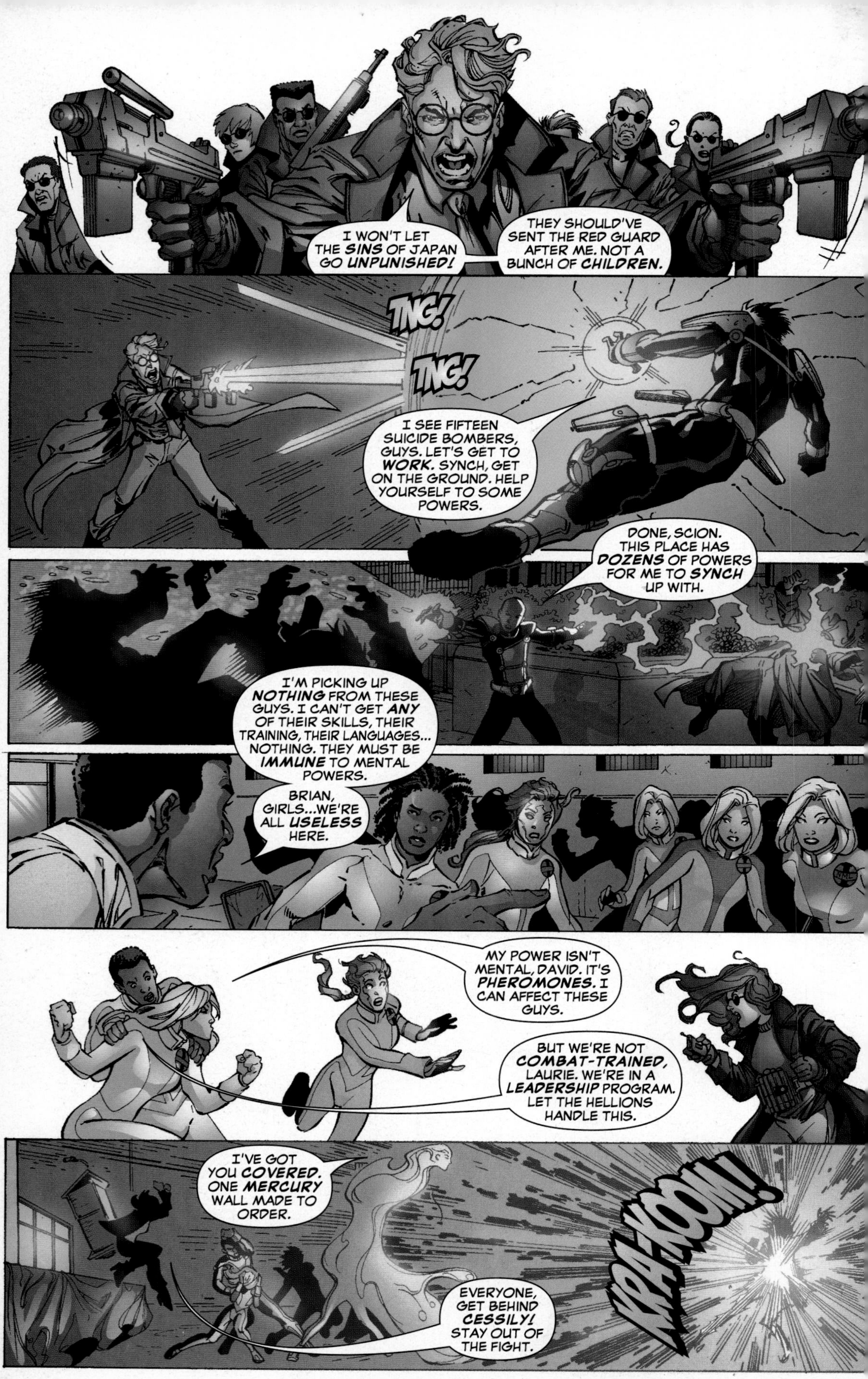
I WON'T LET THE SINS OF JAPAN GO UNPUNISHED!
THEY SHOULD'VE SENT THE RED GUARD AFTER ME. NOT A BUNCH OF CHILDREN.
TNG!
TNG!
I SEE FIFTEEN SUICIDE BOMBERS, GUYS. LET'S GET TO WORK. SYNCH, GET ON THE GROUND. HELP YOURSELF TO SOME POWERS.
DONE, SCION. THIS PLACE HAS DOZENS OF POWERS FOR ME TO SYNCH UP WITH.
I'M PICKING UP NOTHING FROM THESE GUYS. I CAN'T GET ANY OF THEIR SKILLS, THEIR TRAINING, THEIR LANGUAGES... NOTHING. THEY MUST BE IMMUNE TO MENTAL POWERS.
BRIAN, GIRLS...WE'RE ALL USELESS HERE.
MY POWER ISN'T MENTAL, DAVID. IT'S PHEROMONES. I CAN AFFECT THESE GUYS.
BUT WE'RE NOT COMBAT-TRAINED, LAURIE. WE'RE IN A LEADERSHIP PROGRAM. LET THE HELLIONS HANDLE THIS.
I'VE GOT YOU COVERED. ONE MERCURY WALL MADE TO ORDER.
KRA-KOOM!
EVERYONE, GET BEHIND CESSILY! STAY OUT OF THE FIGHT.

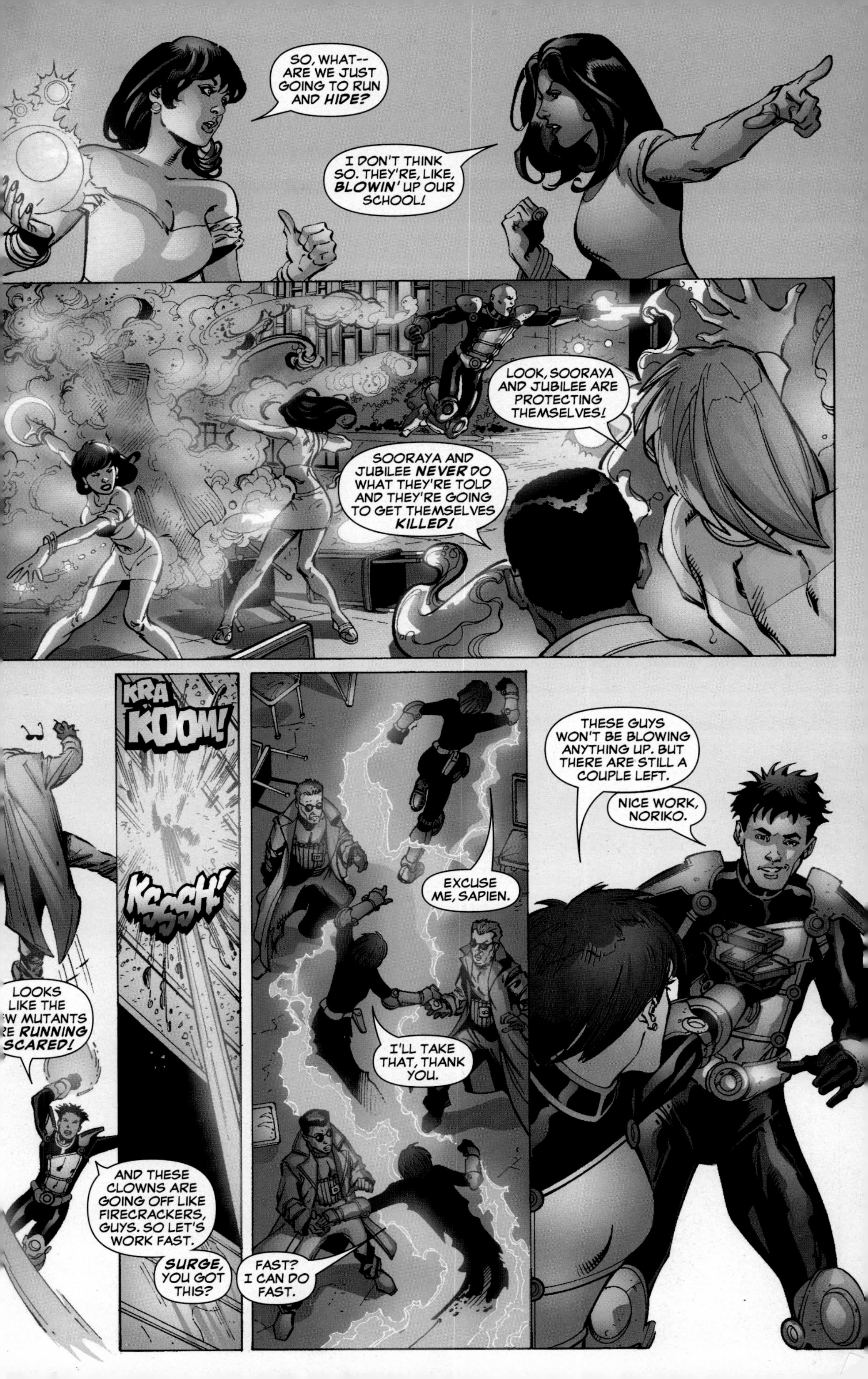
SO, WHAT-- ARE WE JUST GOING TO RUN AND HIDE?
I DON'T THINK SO. THEY'RE, LIKE, BLOWIN' UP OUR SCHOOL!
LOOK, SOORAYA AND JUBILEE ARE PROTECTING THEMSELVES!
SOORAYA AND JUBILEE NEVER DO WHAT THEY'RE TOLD AND THEY'RE GOING TO GET THEMSELVES KILLED!
LOOKS LIKE THE
EW MUTANTS
RE RUNNING SCARED!
AND THESE CLOWNS ARE GOING OFF LIKE FIRECRACKERS, GUYS. SO LET'S WORK FAST.
SURGE, YOU GOT THIS?
KRA KOOM!
KSSSH!
EXCUSE ME, SAPIEN.
I'LL TAKE THAT, THANK YOU.
FAST? I CAN DO FAST.
THESE GUYS WON'T BE BLOWING ANYTHING UP. BUT THERE ARE STILL A COUPLE LEFT.
NICE WORK, NORIKO.

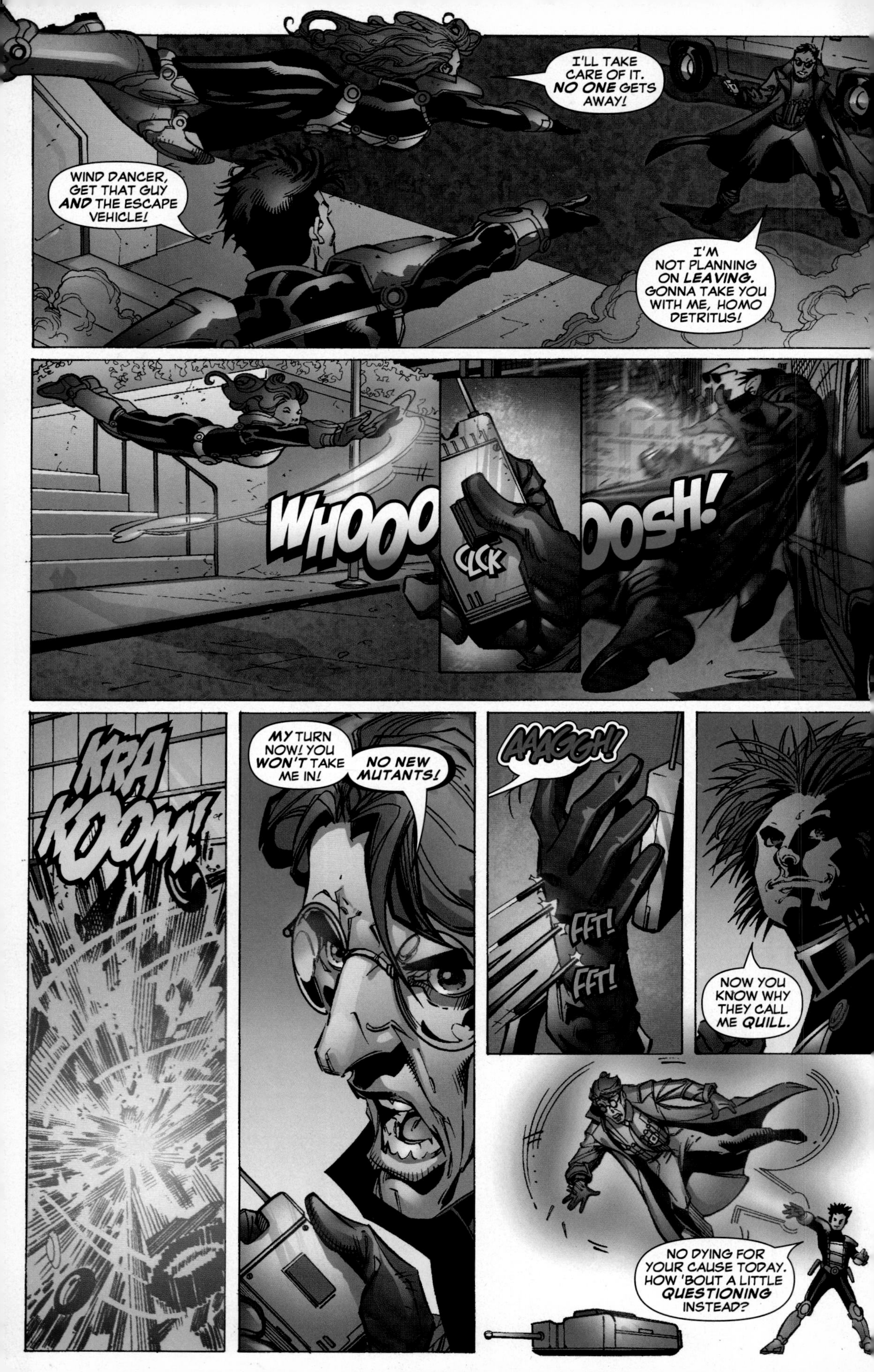
WIND DANCER, GET THAT GUY AND THE ESCAPE VEHICLE!
I'LL TAKE CARE OF IT. NO ONE GETS AWAY!
I'M NOT PLANNING ON LEAVING. GONNA TAKE YOU WITH ME, HOMO DETRITUS!
WHOOO
CLCK
OOSH!
KRA KOOM!
MY TURN NOW! YOU WON'T TAKE ME IN!
NO NEW MUTANTS!
AAAGGH!
FFT!
FFT!
NOW YOU KNOW WHY THEY CALL ME QUILL.
NO DYING FOR YOUR CAUSE TODAY. HOW 'BOUT A LITTLE QUESTIONING INSTEAD?

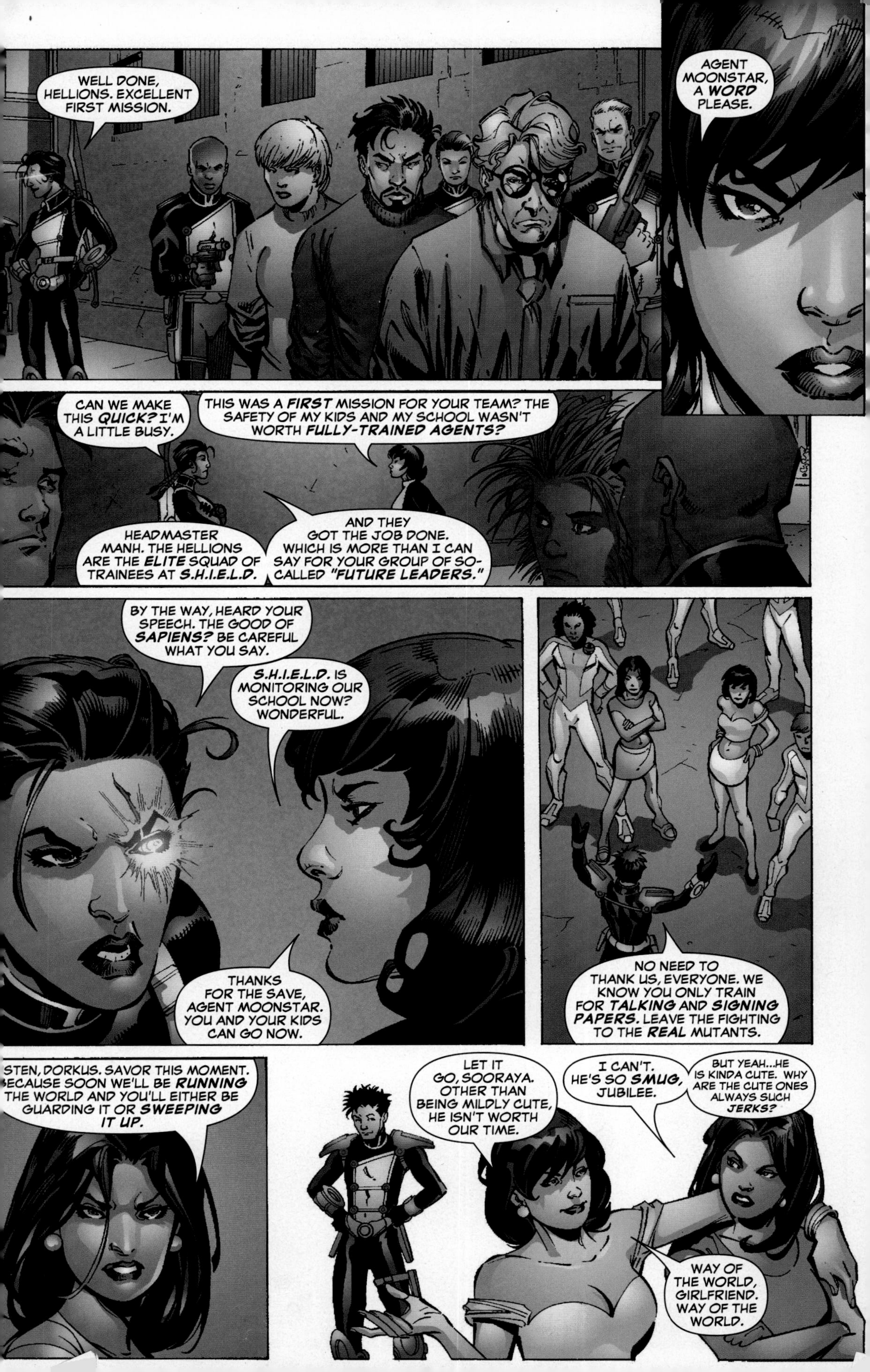
WELL DONE, HELLIONS. EXCELLENT FIRST MISSION.
AGENT MOONSTAR, A WORD PLEASE.
CAN WE MAKE THIS QUICK? I'M A LITTLE BUSY.
THIS WAS A FIRST MISSION FOR YOUR TEAM? THE SAFETY OF MY KIDS AND MY SCHOOL WASN'T WORTH FULLY-TRAINED AGENTS?
HEADMASTER MANH. THE HELLIONS ARE THE ELITE SQUAD OF TRAINEES AT S.H.I.E.L.D.
AND THEY GOT THE JOB DONE. WHICH IS MORE THAN I CAN SAY FOR YOUR GROUP OF SO-CALLED "FUTURE LEADERS."
BY THE WAY, HEARD YOUR SPEECH. THE GOOD OF SAPIENS? BE CAREFUL WHAT YOU SAY.
S.H.I.E.L.D. IS MONITORING OUR SCHOOL NOW? WONDERFUL.
THANKS FOR THE SAVE, AGENT MOONSTAR. YOU AND YOUR KIDS CAN GO NOW.
NO NEED TO THANK US, EVERYONE. WE KNOW YOU ONLY TRAIN FOR TALKING AND SIGNING PAPERS. LEAVE THE FIGHTING TO THE REAL MUTANTS.
STEN, DORKUS. SAVOR THIS MOMENT. BECAUSE SOON WE'LL BE RUNNING THE WORLD AND YOU'LL EITHER BE GUARDING IT OR SWEEPING IT UP.
LET IT GO, SOORAYA. OTHER THAN BEING MILDLY CUTE, HE ISN'T WORTH OUR TIME.
I CAN'T. HE'S SO SMUG, JUBILEE.
BUT YEAH...HE IS KINDA CUTE. WHY ARE THE CUTE ONES ALWAYS SUCH JERKS?
WAY OF THE WORLD, GIRLFRIEND. WAY OF THE WORLD.

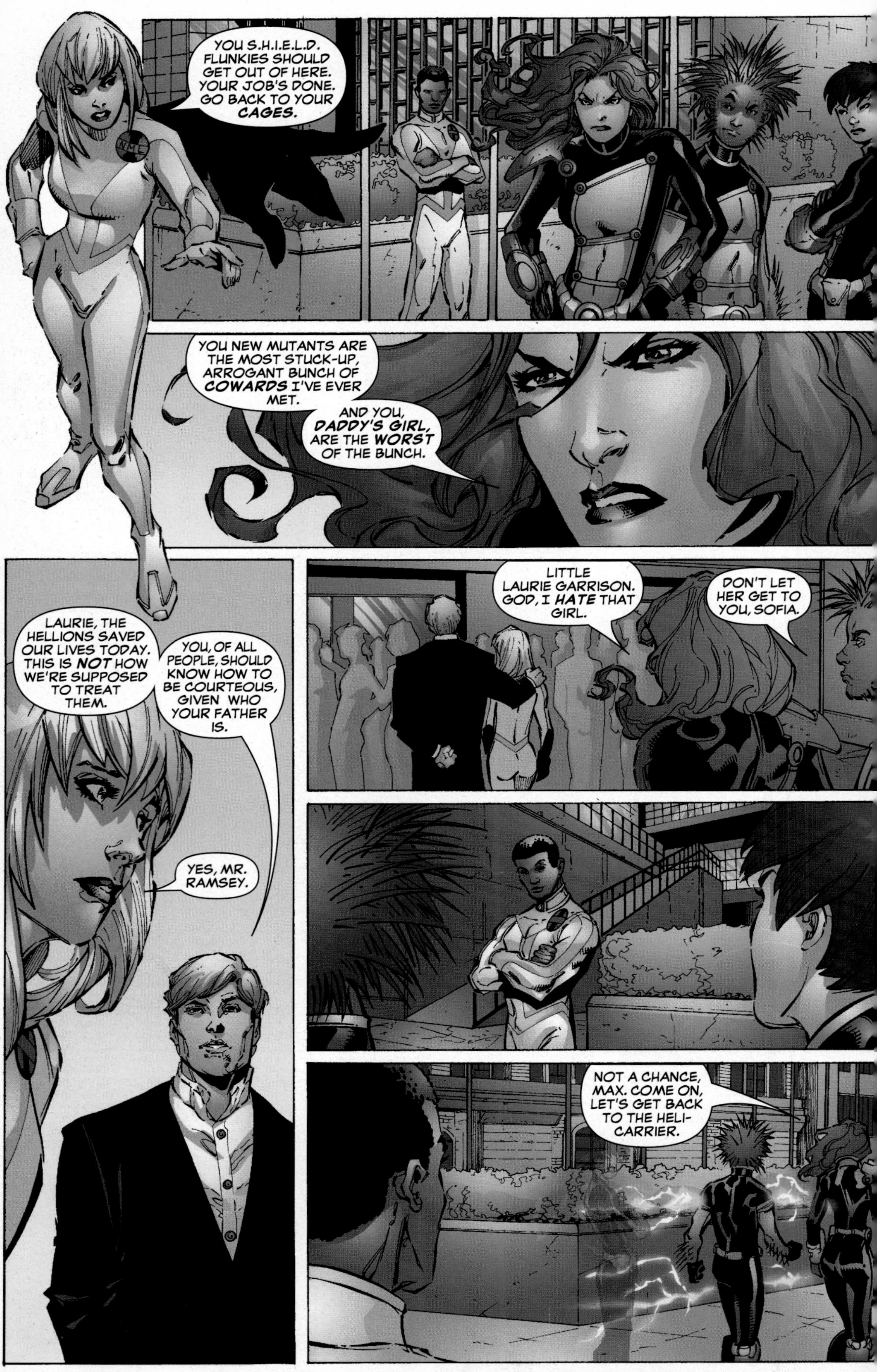

YOU S.H.I.E.L.D. FLUNKIES SHOULD GET OUT OF HERE. YOUR JOB'S DONE. GO BACK TO YOUR CAGES.
YOU NEW MUTANTS ARE THE MOST STUCK-UP, ARROGANT BUNCH OF COWARDS I'VE EVER MET.
AND YOU, DADDY'S GIRL, ARE THE WORST OF THE BUNCH.
LAURIE, THE HELLIONS SAVED OUR LIVES TODAY. THIS IS NOT HOW WE'RE SUPPOSED TO TREAT THEM.
YOU, OF ALL PEOPLE, SHOULD KNOW HOW TO BE COURTEOUS, GIVEN WHO YOUR FATHER IS.
YES, MR. RAMSEY.
LITTLE LAURIE GARRISON. GOD, I HATE THAT GIRL.
DON'T LET HER GET TO YOU, SOFIA.
NOT A CHANCE, MAX. COME ON, LET'S GET BACK TO THE HELI-CARRIER.

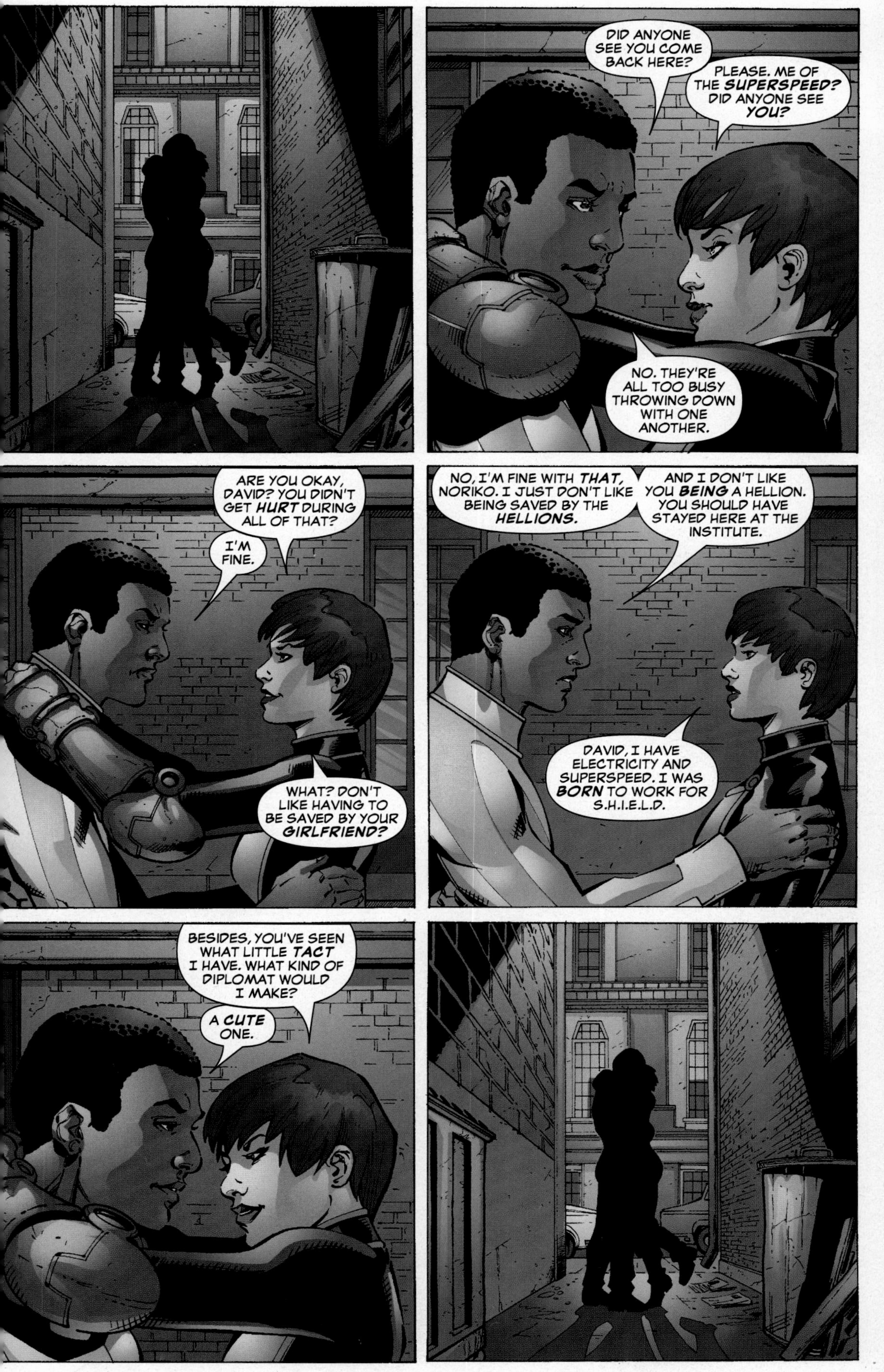
DID ANYONE SEE YOU COME BACK HERE?
PLEASE. ME OF THE SUPERSPEED? DID ANYONE SEE YOU?
NO. THEY'RE ALL TOO BUSY THROWING DOWN WITH ONE ANOTHER.
ARE YOU OKAY, DAVID? YOU DIDN'T GET HURT DURING ALL OF THAT?
I'M FINE.
WHAT? DON'T LIKE HAVING TO BE SAVED BY YOUR GIRLFRIEND?
NO, I'M FINE WITH THAT, NORIKO. I JUST DON'T LIKE BEING SAVED BY THE HELLIONS.
AND I DON'T LIKE YOU BEING A HELLION. YOU SHOULD HAVE STAYED HERE AT THE INSTITUTE.
DAVID, I HAVE ELECTRICITY AND SUPERSPEED. I WAS BORN TO WORK FOR S.H.I.E.L.D.
BESIDES, YOU'VE SEEN WHAT LITTLE TACT I HAVE. WHAT KIND OF DIPLOMAT WOULD I MAKE?
A CUTE ONE.

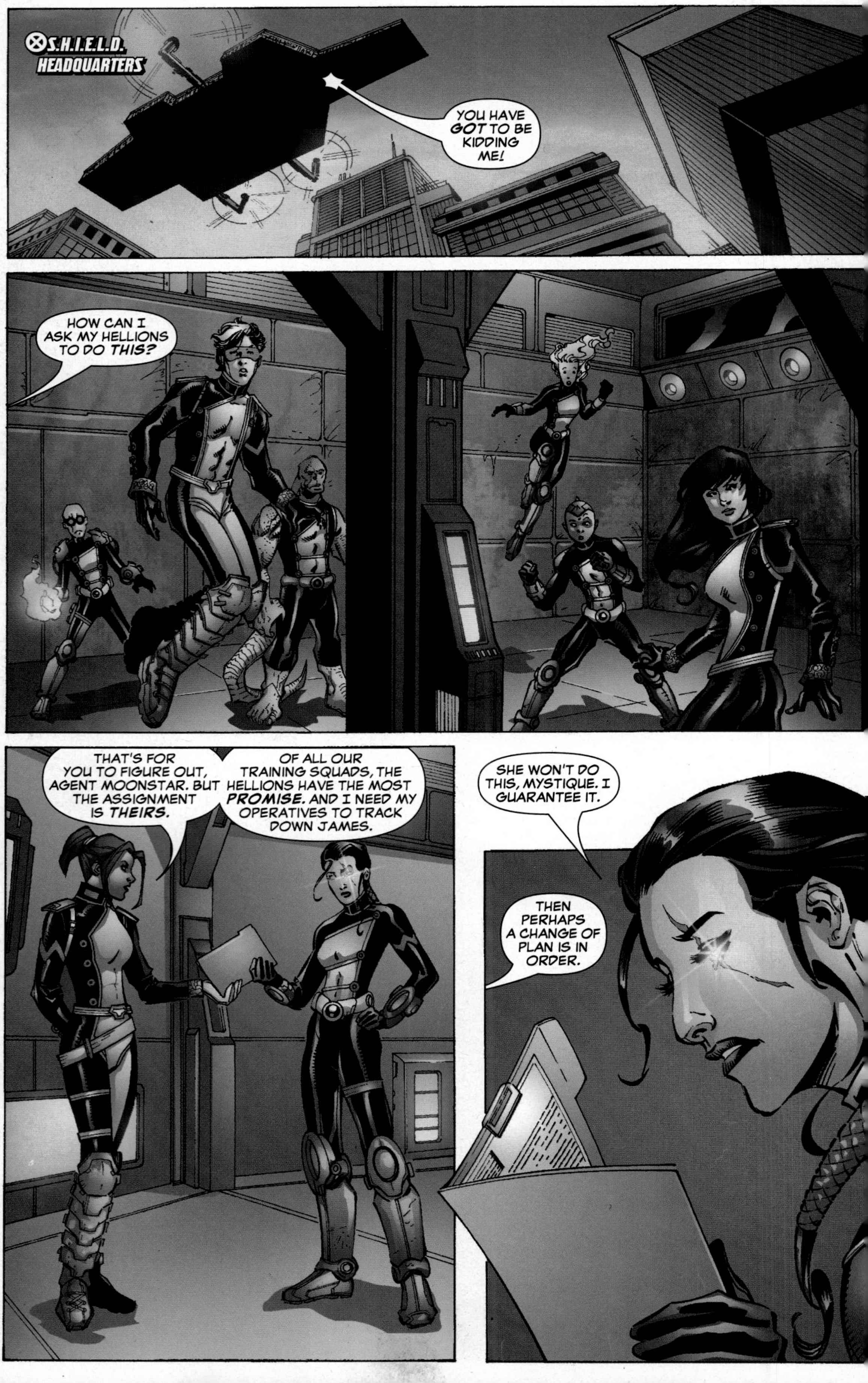
S.H.I.E.L.D. HEADQUARTERS
YOU HAVE GOT TO BE KIDDING ME!
HOW CAN I ASK MY HELLIONS TO DO THIS?
THAT'S FOR YOU TO FIGURE OUT, AGENT MOONSTAR. BUT THE ASSIGNMENT IS THEIRS.
OF ALL OUR TRAINING SQUADS, THE HELLIONS HAVE THE MOST PROMISE. AND I NEED MY OPERATIVES TO TRACK DOWN JAMES.
SHE WON'T DO THIS, MYSTIQUE. I GUARANTEE IT.
THEN PERHAPS A CHANGE OF PLAN IS IN ORDER.

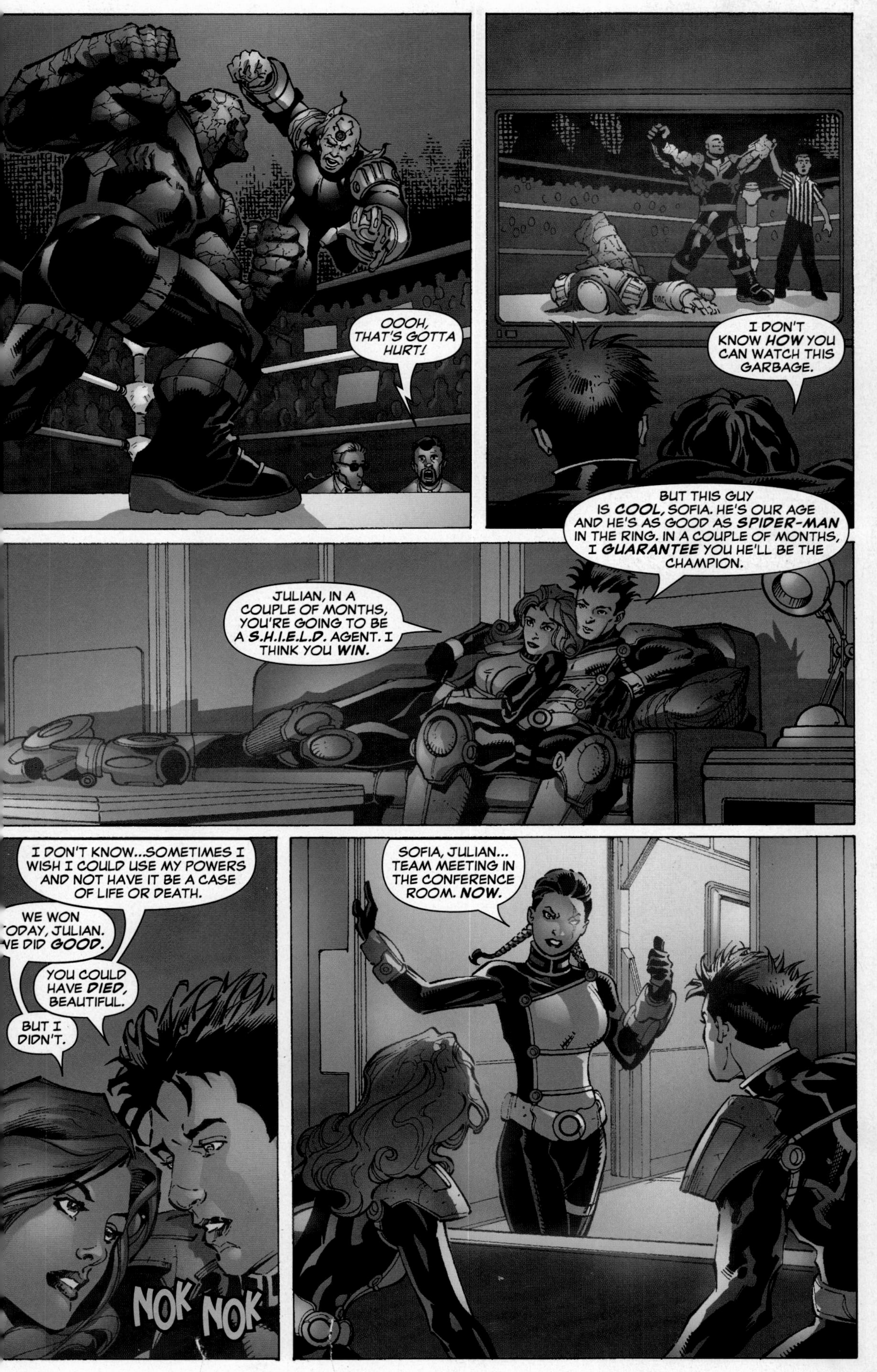
OOOH, THAT'S GOTTA HURT!
I DON'T KNOW HOW YOU CAN WATCH THIS GARBAGE.
BUT THIS GUY IS COOL, SOFIA. HE'S OUR AGE AND HE'S AS GOOD AS SPIDER-MAN IN THE RING. IN A COUPLE OF MONTHS, I GUARANTEE YOU HE'LL BE THE CHAMPION.
JULIAN, IN A COUPLE OF MONTHS, YOU'RE GOING TO BE A S.H.I.E.L.D. AGENT. I THINK YOU WIN.
I DON'T KNOW...SOMETIMES I WISH I COULD USE MY POWERS AND NOT HAVE IT BE A CASE OF LIFE OR DEATH.
WE WON ODAY, JULIAN. VE DID GOOD.
YOU COULD HAVE DIED, BEAUTIFUL.
BUT I DIDN'T.
NOK NOK
SOFIA, JULIAN... TEAM MEETING IN THE CONFERENCE ROOM. NOW.

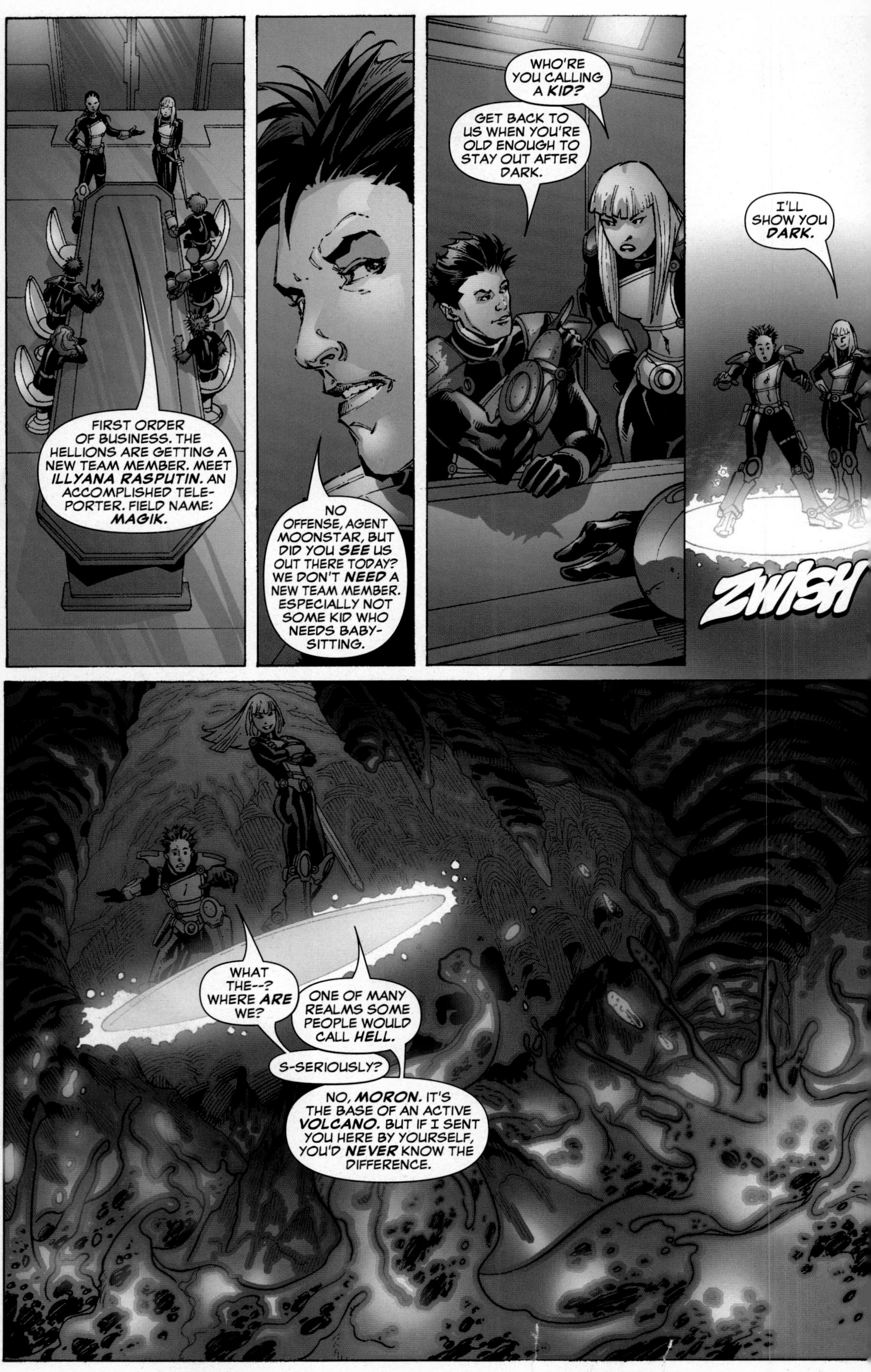
FIRST ORDER OF BUSINESS. THE HELLIONS ARE GETTING A NEW TEAM MEMBER. MEET ILLYANA RASPUTIN. AN ACCOMPLISHED TELE-PORTER. FIELD NAME: MAGIK.
NO OFFENSE, AGENT MOONSTAR, BUT DID YOU SEE US OUT THERE TODAY? WE DON'T NEED A NEW TEAM MEMBER. ESPECIALLY NOT SOME KID WHO NEEDS BABY-SITTING.
WHO'RE YOU CALLING A KID?
GET BACK TO US WHEN YOU'RE OLD ENOUGH TO STAY OUT AFTER DARK.
I'LL SHOW YOU DARK.
ZWISH
WHAT THE--? WHERE ARE WE?
ONE OF MANY REALMS SOME PEOPLE WOULD CALL HELL.
S-SERIOUSLY?
NO, MORON. IT'S THE BASE OF AN ACTIVE VOLCANO. BUT IF I SENT YOU HERE BY YOURSELF, YOU'D NEVER KNOW THE DIFFERENCE.

SATISFIED?

OKAY, GUYS. MAGIK'S IN.

EVERYONE SETTLE DOWN. MAGIK HAS BEEN ADDED TO THE SQUAD BECAUSE WE HAVE A NEW ASSIGNMENT AND SURGE WILL *NOT* BE JOINING YOU.

WHAT? WHY?

AS YOU KNOW, TODAY'S SUICIDE BOMBERS MADE REFERENCE TO JAPAN.

YEAH. WHAT WERE THEY TALKING ABOUT?

WE KNOW WHO SOME OF THE *KEY* MEMBERS ARE, BUT WE DON'T KNOW WHERE IN JAPAN THEY'RE LOCATED. IT WILL BE YOUR JOB TO *FIND* THEM AND SHUT THEM *DOWN*.

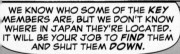

WE BELIEVE THEY'RE CONNECTED TO A HUMAN RESISTANCE GROUP OVER THERE. EMPEROR SUNFIRE IS *NOT* PLEASED WITH THE TROUBLE THEY ARE CAUSING HIM.

WAIT, I DON'T GET THIS! I *KNOW* EMPEROR SUNFIRE. AND I SPEAK JAPANESE. *I'M* THE ONE WHO *HAS* TO GO!

JUST TAKE A LOOK AT THE FOLDER, NORIKO.

THEIR LEADER IS SEIJI ASHIDA. YOUR *FATHER*.

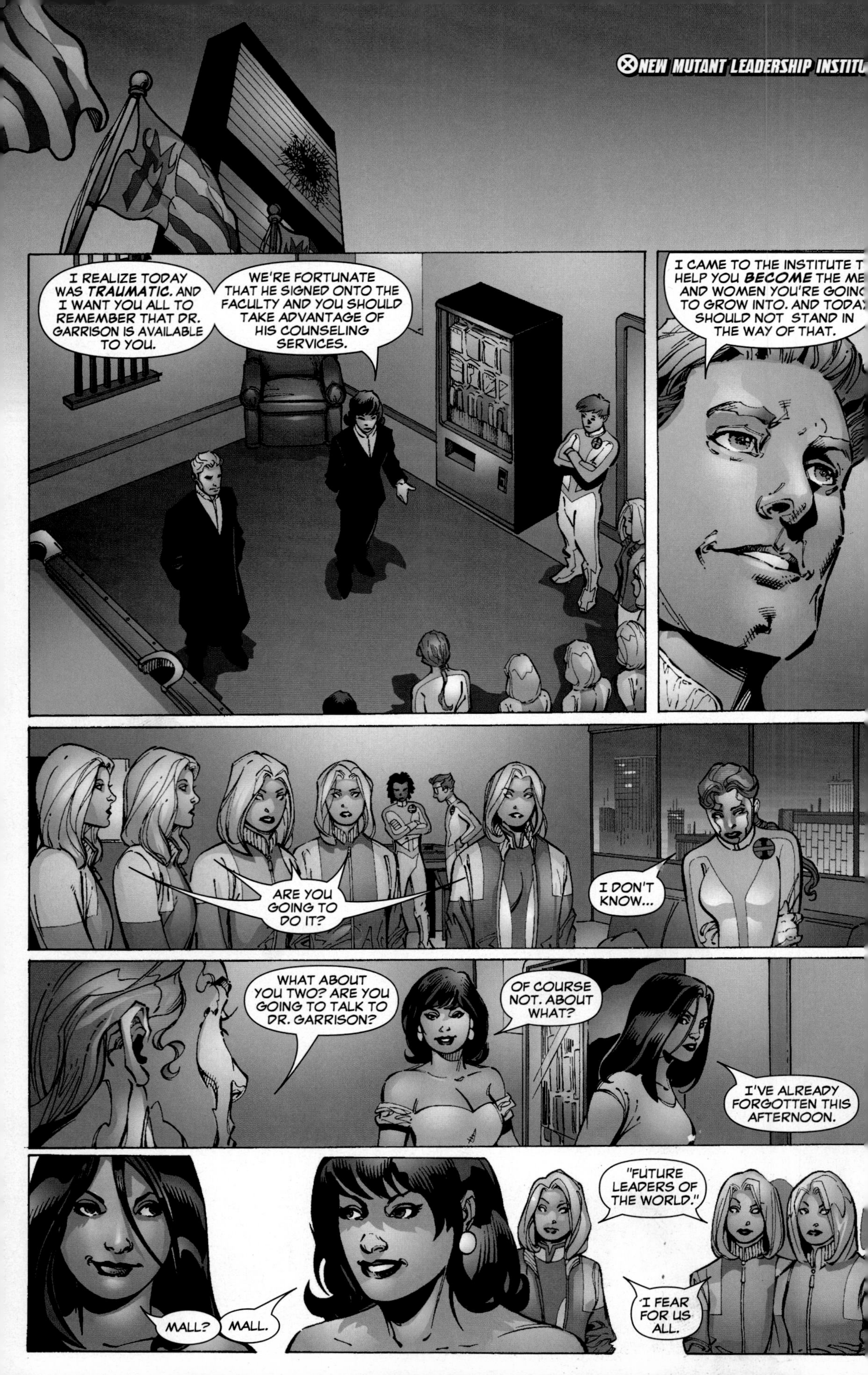
NEW MUTANT LEADERSHIP INSTITU
I REALIZE TODAY WAS TRAUMATIC. AND I WANT YOU ALL TO REMEMBER THAT DR. GARRISON IS AVAILABLE TO YOU.
WE'RE FORTUNATE THAT HE SIGNED ONTO THE FACULTY AND YOU SHOULD TAKE ADVANTAGE OF HIS COUNSELING SERVICES.
I CAME TO THE INSTITUTE T HELP YOU BECOME THE ME AND WOMEN YOU'RE GOIN TO GROW INTO. AND TODA SHOULD NOT STAND IN THE WAY OF THAT.
ARE YOU GOING TO DO IT?
I DON'T KNOW...
WHAT ABOUT YOU TWO? ARE YOU GOING TO TALK TO DR. GARRISON?
OF COURSE NOT. ABOUT WHAT?
I'VE ALREADY FORGOTTEN THIS AFTERNOON.
MALL?
MALL.
"FUTURE LEADERS OF THE WORLD."
"I FEAR FOR US ALL.

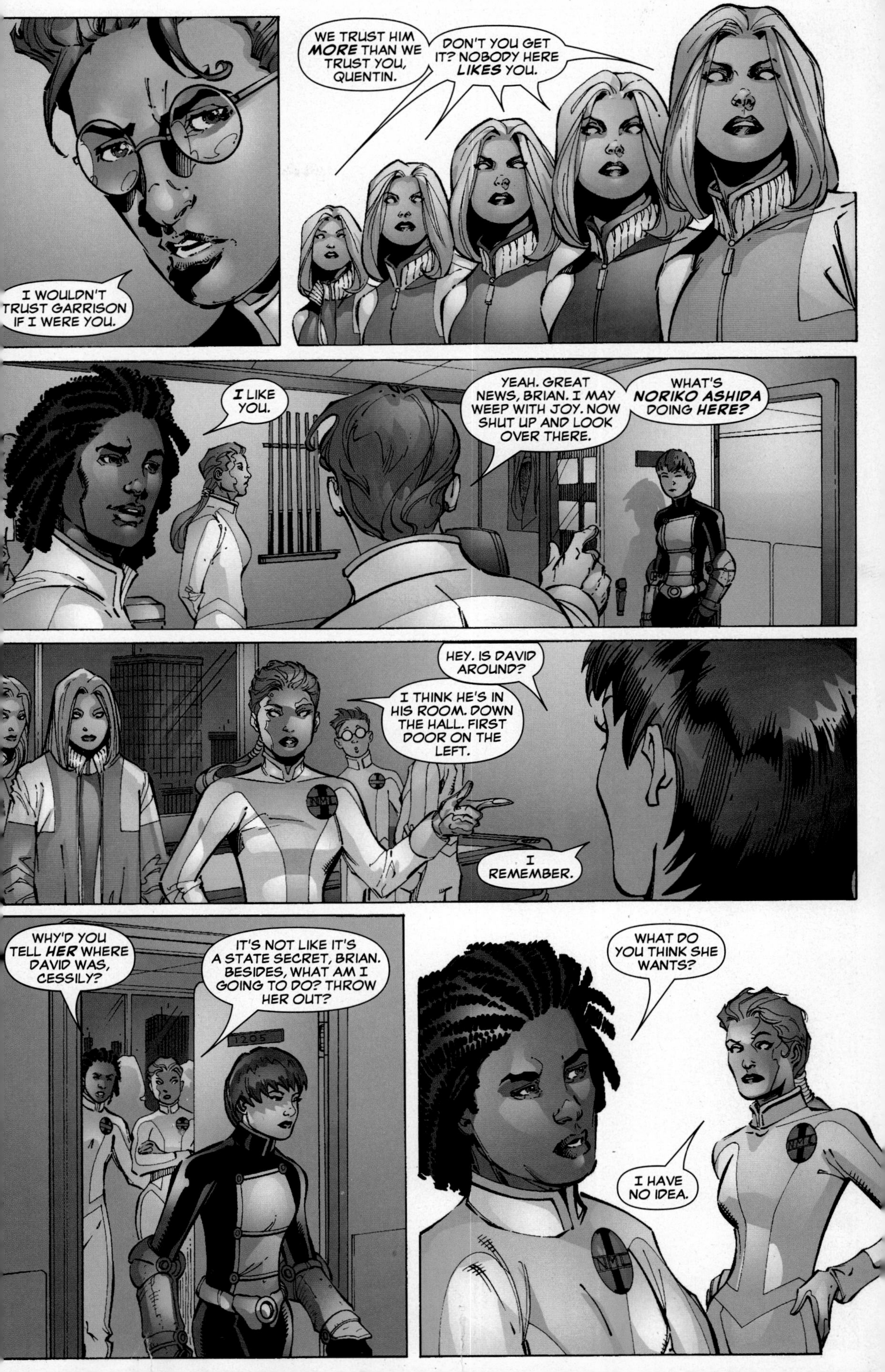
I WOULDN'T TRUST GARRISON IF I WERE YOU.
WE TRUST HIM MORE THAN WE TRUST YOU, QUENTIN.
DON'T YOU GET IT? NOBODY HERE LIKES YOU.
I LIKE YOU.
YEAH. GREAT NEWS, BRIAN. I MAY WEEP WITH JOY. NOW SHUT UP AND LOOK OVER THERE.
WHAT'S NORIKO ASHIDA DOING HERE?
HEY. IS DAVID AROUND?
I THINK HE'S IN HIS ROOM. DOWN THE HALL. FIRST DOOR ON THE LEFT.
I REMEMBER.
WHY'D YOU TELL HER WHERE DAVID WAS, CESSILY?
IT'S NOT LIKE IT'S A STATE SECRET, BRIAN. BESIDES, WHAT AM I GOING TO DO? THROW HER OUT?
1205
WHAT DO YOU THINK SHE WANTS?
I HAVE NO IDEA.

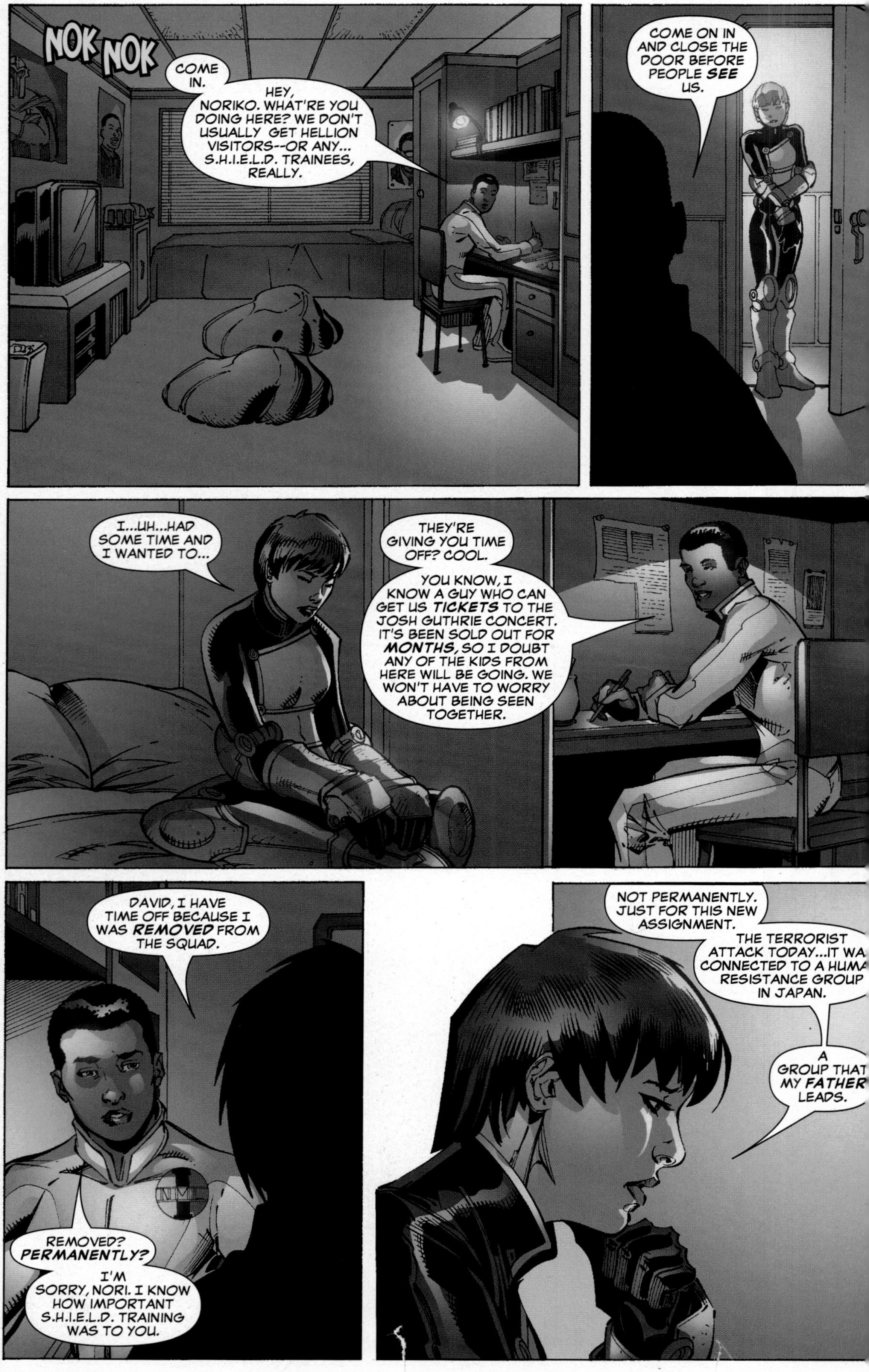
NOK NOK
COME IN.
HEY, NORIKO. WHAT'RE YOU DOING HERE? WE DON'T USUALLY GET HELLION VISITORS--OR ANY... S.H.I.E.L.D. TRAINEES, REALLY.
COME ON IN AND CLOSE THE DOOR BEFORE PEOPLE SEE US.
I...UH...HAD SOME TIME AND I WANTED TO...
THEY'RE GIVING YOU TIME OFF? COOL.
YOU KNOW, I KNOW A GUY WHO CAN GET US TICKETS TO THE JOSH GUTHRIE CONCERT. IT'S BEEN SOLD OUT FOR MONTHS, SO I DOUBT ANY OF THE KIDS FROM HERE WILL BE GOING. WE WON'T HAVE TO WORRY ABOUT BEING SEEN TOGETHER.
DAVID, I HAVE TIME OFF BECAUSE I WAS REMOVED FROM THE SQUAD.
REMOVED? PERMANENTLY?
I'M SORRY, NORI. I KNOW HOW IMPORTANT S.H.I.E.L.D. TRAINING WAS TO YOU.
NOT PERMANENTLY. JUST FOR THIS NEW ASSIGNMENT.
THE TERRORIST ATTACK TODAY...IT WA CONNECTED TO A HUMA RESISTANCE GROUP IN JAPAN.
A GROUP THAT MY FATHER LEADS.

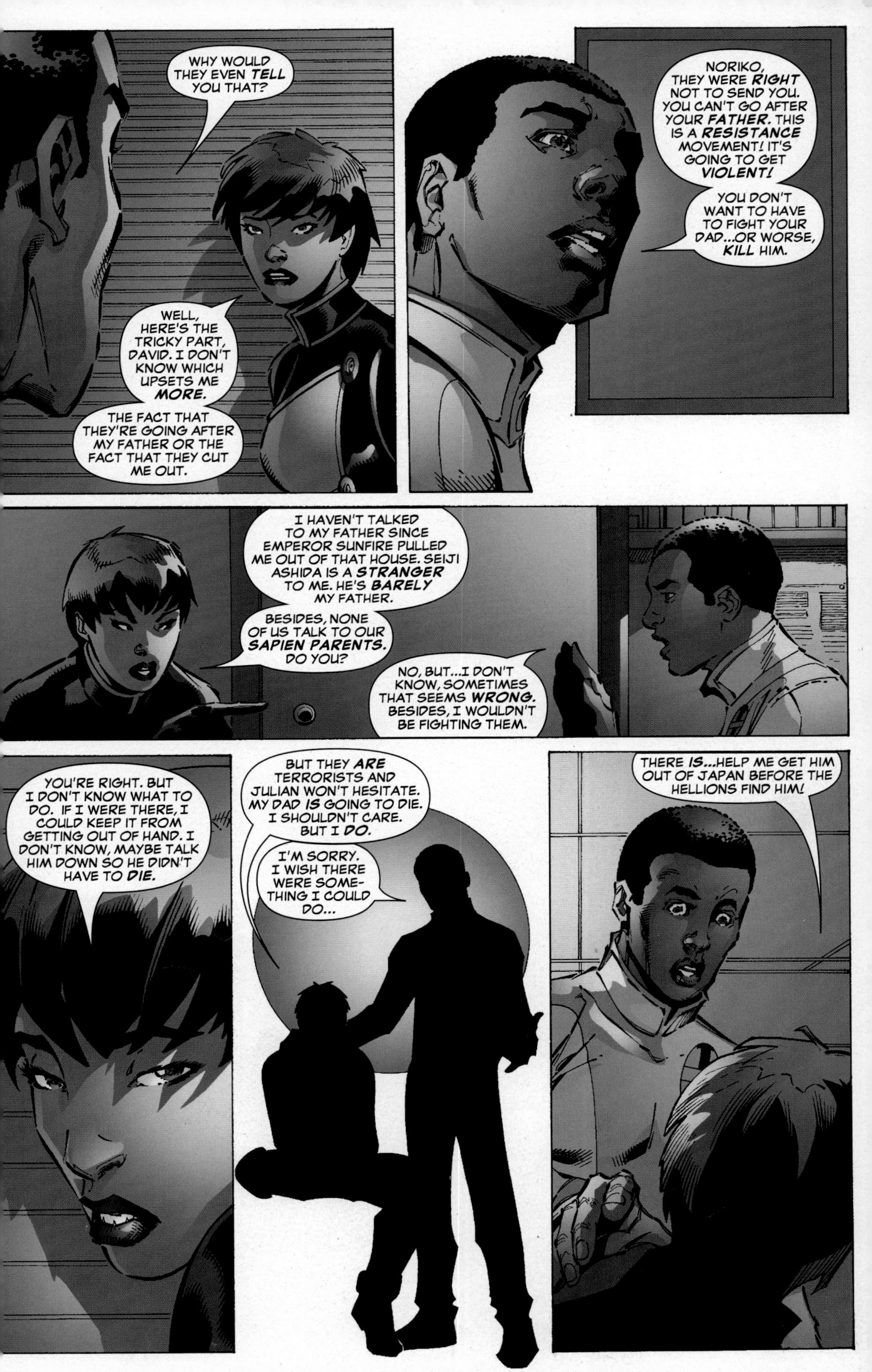
WHY WOULD THEY EVEN TELL YOU THAT?
WELL, HERE'S THE TRICKY PART, DAVID. I DON'T KNOW WHICH UPSETS ME MORE.
THE FACT THAT THEY'RE GOING AFTER MY FATHER OR THE FACT THAT THEY CUT ME OUT.
NORIKO, THEY WERE RIGHT NOT TO SEND YOU. YOU CAN'T GO AFTER YOUR FATHER. THIS IS A RESISTANCE MOVEMENT! IT'S GOING TO GET VIOLENT!
YOU DON'T WANT TO HAVE TO FIGHT YOUR DAD...OR WORSE, KILL HIM.
I HAVEN'T TALKED TO MY FATHER SINCE EMPEROR SUNFIRE PULLED ME OUT OF THAT HOUSE. SEIJI ASHIDA IS A STRANGER TO ME. HE'S BARELY MY FATHER.
BESIDES, NONE OF US TALK TO OUR SAPIEN PARENTS. DO YOU?
NO, BUT...I DON'T KNOW, SOMETIMES THAT SEEMS WRONG. BESIDES, I WOULDN'T BE FIGHTING THEM.
YOU'RE RIGHT. BUT I DON'T KNOW WHAT TO DO. IF I WERE THERE, I COULD KEEP IT FROM GETTING OUT OF HAND. I DON'T KNOW, MAYBE TALK HIM DOWN SO HE DIDN'T HAVE TO DIE.
BUT THEY ARE TERRORISTS AND JULIAN WON'T HESITATE. MY DAD IS GOING TO DIE. I SHOULDN'T CARE. BUT I DO.
I'M SORRY. I WISH THERE WERE SOME-THING I COULD DO...
THERE IS...HELP ME GET HIM OUT OF JAPAN BEFORE THE HELLIONS FIND HIM!

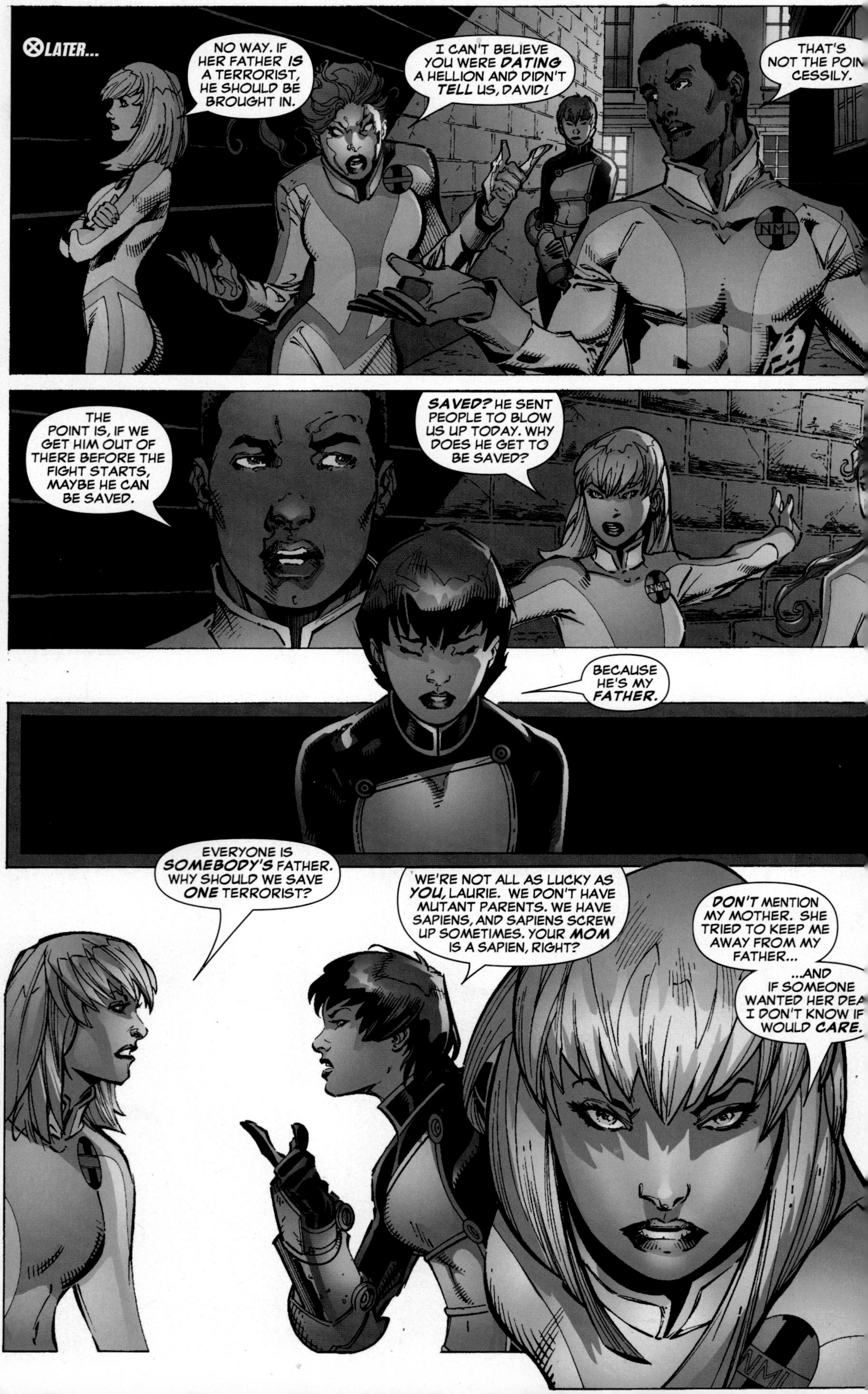
LATER...
NO WAY. IF HER FATHER IS A TERRORIST, HE SHOULD BE BROUGHT IN.
I CAN'T BELIEVE YOU WERE DATING A HELLION AND DIDN'T TELL US, DAVID!
THAT'S NOT THE POIN CESSILY.
THE POINT IS, IF WE GET HIM OUT OF THERE BEFORE THE FIGHT STARTS, MAYBE HE CAN BE SAVED.
SAVED? HE SENT PEOPLE TO BLOW US UP TODAY. WHY DOES HE GET TO BE SAVED?
BECAUSE HE'S MY FATHER.
EVERYONE IS SOMEBODY'S FATHER. WHY SHOULD WE SAVE ONE TERRORIST?
WE'RE NOT ALL AS LUCKY AS YOU, LAURIE. WE DON'T HAVE MUTANT PARENTS. WE HAVE SAPIENS, AND SAPIENS SCREW UP SOMETIMES. YOUR MOM IS A SAPIEN, RIGHT?
DON'T MENTION MY MOTHER. SHE TRIED TO KEEP ME AWAY FROM MY FATHER...
...AND IF SOMEONE WANTED HER DEA I DON'T KNOW IF WOULD CARE.

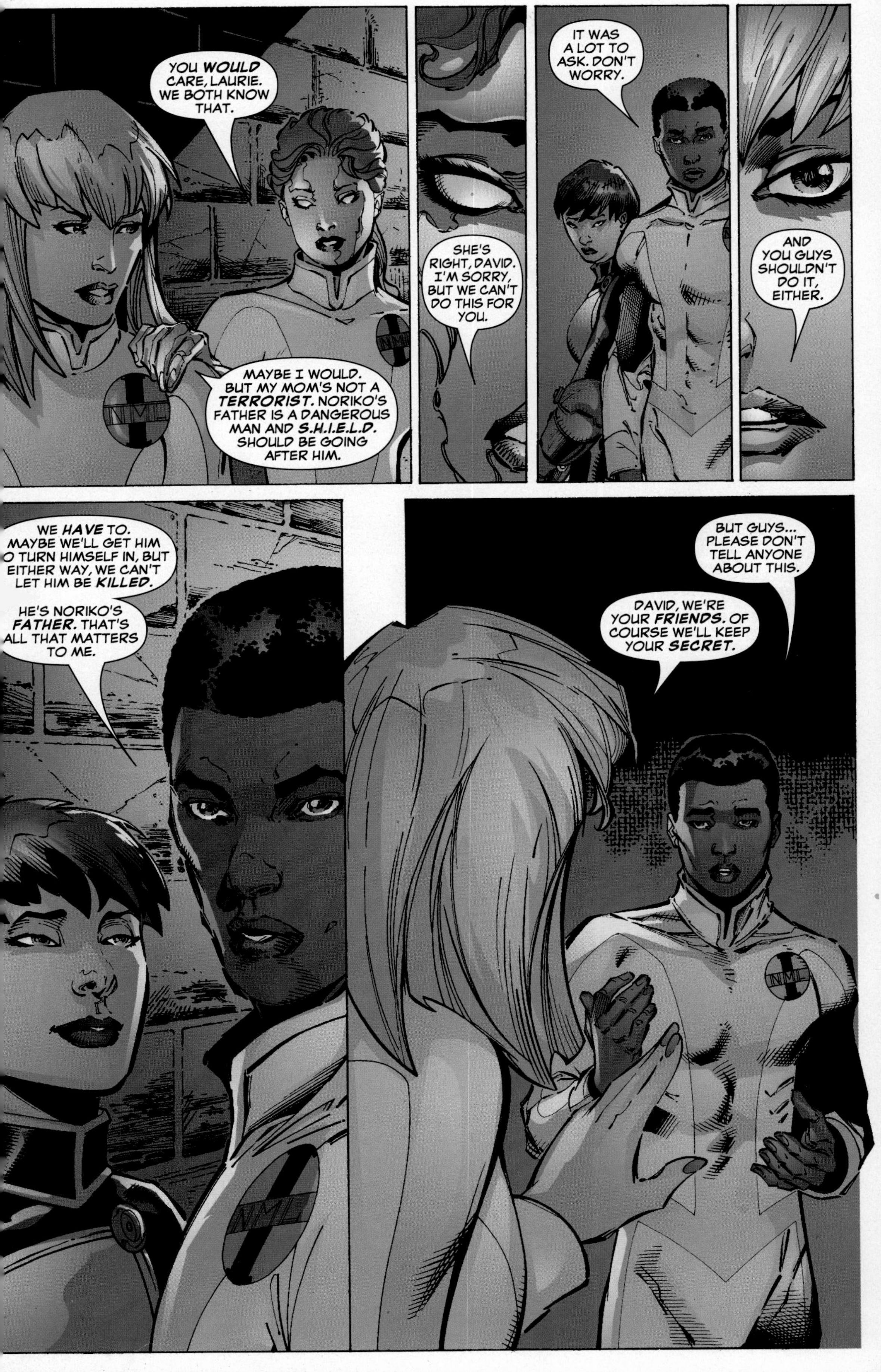
YOU WOULD CARE, LAURIE. WE BOTH KNOW THAT.
MAYBE I WOULD. BUT MY MOM'S NOT A TERRORIST. NORIKO'S FATHER IS A DANGEROUS MAN AND S.H.I.E.L.D. SHOULD BE GOING AFTER HIM.
SHE'S RIGHT, DAVID. I'M SORRY, BUT WE CAN'T DO THIS FOR YOU.
IT WAS A LOT TO ASK. DON'T WORRY.
AND YOU GUYS SHOULDN'T DO IT, EITHER.
WE HAVE TO. MAYBE WE'LL GET HIM O TURN HIMSELF IN, BUT EITHER WAY, WE CAN'T LET HIM BE KILLED.
HE'S NORIKO'S FATHER. THAT'S ALL THAT MATTERS TO ME.
BUT GUYS... PLEASE DON'T TELL ANYONE ABOUT THIS.
DAVID, WE'RE YOUR FRIENDS. OF COURSE WE'LL KEEP YOUR SECRET.

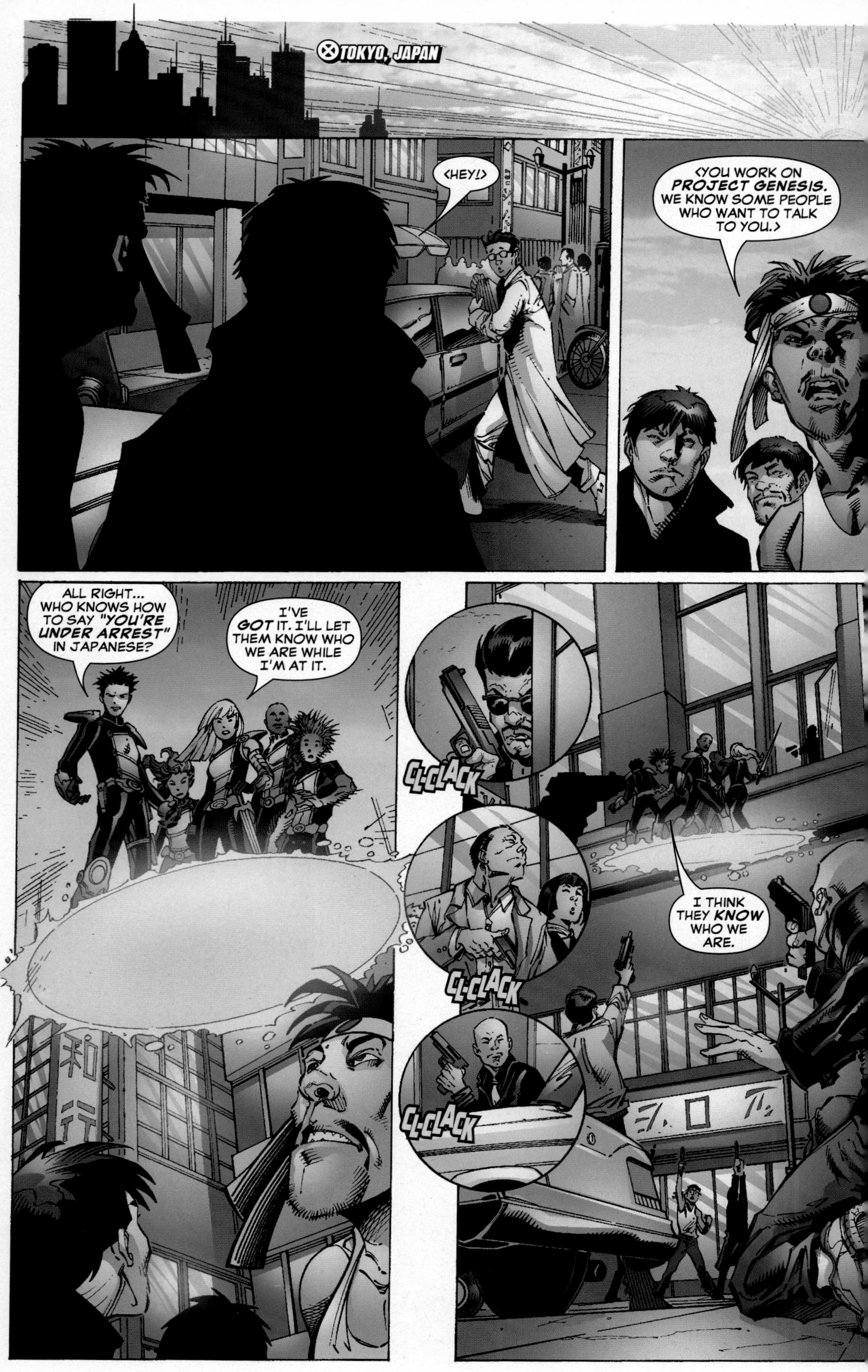
TOKYO, JAPAN
<HEY!>
<YOU WORK ON PROJECT GENESIS. WE KNOW SOME PEOPLE WHO WANT TO TALK TO YOU.>
ALL RIGHT... WHO KNOWS HOW TO SAY "YOU'RE UNDER ARREST" IN JAPANESE?
I'VE GOT IT. I'LL LET THEM KNOW WHO WE ARE WHILE I'M AT IT.
CL-CLACK
CL-CLACK
CL-CLACK
I THINK THEY KNOW WHO WE ARE.

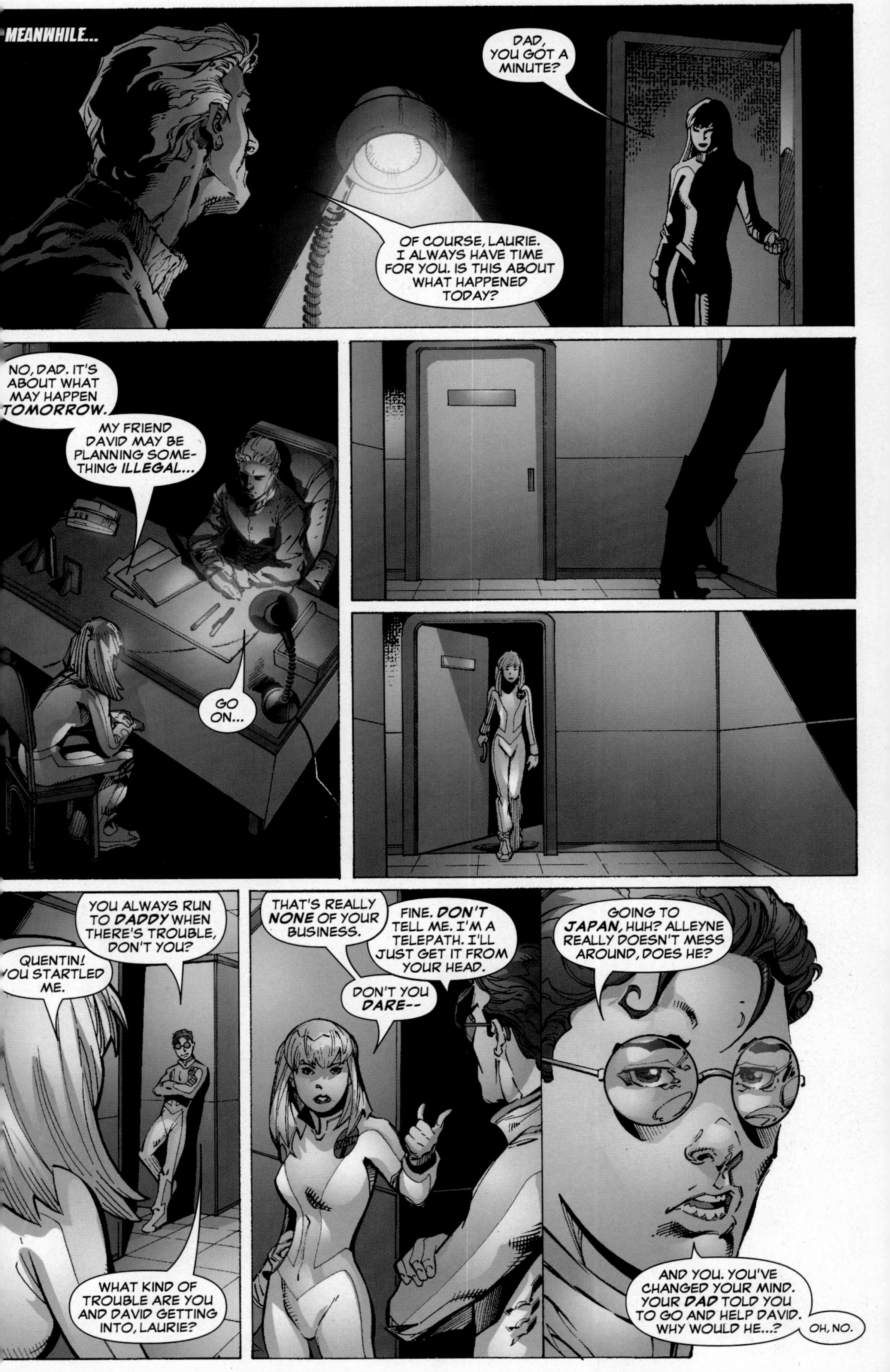
MEANWHILE...
DAD, YOU GOT A MINUTE?
OF COURSE, LAURIE. I ALWAYS HAVE TIME FOR YOU. IS THIS ABOUT WHAT HAPPENED TODAY?
NO, DAD. IT'S ABOUT WHAT MAY HAPPEN TOMORROW.
MY FRIEND DAVID MAY BE PLANNING SOMETHING ILLEGAL...
GO ON...
YOU ALWAYS RUN TO DADDY WHEN THERE'S TROUBLE, DON'T YOU?
QUENTIN! YOU STARTLED ME.
WHAT KIND OF TROUBLE ARE YOU AND DAVID GETTING INTO, LAURIE?
THAT'S REALLY NONE OF YOUR BUSINESS.
FINE. DON'T TELL ME. I'M A TELEPATH. I'LL JUST GET IT FROM YOUR HEAD.
DON'T YOU DARE--
GOING TO JAPAN, HUH? ALLEYNE REALLY DOESN'T MESS AROUND, DOES HE?
AND YOU. YOU'VE CHANGED YOUR MIND. YOUR DAD TOLD YOU TO GO AND HELP DAVID. WHY WOULD HE...?
OH, NO.

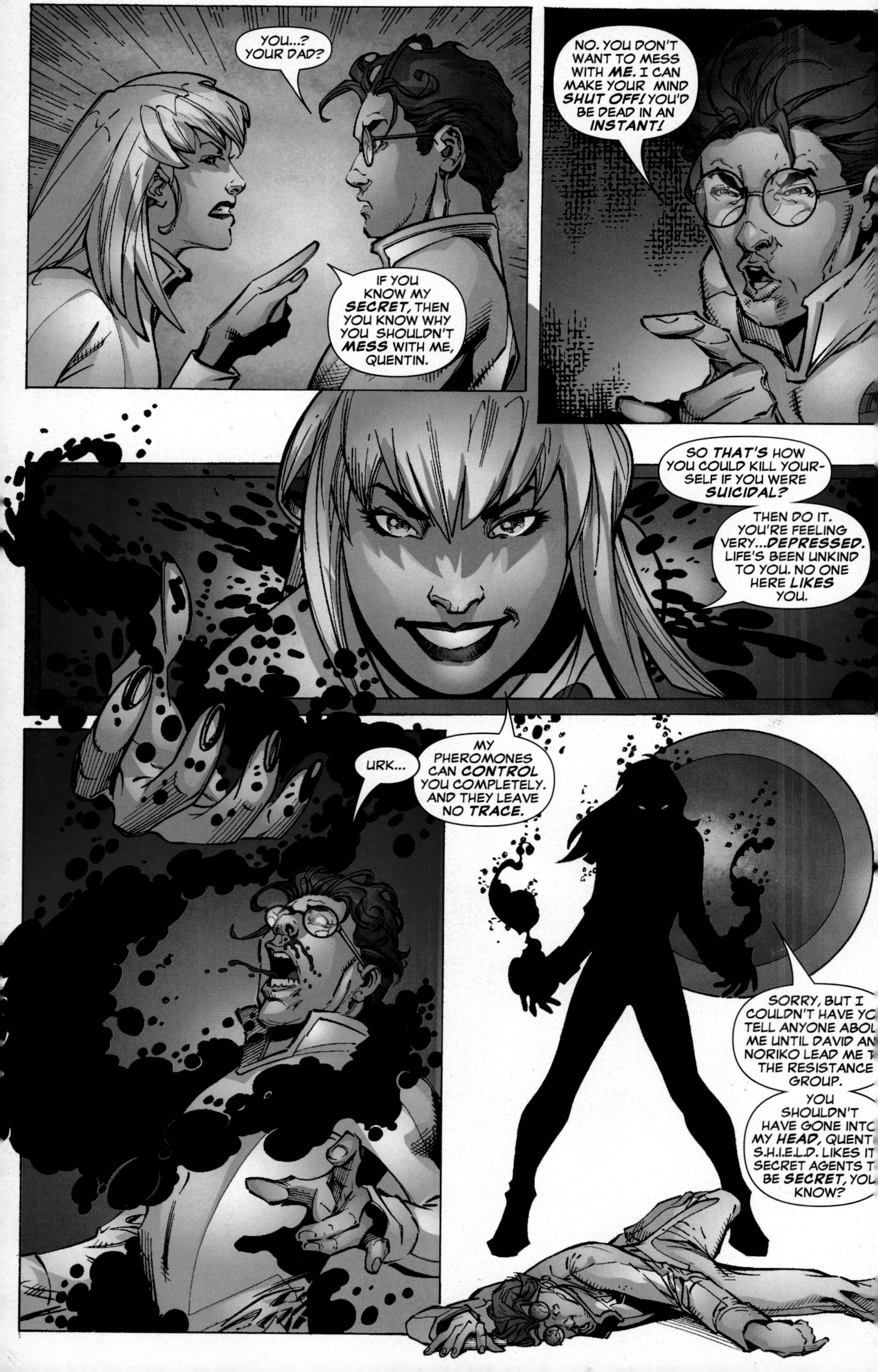
YOU...? YOUR DAD?
IF YOU KNOW MY SECRET, THEN YOU KNOW WHY YOU SHOULDN'T MESS WITH ME, QUENTIN.
NO. YOU DON'T WANT TO MESS WITH ME. I CAN MAKE YOUR MIND SHUT OFF! YOU'D BE DEAD IN AN INSTANT!
SO THAT'S HOW YOU COULD KILL YOUR-SELF IF YOU WERE SUICIDAL?
THEN DO IT. YOU'RE FEELING VERY...DEPRESSED. LIFE'S BEEN UNKIND TO YOU. NO ONE HERE LIKES YOU.
URK...
MY PHEROMONES CAN CONTROL YOU COMPLETELY. AND THEY LEAVE NO TRACE.
SORRY, BUT I COULDN'T HAVE YO TELL ANYONE ABOU ME UNTIL DAVID AN NORIKO LEAD ME T THE RESISTANCE GROUP.
YOU SHOULDN'T HAVE GONE INTO MY HEAD, QUENTI S.H.I.E.L.D. LIKES IT SECRET AGENTS T BE SECRET, YOU KNOW?

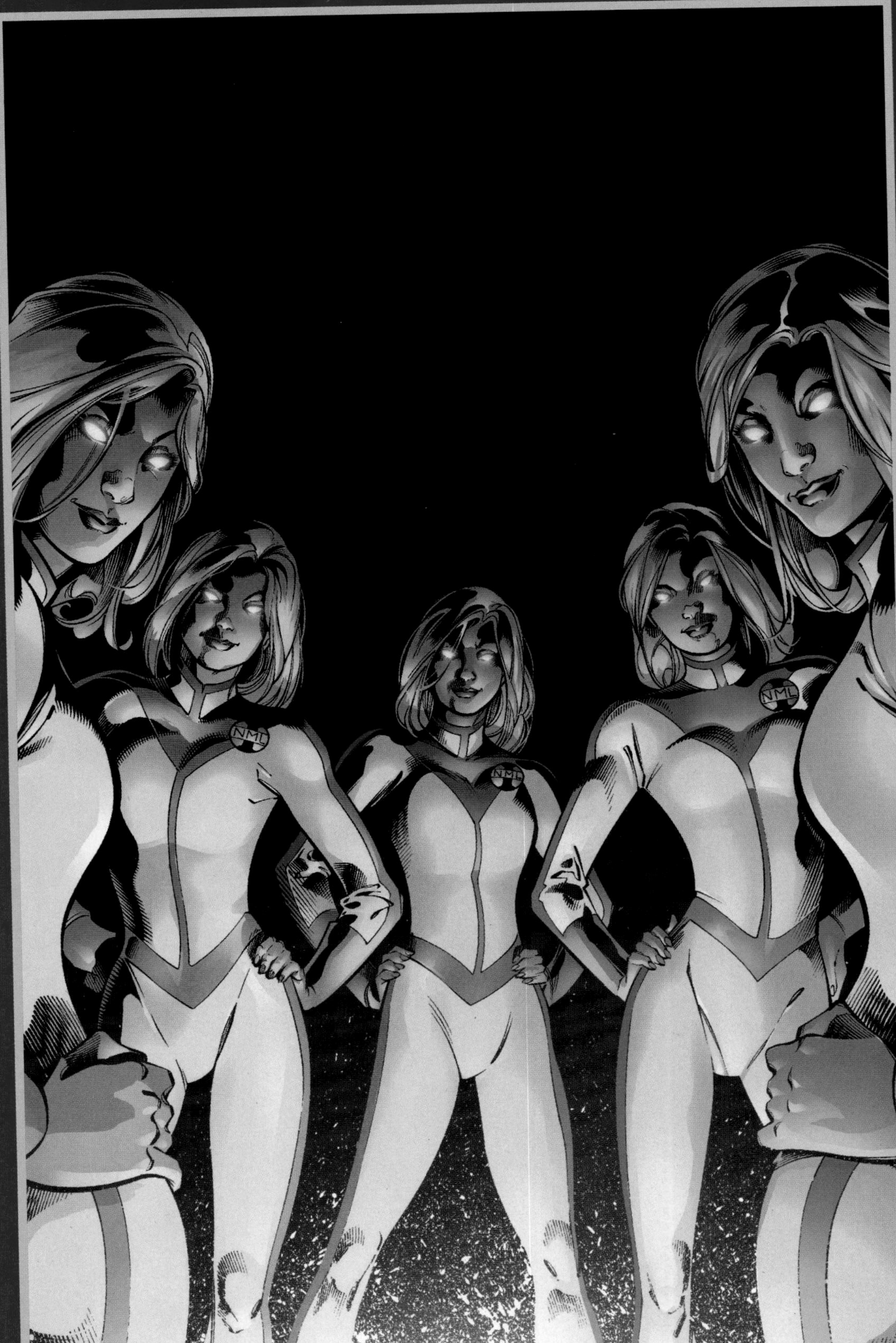
NML
NML
NML

NEW X-MEN: ACADEMY X #17

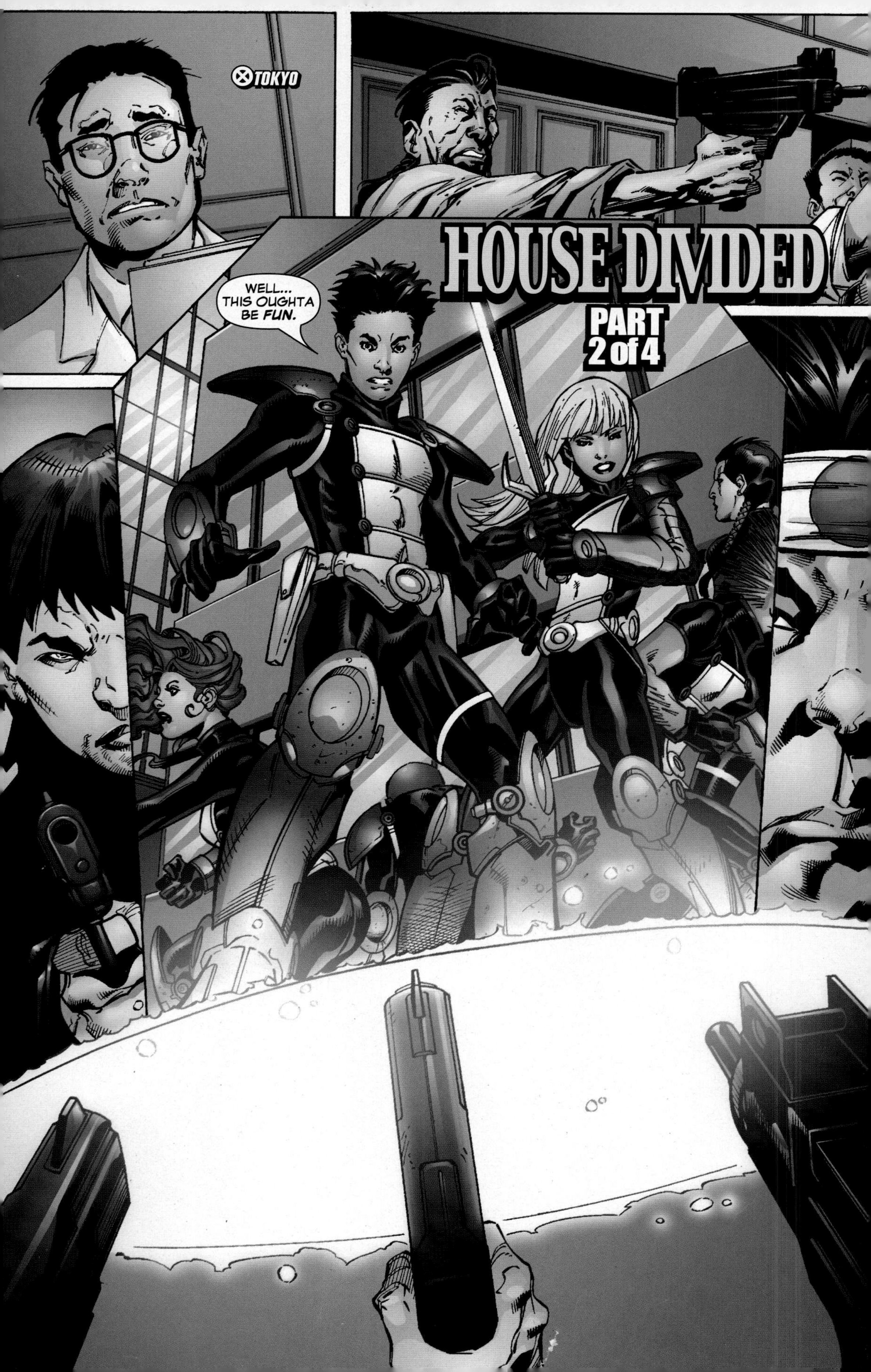
TOKYO
HOUSE DIVIDED
PART 2 of 4
WELL... THIS OUGHTA BE *FUN*.

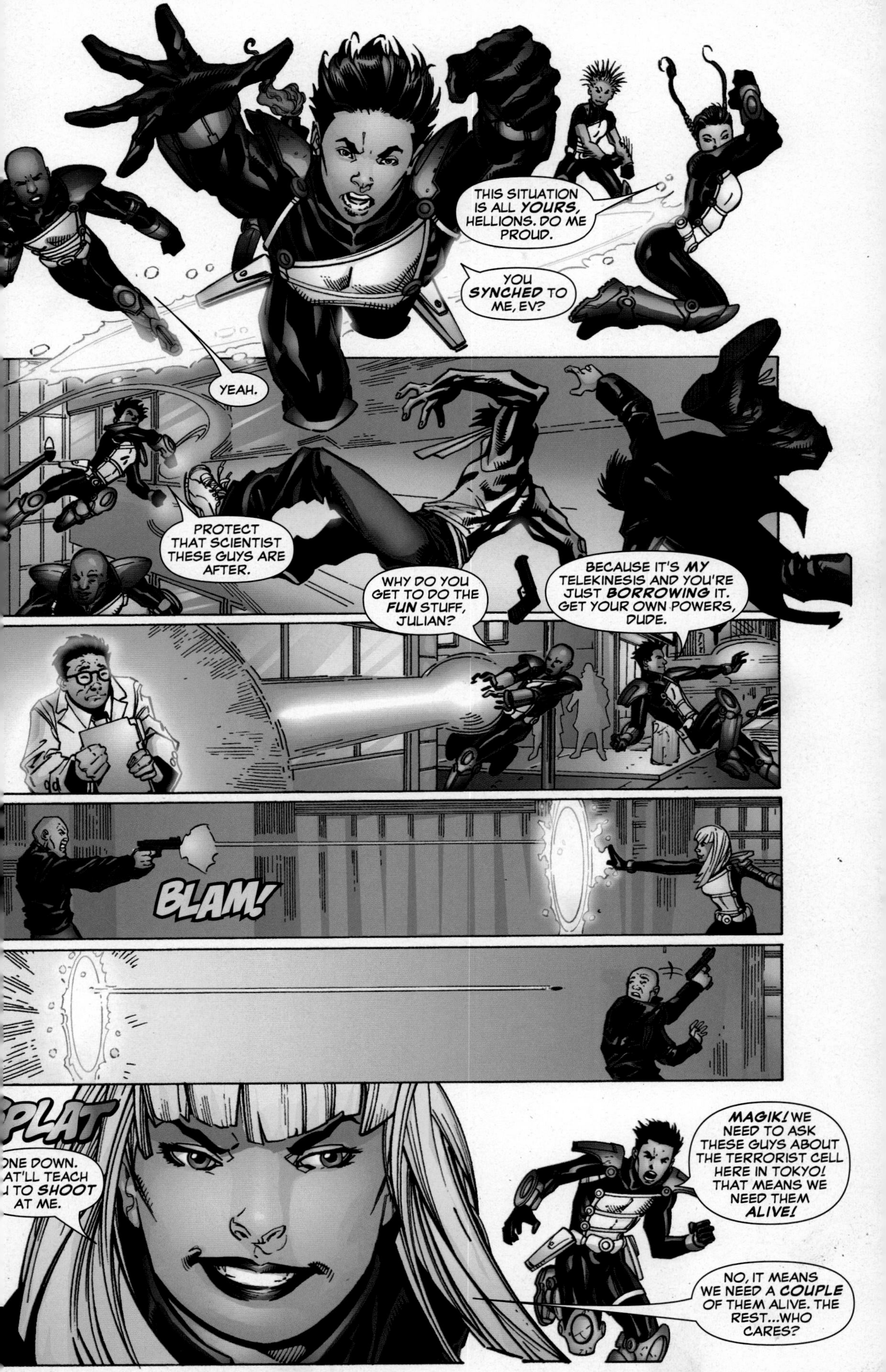
THIS SITUATION IS ALL **YOURS,** HELLIONS. DO ME PROUD.
YOU **SYNCHED** TO ME, EV?
YEAH.
PROTECT THAT SCIENTIST THESE GUYS ARE AFTER.
WHY DO YOU GET TO DO THE **FUN** STUFF, JULIAN?
BECAUSE IT'S **MY** TELEKINESIS AND YOU'RE JUST **BORROWING** IT. GET YOUR OWN POWERS, DUDE.
BLAM!
PLAT
ONE DOWN. AT'LL TEACH U TO **SHOOT** AT ME.
MAGIK! WE NEED TO ASK THESE GUYS ABOUT THE TERRORIST CELL HERE IN TOKYO! THAT MEANS WE NEED THEM **ALIVE!**
NO, IT MEANS WE NEED A **COUPLE** OF THEM ALIVE. THE REST...WHO CARES?

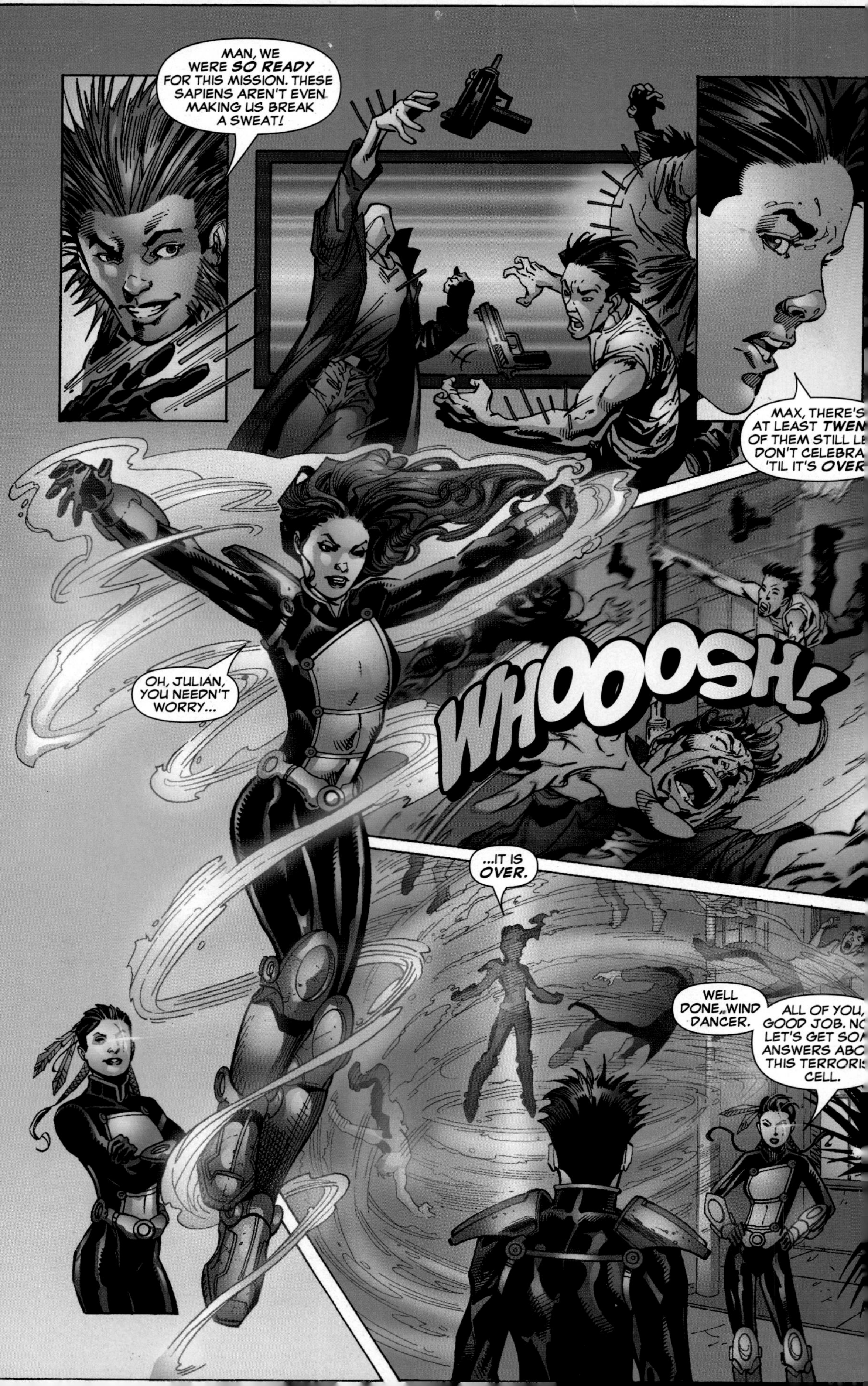
MAN, WE WERE ***SO READY*** FOR THIS MISSION. THESE SAPIENS AREN'T EVEN MAKING US BREAK A SWEAT!
MAX, THERE'S AT LEAST ***TWEN*** OF THEM STILL LE DON'T CELEBRA 'TIL IT'S ***OVER***
OH, JULIAN, YOU NEEDN'T WORRY...
WHOOOOSH!
...IT IS ***OVER.***
WELL DONE, WIND DANCER.
ALL OF YOU, GOOD JOB. NO LET'S GET SOM ANSWERS ABO THIS TERRORIS CELL.

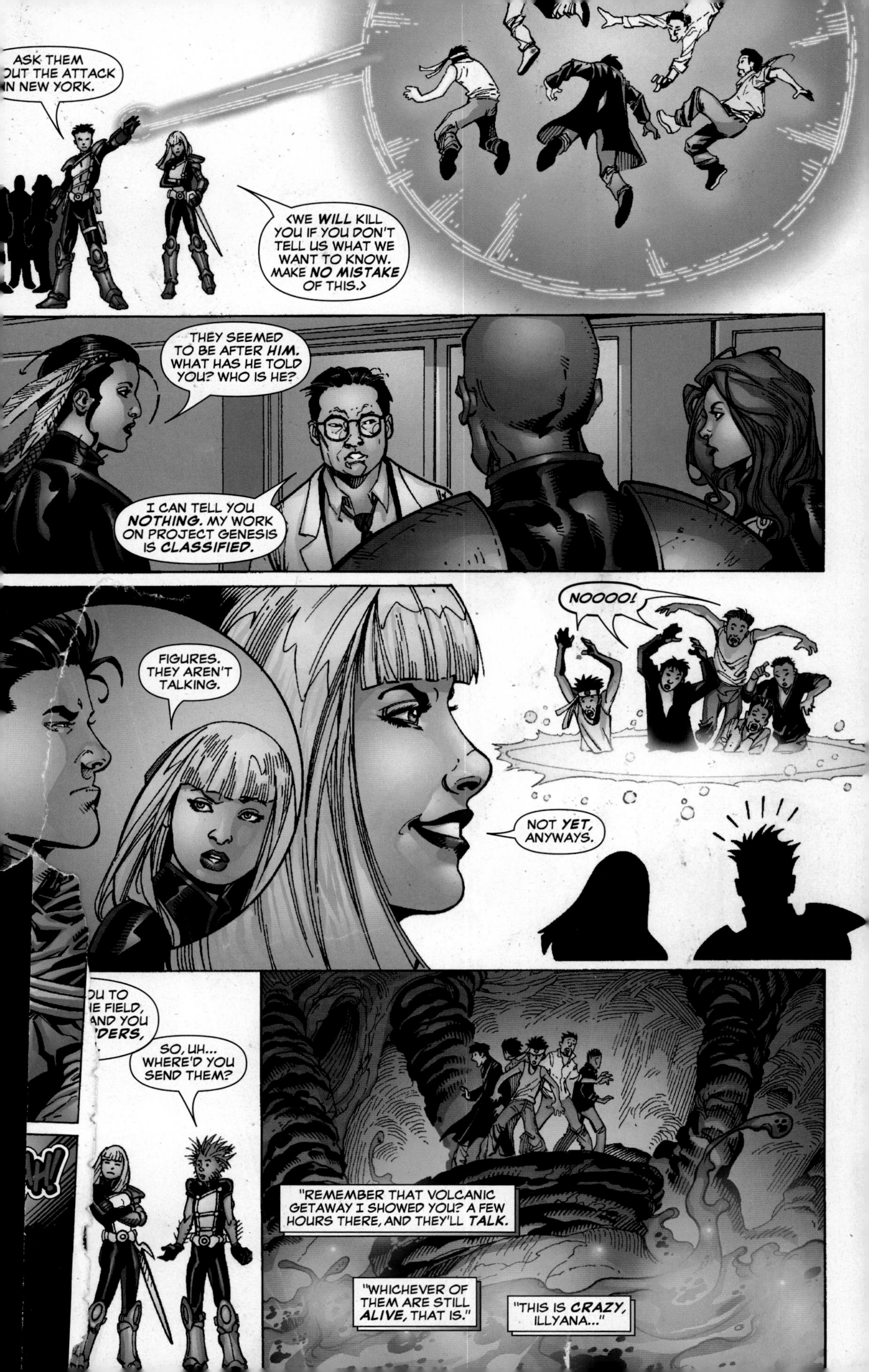
ASK THEM
OUT THE ATTACK
N NEW YORK.
<WE WILL KILL YOU IF YOU DON'T TELL US WHAT WE WANT TO KNOW. MAKE NO MISTAKE OF THIS.>
THEY SEEMED TO BE AFTER HIM. WHAT HAS HE TOLD YOU? WHO IS HE?
I CAN TELL YOU NOTHING. MY WORK ON PROJECT GENESIS IS CLASSIFIED.
FIGURES. THEY AREN'T TALKING.
NOOOO!
NOT YET, ANYWAYS.
OU TO
E FIELD,
AND YOU
DERS,
AH!
SO, UH... WHERE'D YOU SEND THEM?
"REMEMBER THAT VOLCANIC GETAWAY I SHOWED YOU? A FEW HOURS THERE, AND THEY'LL TALK.
"WHICHEVER OF THEM ARE STILL ALIVE, THAT IS."
"THIS IS CRAZY, ILLYANA..."

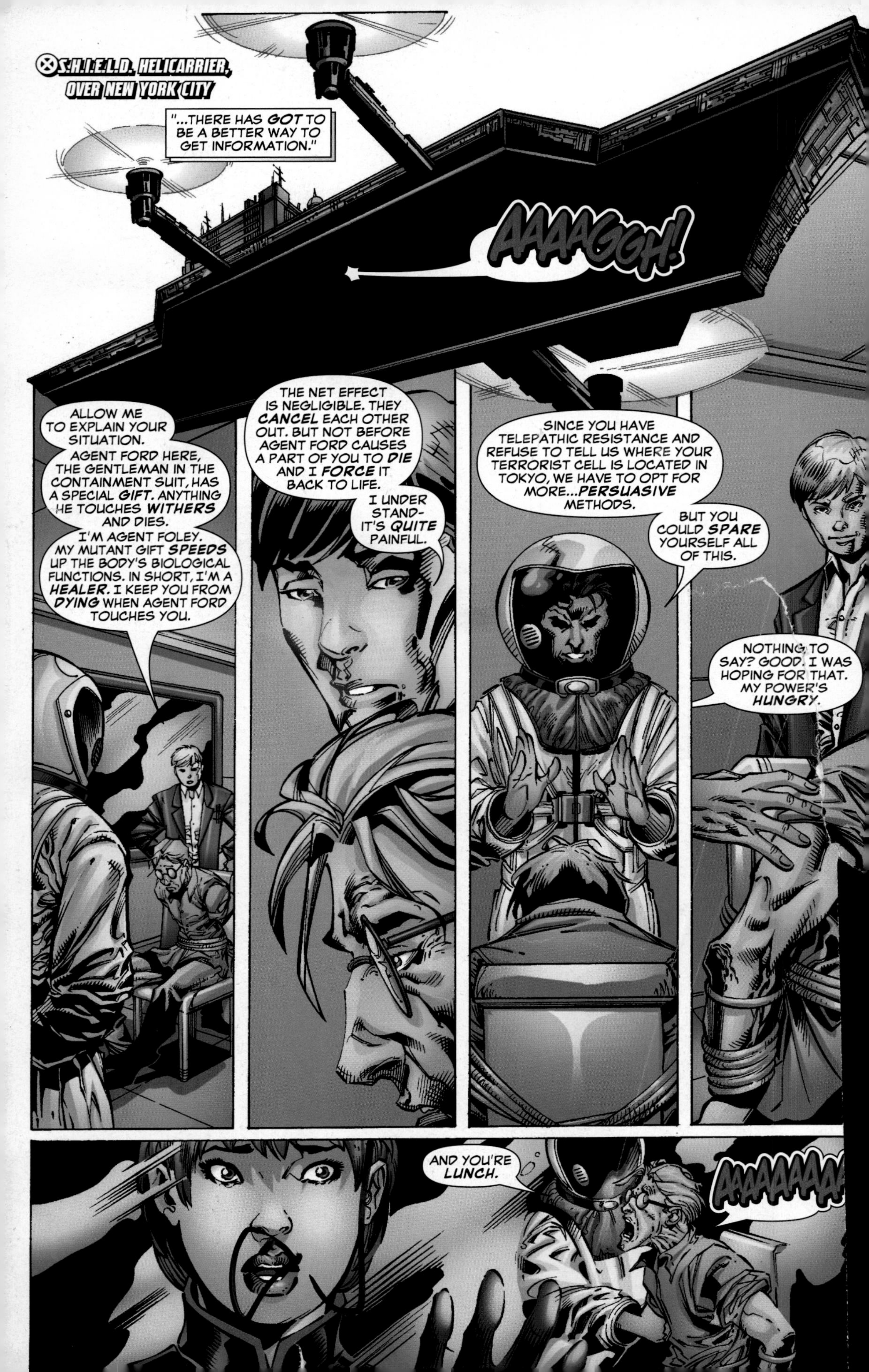
S.H.I.E.L.D. HELICARRIER, OVER NEW YORK CITY
"...THERE HAS GOT TO BE A BETTER WAY TO GET INFORMATION."
AAAAGGH!
ALLOW ME TO EXPLAIN YOUR SITUATION.
AGENT FORD HERE, THE GENTLEMAN IN THE CONTAINMENT SUIT, HAS A SPECIAL GIFT. ANYTHING HE TOUCHES WITHERS AND DIES.
I'M AGENT FOLEY. MY MUTANT GIFT SPEEDS UP THE BODY'S BIOLOGICAL FUNCTIONS. IN SHORT, I'M A HEALER. I KEEP YOU FROM DYING WHEN AGENT FORD TOUCHES YOU.
THE NET EFFECT IS NEGLIGIBLE. THEY CANCEL EACH OTHER OUT. BUT NOT BEFORE AGENT FORD CAUSES A PART OF YOU TO DIE AND I FORCE IT BACK TO LIFE.
I UNDERSTAND-IT'S QUITE PAINFUL.
SINCE YOU HAVE TELEPATHIC RESISTANCE AND REFUSE TO TELL US WHERE YOUR TERRORIST CELL IS LOCATED IN TOKYO, WE HAVE TO OPT FOR MORE...PERSUASIVE METHODS.
BUT YOU COULD SPARE YOURSELF ALL OF THIS.
NOTHING TO SAY? GOOD. I WAS HOPING FOR THAT. MY POWER'S HUNGRY.
AND YOU'RE LUNCH.
AAAAAAAA

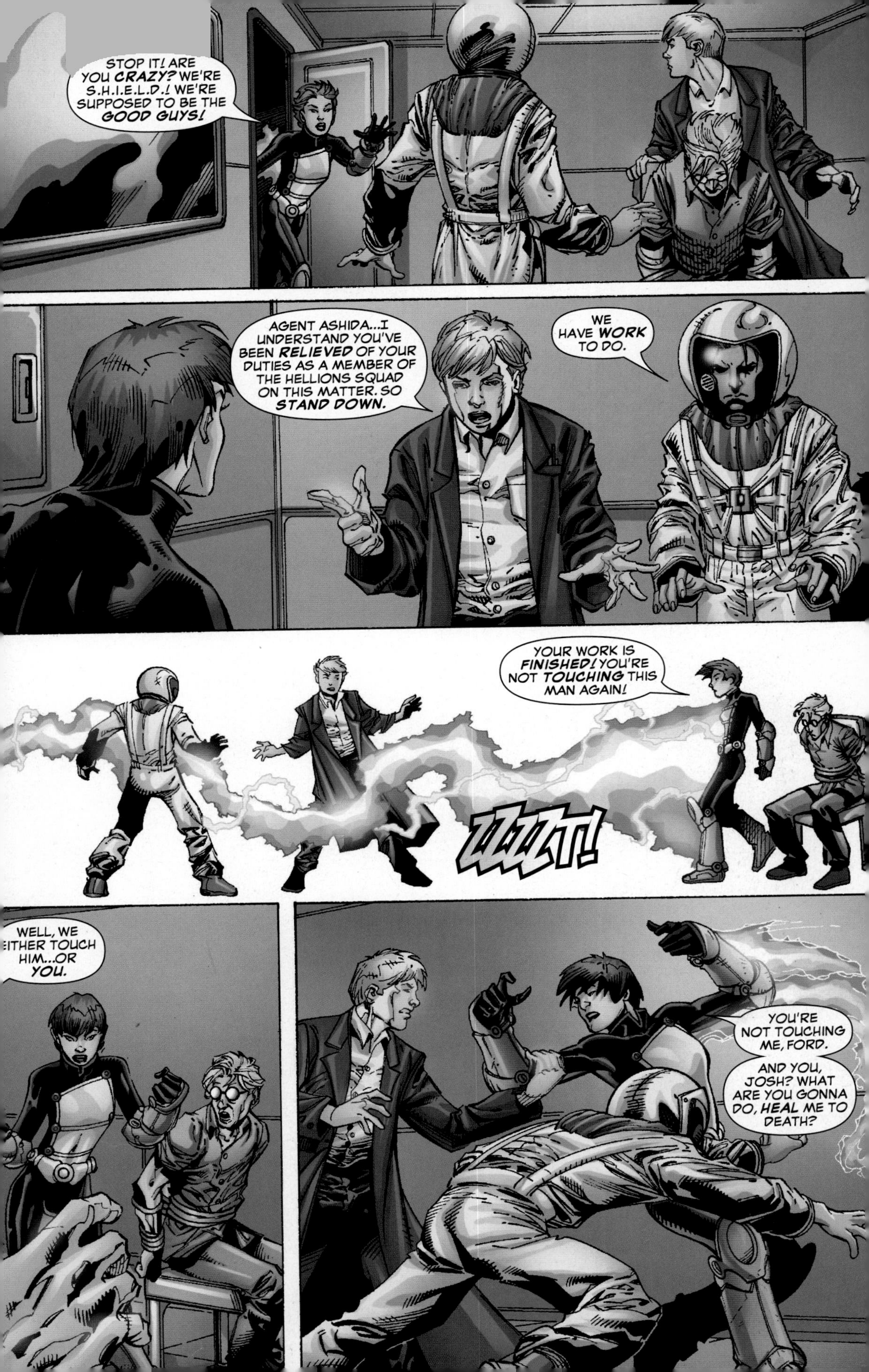
STOP IT! ARE YOU CRAZY? WE'RE S.H.I.E.L.D.! WE'RE SUPPOSED TO BE THE GOOD GUYS!
AGENT ASHIDA...I UNDERSTAND YOU'VE BEEN RELIEVED OF YOUR DUTIES AS A MEMBER OF THE HELLIONS SQUAD ON THIS MATTER. SO STAND DOWN.
WE HAVE WORK TO DO.
YOUR WORK IS FINISHED! YOU'RE NOT TOUCHING THIS MAN AGAIN!
ZZZZT!
WELL, WE EITHER TOUCH HIM...OR YOU.
YOU'RE NOT TOUCHING ME, FORD.
AND YOU, JOSH? WHAT ARE YOU GONNA DO, HEAL ME TO DEATH?

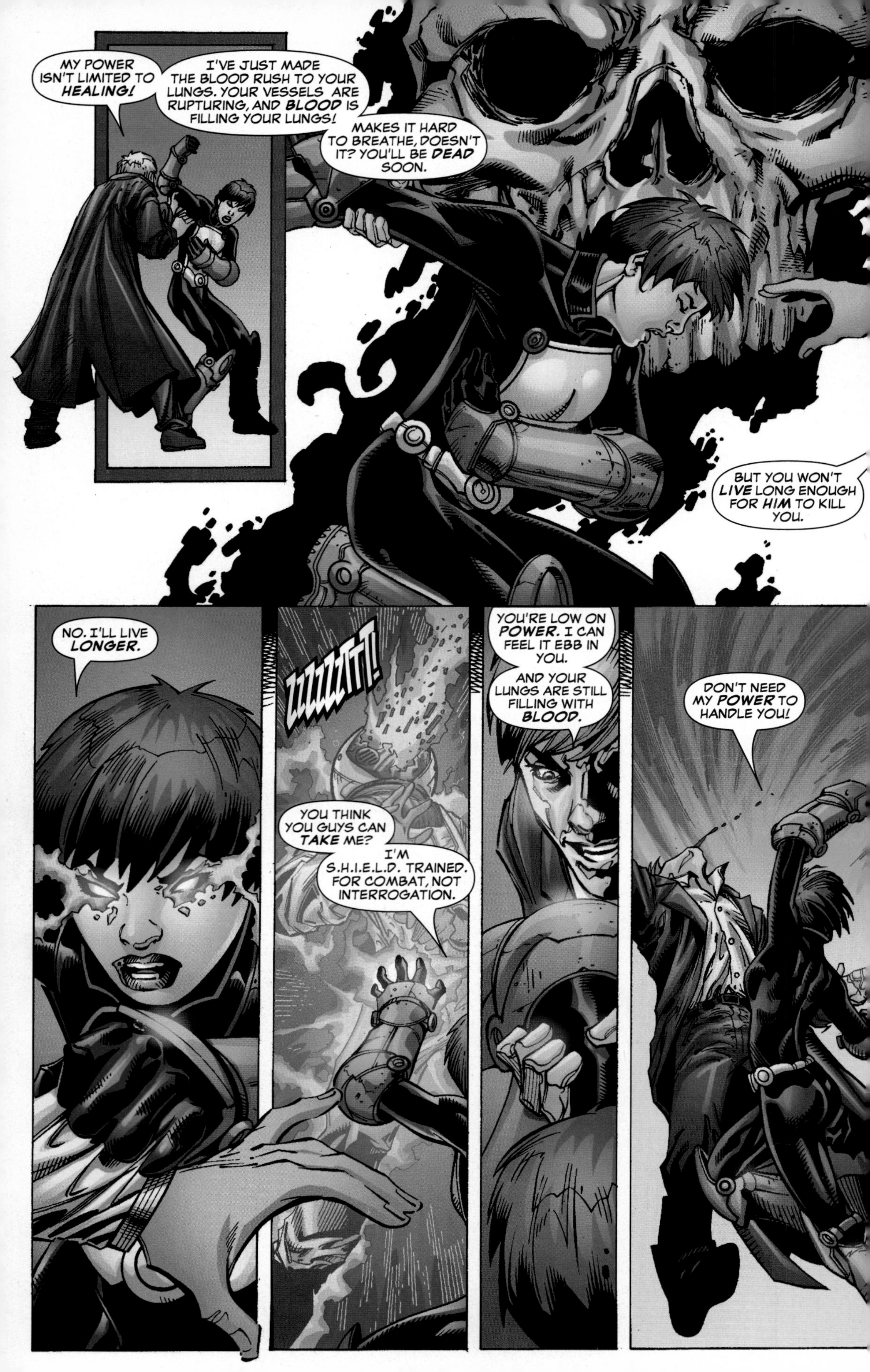
MY POWER ISN'T LIMITED TO HEALING!
I'VE JUST MADE THE BLOOD RUSH TO YOUR LUNGS. YOUR VESSELS ARE RUPTURING, AND BLOOD IS FILLING YOUR LUNGS!
MAKES IT HARD TO BREATHE, DOESN'T IT? YOU'LL BE DEAD SOON.
BUT YOU WON'T LIVE LONG ENOUGH FOR HIM TO KILL YOU.
NO. I'LL LIVE LONGER.
ZZZZZZTTT!
YOU THINK YOU GUYS CAN TAKE ME?
I'M S.H.I.E.L.D. TRAINED. FOR COMBAT, NOT INTERROGATION.
YOU'RE LOW ON POWER. I CAN FEEL IT EBB IN YOU.
AND YOUR LUNGS ARE STILL FILLING WITH BLOOD.
DON'T NEED MY POWER TO HANDLE YOU!

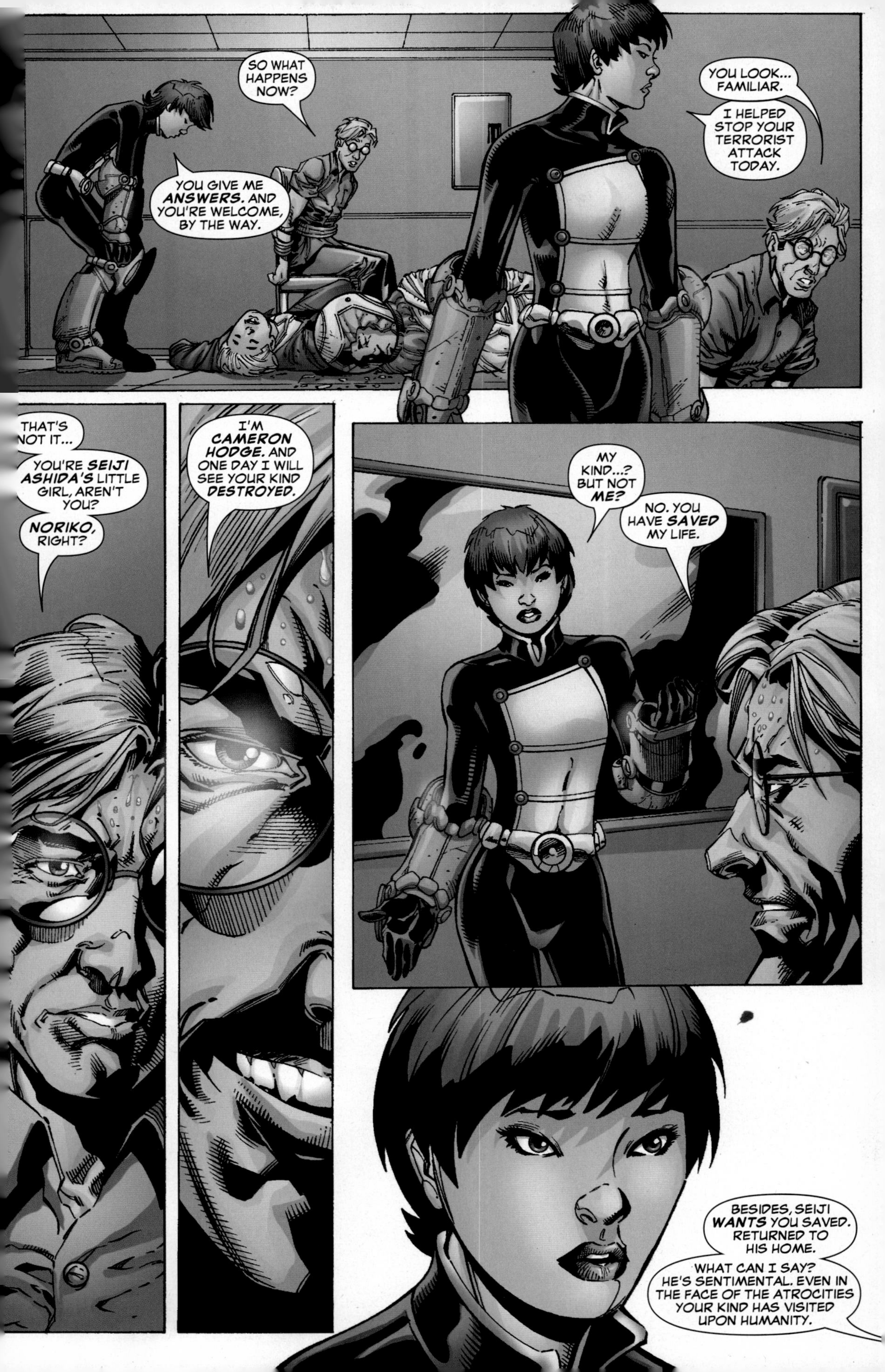
SO WHAT HAPPENS NOW?
YOU GIVE ME ANSWERS. AND YOU'RE WELCOME, BY THE WAY.
YOU LOOK... FAMILIAR.
I HELPED STOP YOUR TERRORIST ATTACK TODAY.
THAT'S NOT IT...
YOU'RE SEIJI ASHIDA'S LITTLE GIRL, AREN'T YOU?
NORIKO, RIGHT?
I'M CAMERON HODGE. AND ONE DAY I WILL SEE YOUR KIND DESTROYED.
MY KIND...? BUT NOT ME?
NO. YOU HAVE SAVED MY LIFE.
BESIDES, SEIJI WANTS YOU SAVED. RETURNED TO HIS HOME.
WHAT CAN I SAY? HE'S SENTIMENTAL. EVEN IN THE FACE OF THE ATROCITIES YOUR KIND HAS VISITED UPON HUMANITY.

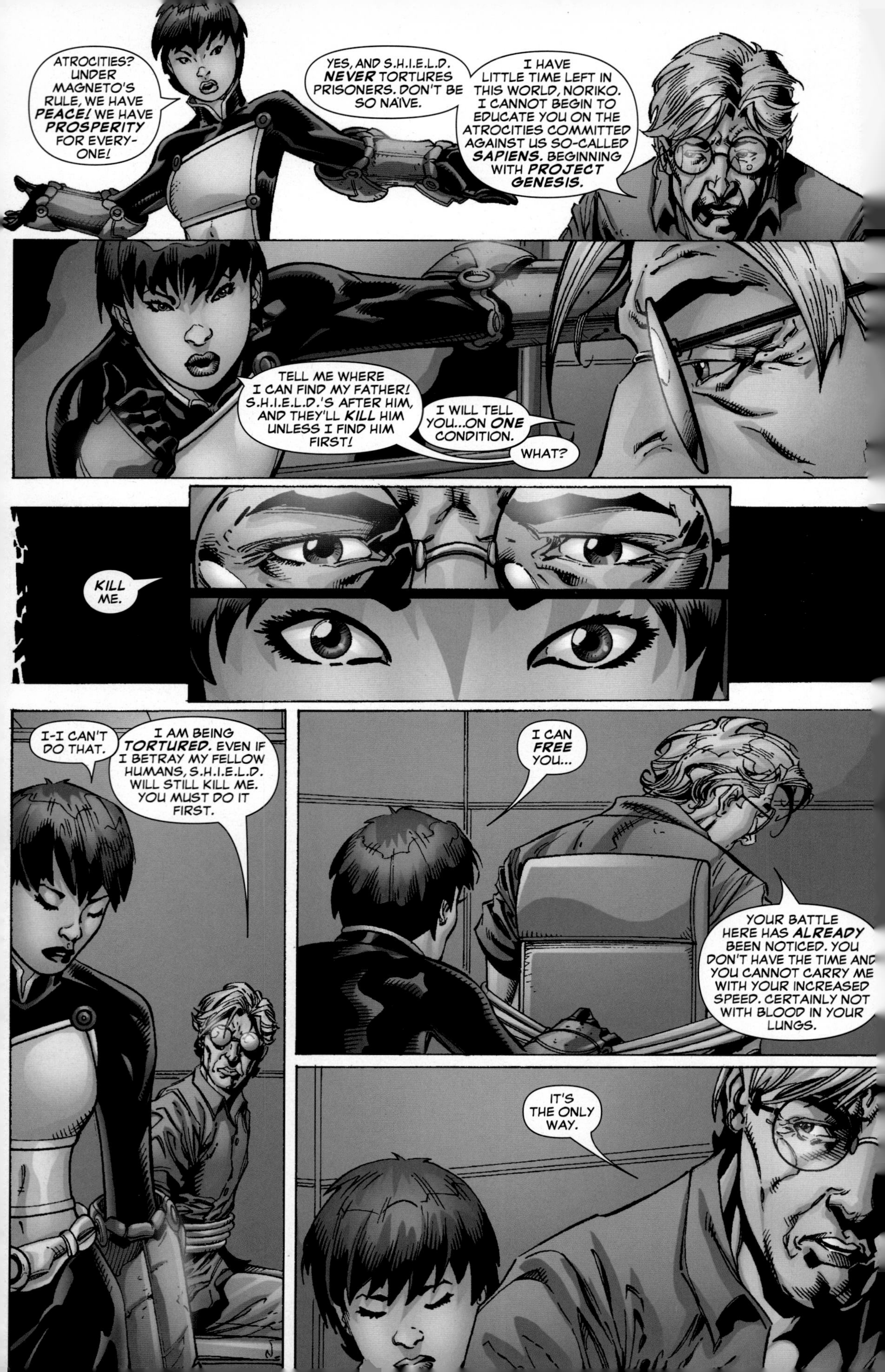
ATROCITIES? UNDER MAGNETO'S RULE, WE HAVE PEACE! WE HAVE PROSPERITY FOR EVERY-ONE!
YES, AND S.H.I.E.L.D. NEVER TORTURES PRISONERS. DON'T BE SO NAÏVE.
I HAVE LITTLE TIME LEFT IN THIS WORLD, NORIKO. I CANNOT BEGIN TO EDUCATE YOU ON THE ATROCITIES COMMITTED AGAINST US SO-CALLED SAPIENS. BEGINNING WITH PROJECT GENESIS.
TELL ME WHERE I CAN FIND MY FATHER! S.H.I.E.L.D.'S AFTER HIM, AND THEY'LL KILL HIM UNLESS I FIND HIM FIRST!
I WILL TELL YOU...ON ONE CONDITION.
WHAT?
KILL ME.
I-I CAN'T DO THAT.
I AM BEING TORTURED. EVEN IF I BETRAY MY FELLOW HUMANS, S.H.I.E.L.D. WILL STILL KILL ME. YOU MUST DO IT FIRST.
I CAN FREE YOU...
YOUR BATTLE HERE HAS ALREADY BEEN NOTICED. YOU DON'T HAVE THE TIME AND YOU CANNOT CARRY ME WITH YOUR INCREASED SPEED. CERTAINLY NOT WITH BLOOD IN YOUR LUNGS.
IT'S THE ONLY WAY.

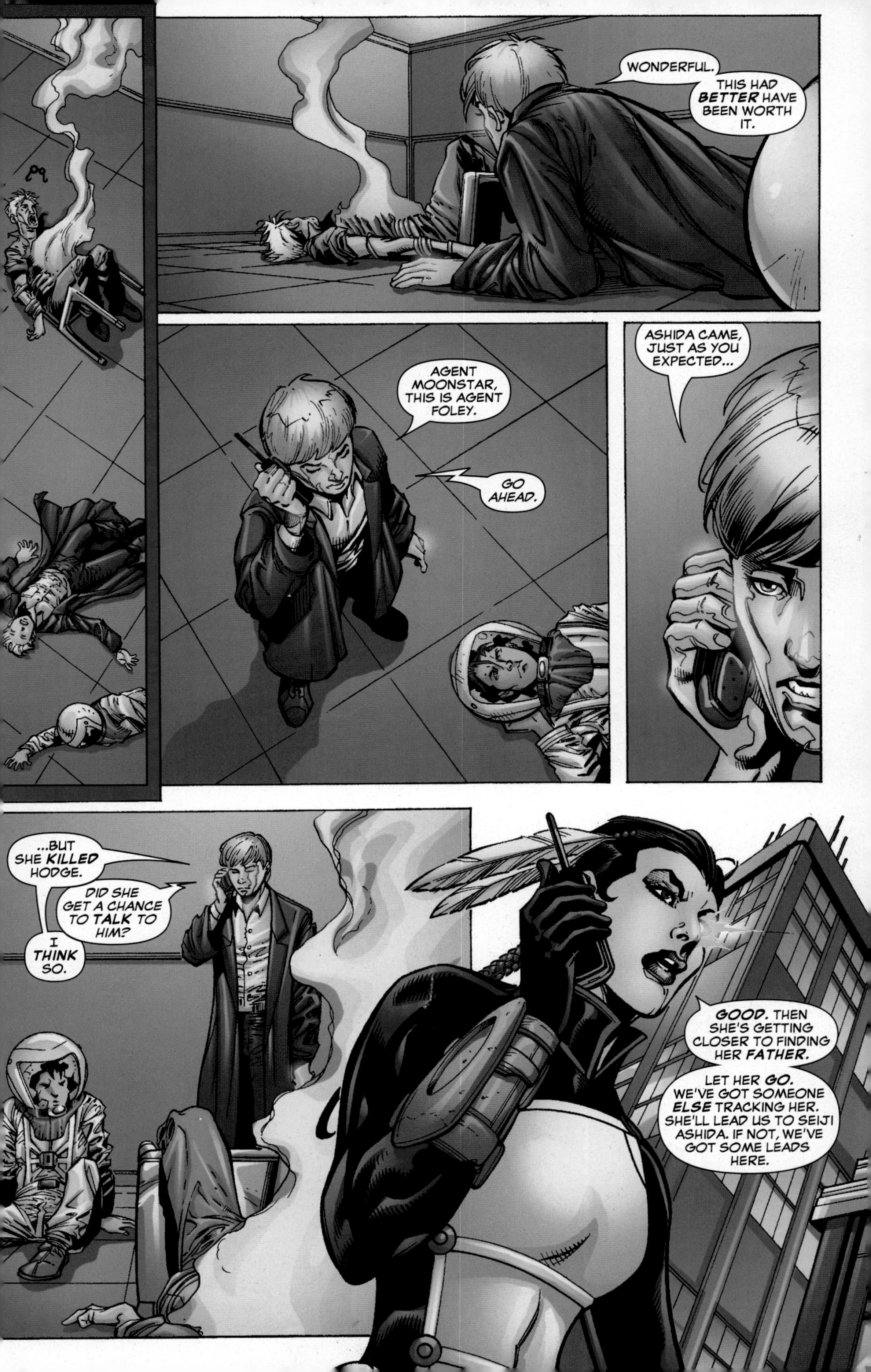
WONDERFUL.
THIS HAD BETTER HAVE BEEN WORTH IT.
AGENT MOONSTAR, THIS IS AGENT FOLEY.
GO AHEAD.
ASHIDA CAME, JUST AS YOU EXPECTED...
...BUT SHE KILLED HODGE.
DID SHE GET A CHANCE TO TALK TO HIM?
I THINK SO.
GOOD. THEN SHE'S GETTING CLOSER TO FINDING HER FATHER.
LET HER GO. WE'VE GOT SOMEONE ELSE TRACKING HER. SHE'LL LEAD US TO SEIJI ASHIDA. IF NOT, WE'VE GOT SOME LEADS HERE.

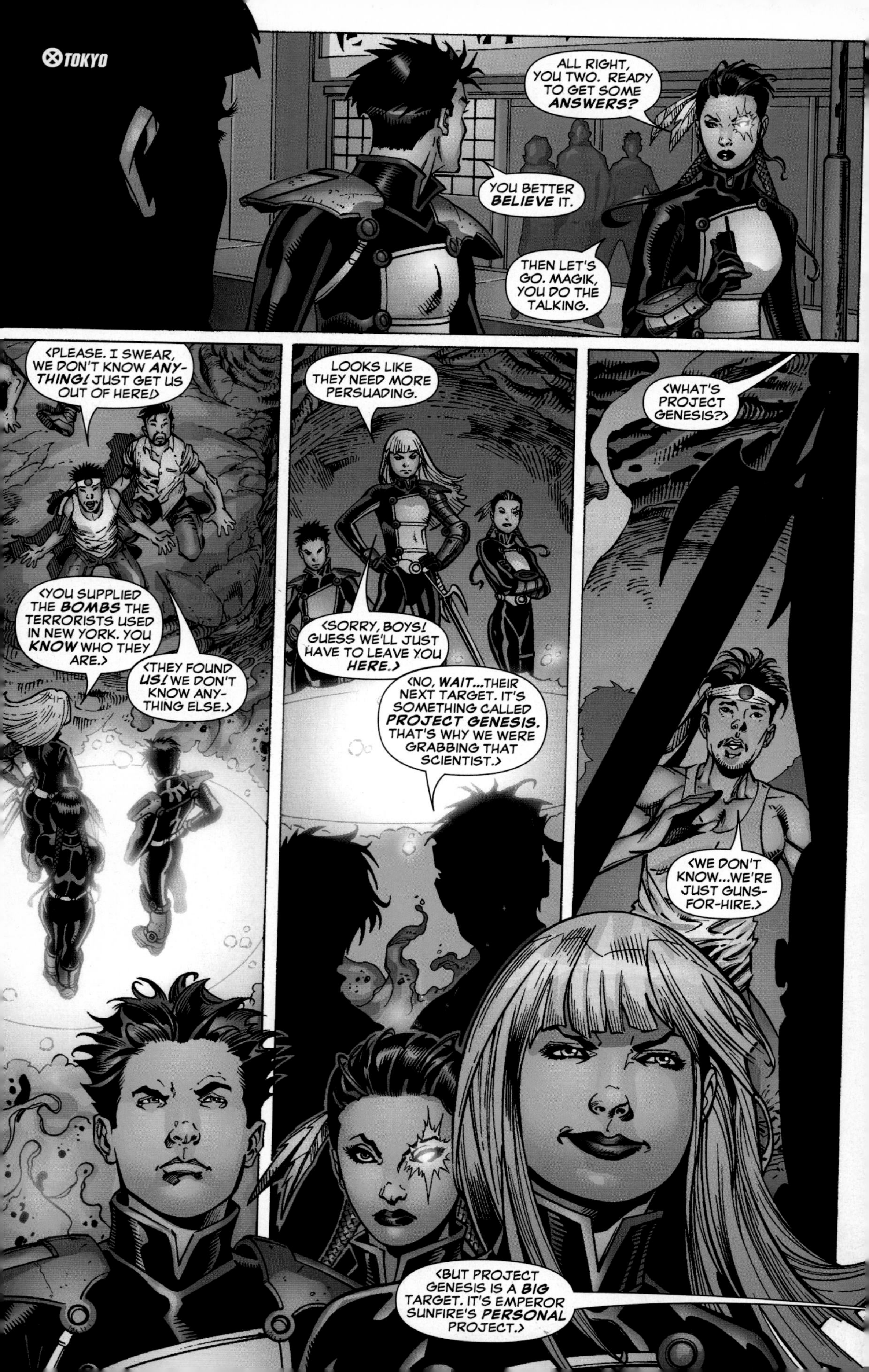
TOKYO
ALL RIGHT, YOU TWO. READY TO GET SOME ANSWERS?
YOU BETTER BELIEVE IT.
THEN LET'S GO. MAGIK, YOU DO THE TALKING.
<PLEASE. I SWEAR, WE DON'T KNOW ANYTHING! JUST GET US OUT OF HERE!>
<YOU SUPPLIED THE BOMBS THE TERRORISTS USED IN NEW YORK. YOU KNOW WHO THEY ARE.>
<THEY FOUND US! WE DON'T KNOW ANYTHING ELSE.>
LOOKS LIKE THEY NEED MORE PERSUADING.
<SORRY, BOYS! GUESS WE'LL JUST HAVE TO LEAVE YOU HERE.>
<NO, WAIT...THEIR NEXT TARGET. IT'S SOMETHING CALLED PROJECT GENESIS. THAT'S WHY WE WERE GRABBING THAT SCIENTIST.>
<WHAT'S PROJECT GENESIS?>
<WE DON'T KNOW...WE'RE JUST GUNS-FOR-HIRE.>
<BUT PROJECT GENESIS IS A BIG TARGET. IT'S EMPEROR SUNFIRE'S PERSONAL PROJECT.>

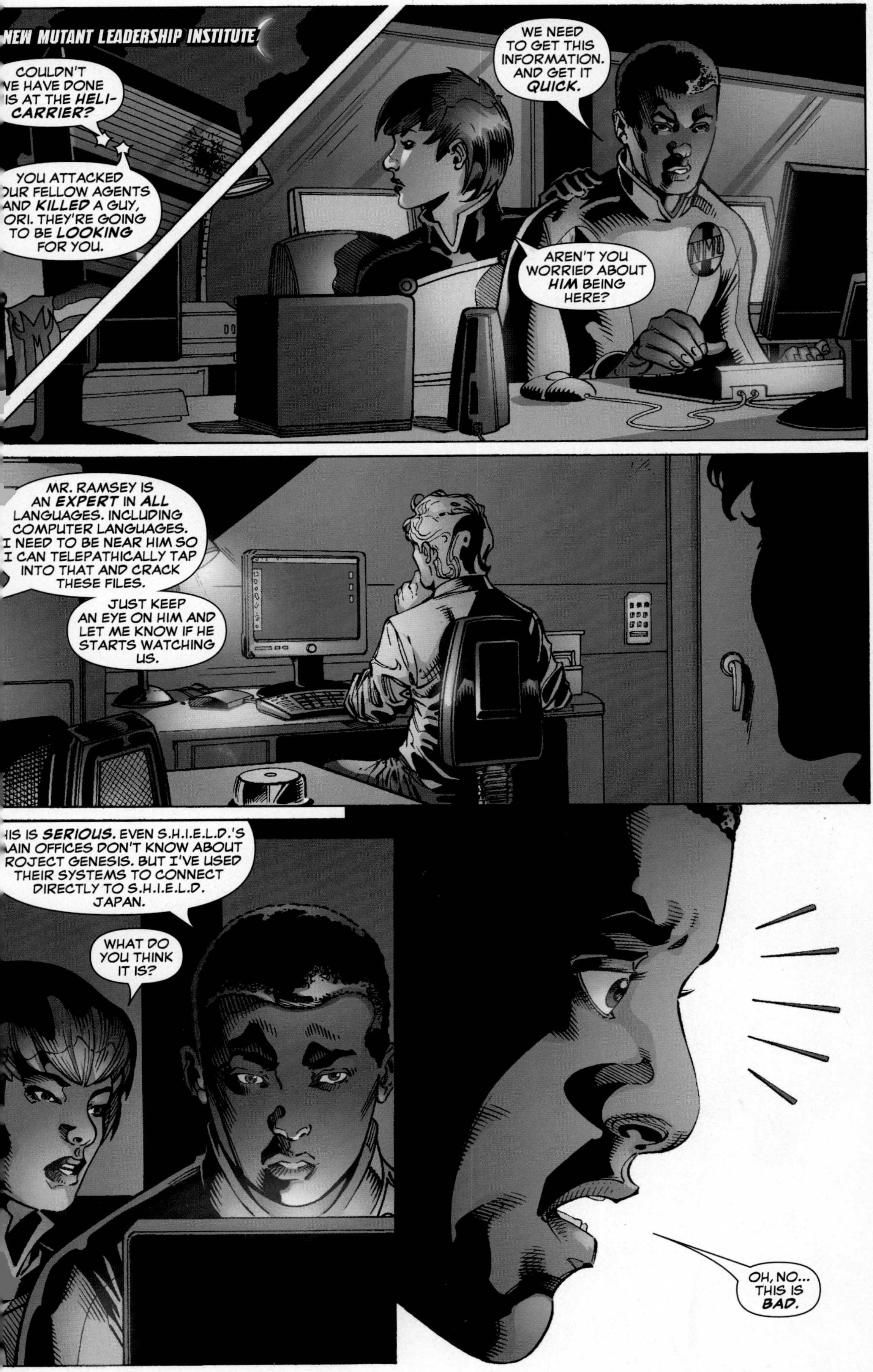
NEW MUTANT LEADERSHIP INSTITUTE
COULDN'T VE HAVE DONE IS AT THE HELI-CARRIER?
YOU ATTACKED OUR FELLOW AGENTS AND KILLED A GUY, ORI. THEY'RE GOING TO BE LOOKING FOR YOU.
WE NEED TO GET THIS INFORMATION. AND GET IT QUICK.
AREN'T YOU WORRIED ABOUT HIM BEING HERE?
MR. RAMSEY IS AN EXPERT IN ALL LANGUAGES. INCLUDING COMPUTER LANGUAGES. I NEED TO BE NEAR HIM SO I CAN TELEPATHICALLY TAP INTO THAT AND CRACK THESE FILES.
JUST KEEP AN EYE ON HIM AND LET ME KNOW IF HE STARTS WATCHING US.
HIS IS SERIOUS. EVEN S.H.I.E.L.D.'S AIN OFFICES DON'T KNOW ABOUT ROJECT GENESIS. BUT I'VE USED THEIR SYSTEMS TO CONNECT DIRECTLY TO S.H.I.E.L.D. JAPAN.
WHAT DO YOU THINK IT IS?
OH, NO... THIS IS BAD.

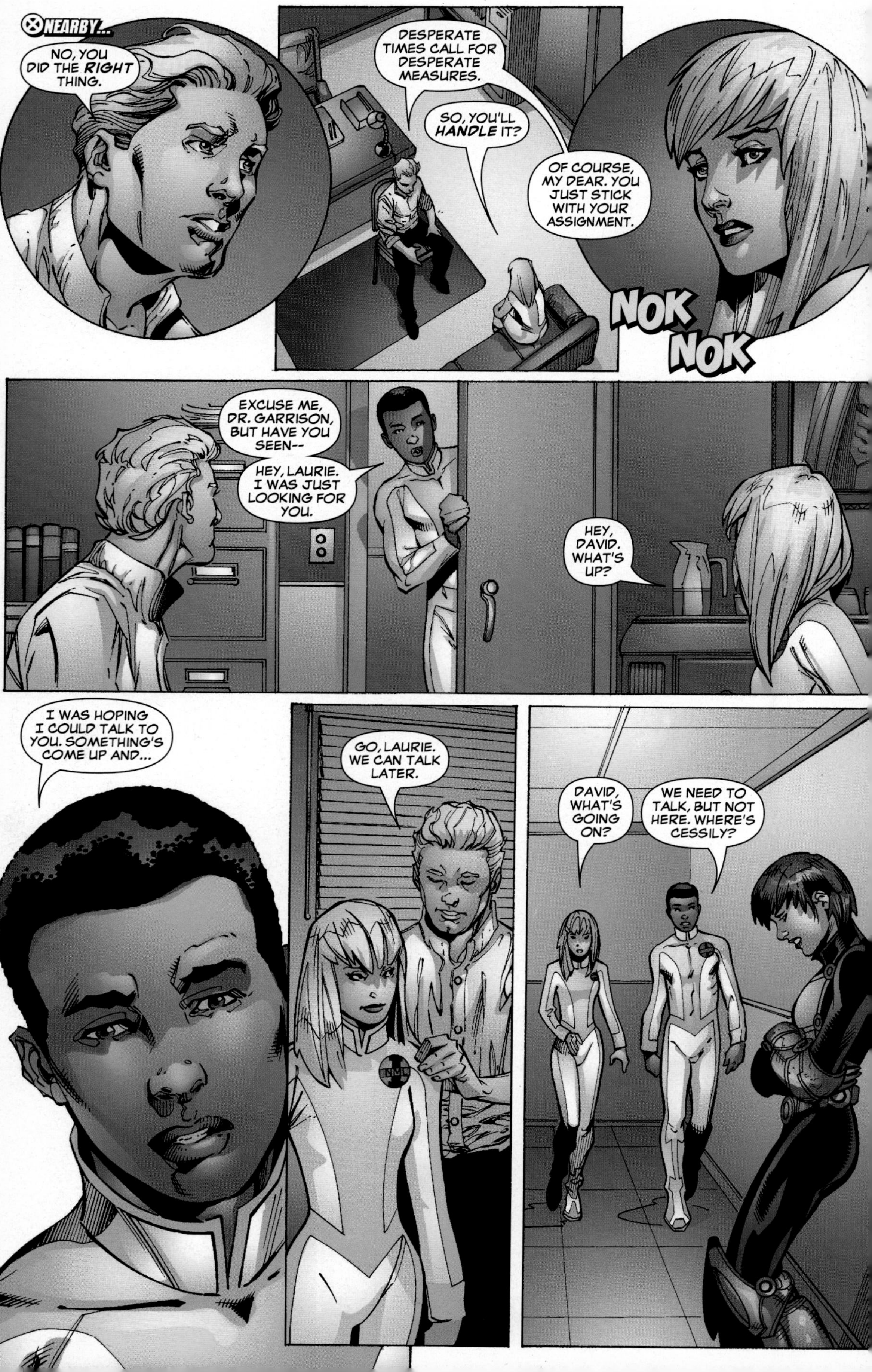
NEARBY...
NO, YOU DID THE RIGHT THING.
DESPERATE TIMES CALL FOR DESPERATE MEASURES.
SO, YOU'LL HANDLE IT?
OF COURSE, MY DEAR. YOU JUST STICK WITH YOUR ASSIGNMENT.
NOK NOK
EXCUSE ME, DR. GARRISON, BUT HAVE YOU SEEN--
HEY, LAURIE. I WAS JUST LOOKING FOR YOU.
HEY, DAVID. WHAT'S UP?
I WAS HOPING I COULD TALK TO YOU. SOMETHING'S COME UP AND...
GO, LAURIE. WE CAN TALK LATER.
DAVID, WHAT'S GOING ON?
WE NEED TO TALK, BUT NOT HERE. WHERE'S CESSILY?

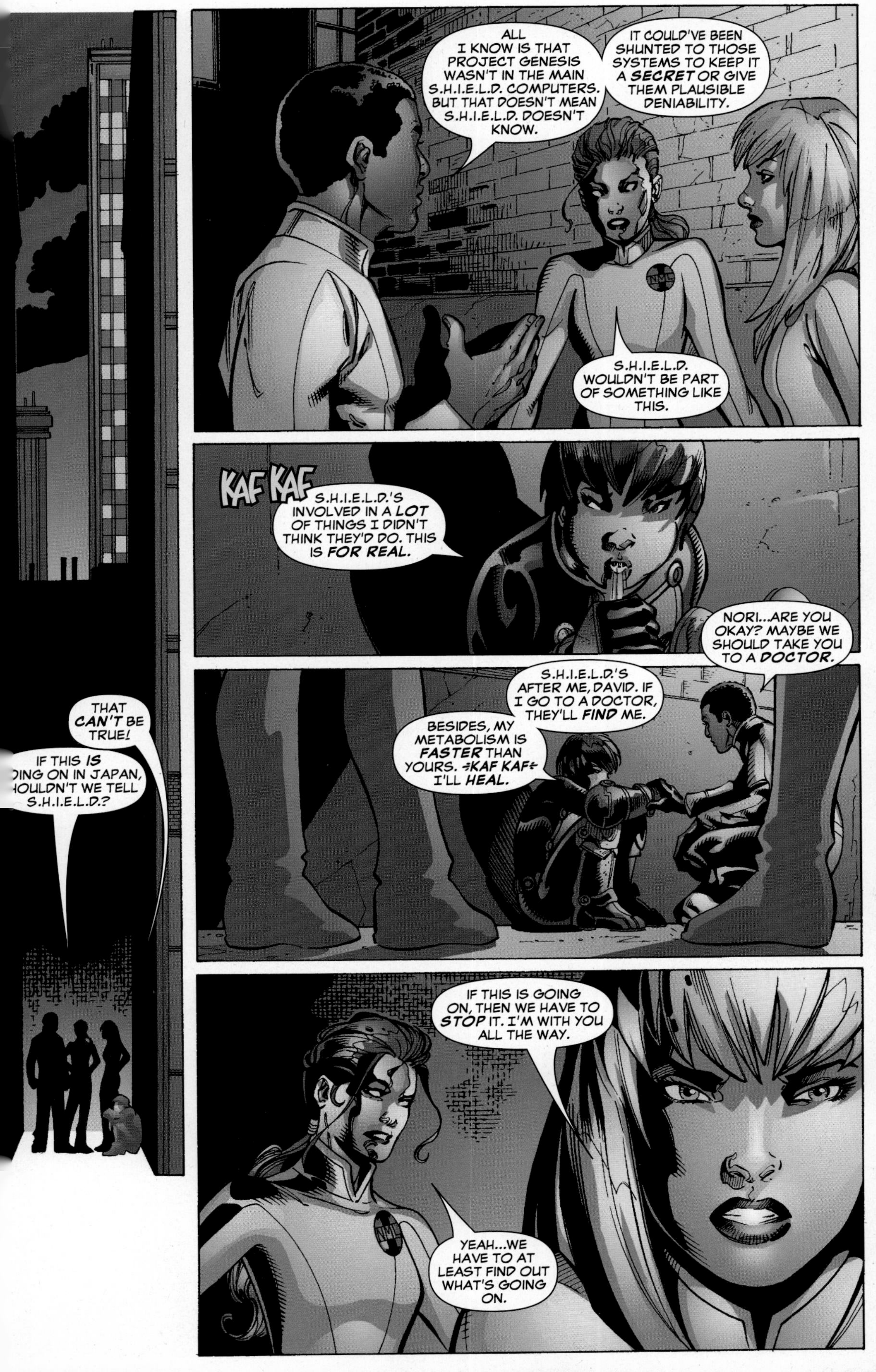
THAT CAN'T BE TRUE!
IF THIS IS OING ON IN JAPAN, HOULDN'T WE TELL S.H.I.E.L.D.?
ALL I KNOW IS THAT PROJECT GENESIS WASN'T IN THE MAIN S.H.I.E.L.D. COMPUTERS. BUT THAT DOESN'T MEAN S.H.I.E.L.D. DOESN'T KNOW.
IT COULD'VE BEEN SHUNTED TO THOSE SYSTEMS TO KEEP IT A SECRET OR GIVE THEM PLAUSIBLE DENIABILITY.
S.H.I.E.L.D. WOULDN'T BE PART OF SOMETHING LIKE THIS.
KAF KAF
S.H.I.E.L.D.'S INVOLVED IN A LOT OF THINGS I DIDN'T THINK THEY'D DO. THIS IS FOR REAL.
NORI...ARE YOU OKAY? MAYBE WE SHOULD TAKE YOU TO A DOCTOR.
S.H.I.E.L.D.'S AFTER ME, DAVID. IF I GO TO A DOCTOR, THEY'LL FIND ME.
BESIDES, MY METABOLISM IS FASTER THAN YOURS. ≠KAF KAF≠ I'LL HEAL.
IF THIS IS GOING ON, THEN WE HAVE TO STOP IT. I'M WITH YOU ALL THE WAY.
YEAH...WE HAVE TO AT LEAST FIND OUT WHAT'S GOING ON.

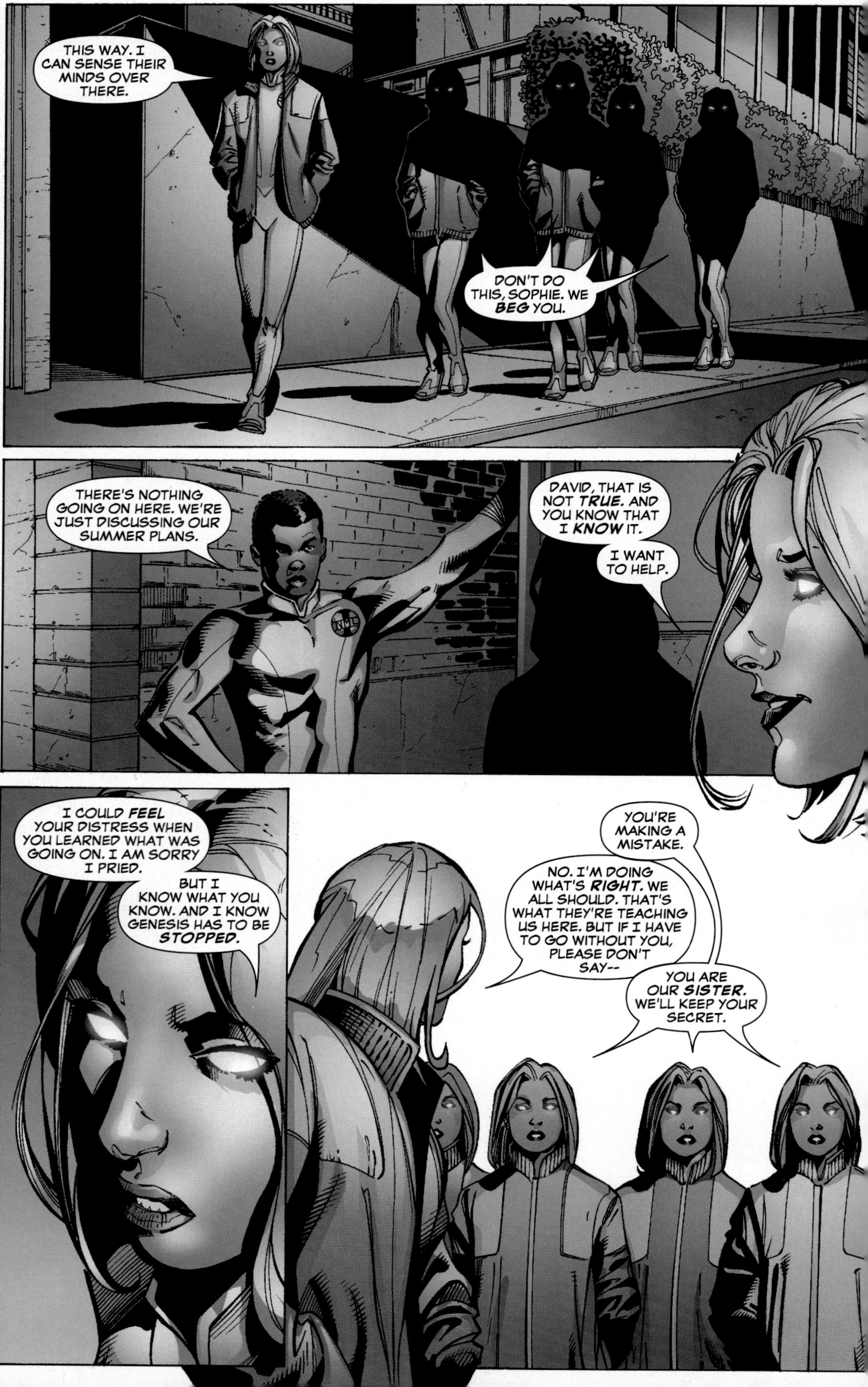
THIS WAY. I CAN SENSE THEIR MINDS OVER THERE.
DON'T DO THIS, SOPHIE. WE **BEG** YOU.
THERE'S NOTHING GOING ON HERE. WE'RE JUST DISCUSSING OUR SUMMER PLANS.
DAVID, THAT IS NOT **TRUE.** AND YOU KNOW THAT I **KNOW** IT.
I WANT TO HELP.
I COULD **FEEL** YOUR DISTRESS WHEN YOU LEARNED WHAT WAS GOING ON. I AM SORRY I PRIED.
BUT I KNOW WHAT YOU KNOW. AND I KNOW GENESIS HAS TO BE **STOPPED.**
YOU'RE MAKING A MISTAKE.
NO. I'M DOING WHAT'S **RIGHT.** WE ALL SHOULD. THAT'S WHAT THEY'RE TEACHING US HERE. BUT IF I HAVE TO GO WITHOUT YOU, PLEASE DON'T SAY--
YOU ARE OUR **SISTER.** WE'LL KEEP YOUR SECRET.

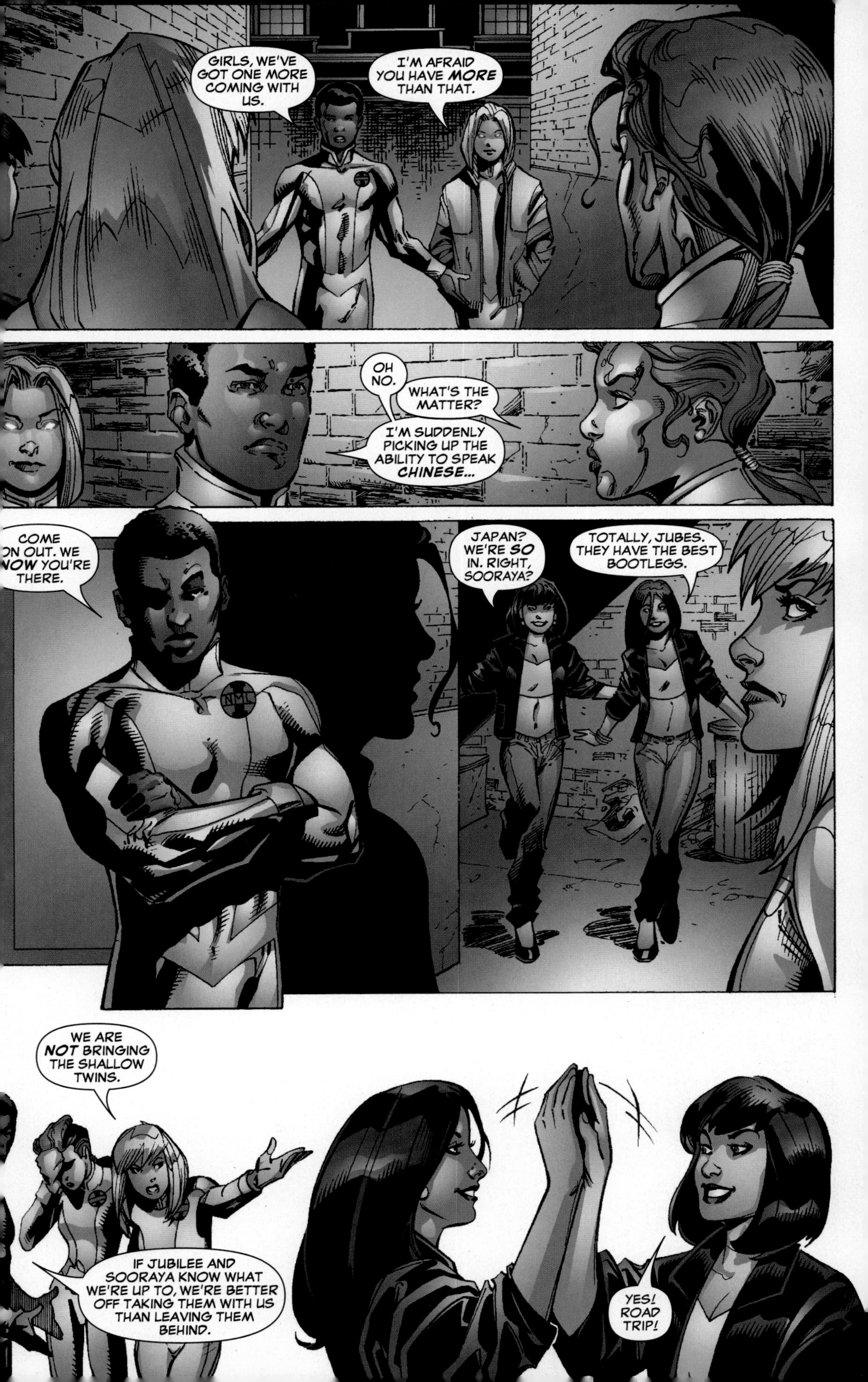

GIRLS, WE'VE GOT ONE MORE COMING WITH US.
I'M AFRAID YOU HAVE *MORE* THAN THAT.
OH NO.
WHAT'S THE MATTER?
I'M SUDDENLY PICKING UP THE ABILITY TO SPEAK *CHINESE*...
COME ON OUT. WE *NOW* YOU'RE THERE.
JAPAN? WE'RE *SO* IN. RIGHT, SOORAYA?
TOTALLY, JUBES. THEY HAVE THE BEST BOOTLEGS.
WE ARE *NOT* BRINGING THE SHALLOW TWINS.
IF JUBILEE AND SOORAYA KNOW WHAT WE'RE UP TO, WE'RE BETTER OFF TAKING THEM WITH US THAN LEAVING THEM BEHIND.
YES! ROAD TRIP!

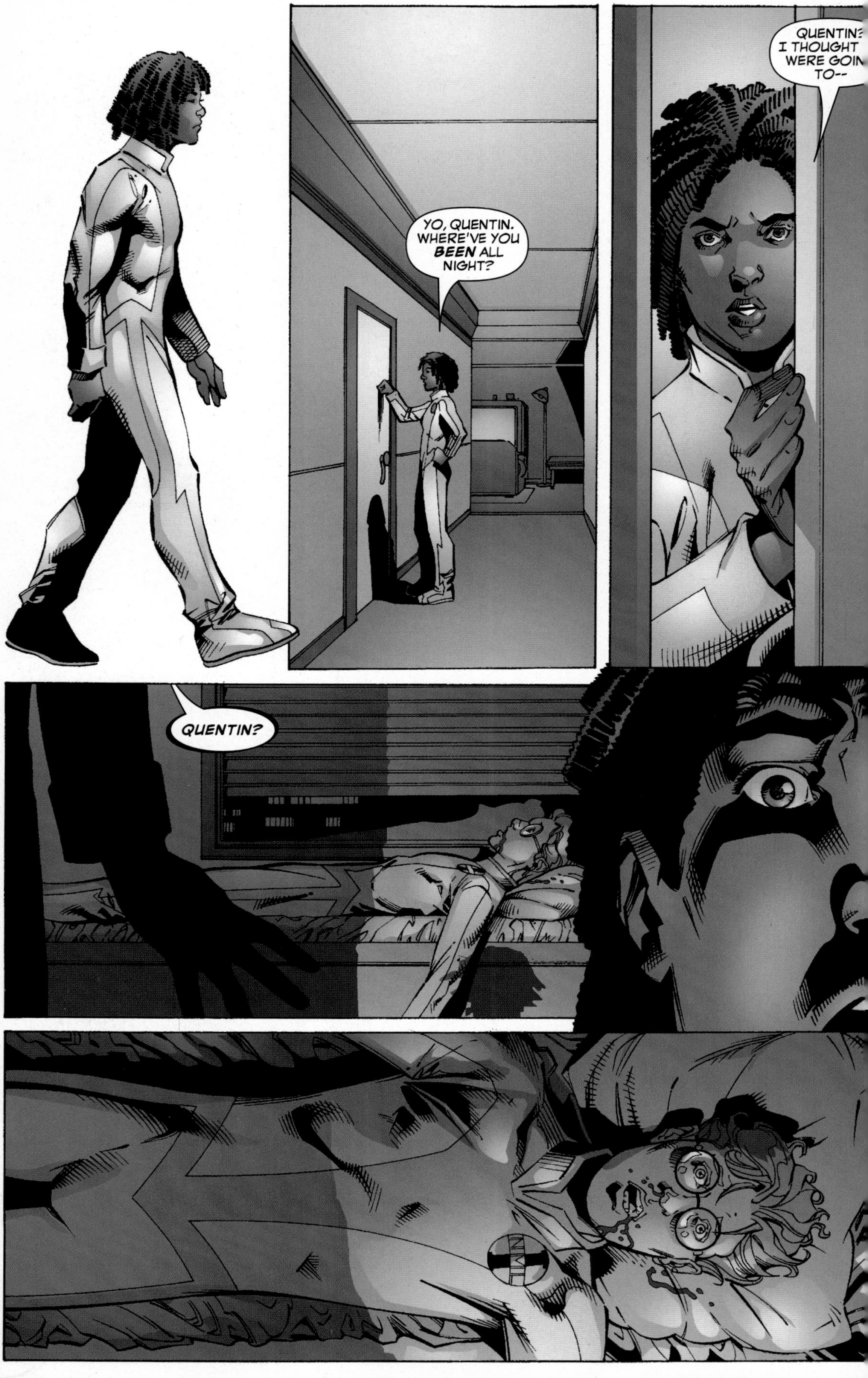
YO, QUENTIN. WHERE'VE YOU **BEEN** ALL NIGHT?
QUENTIN? I THOUGHT WERE GOIN TO--
QUENTIN?

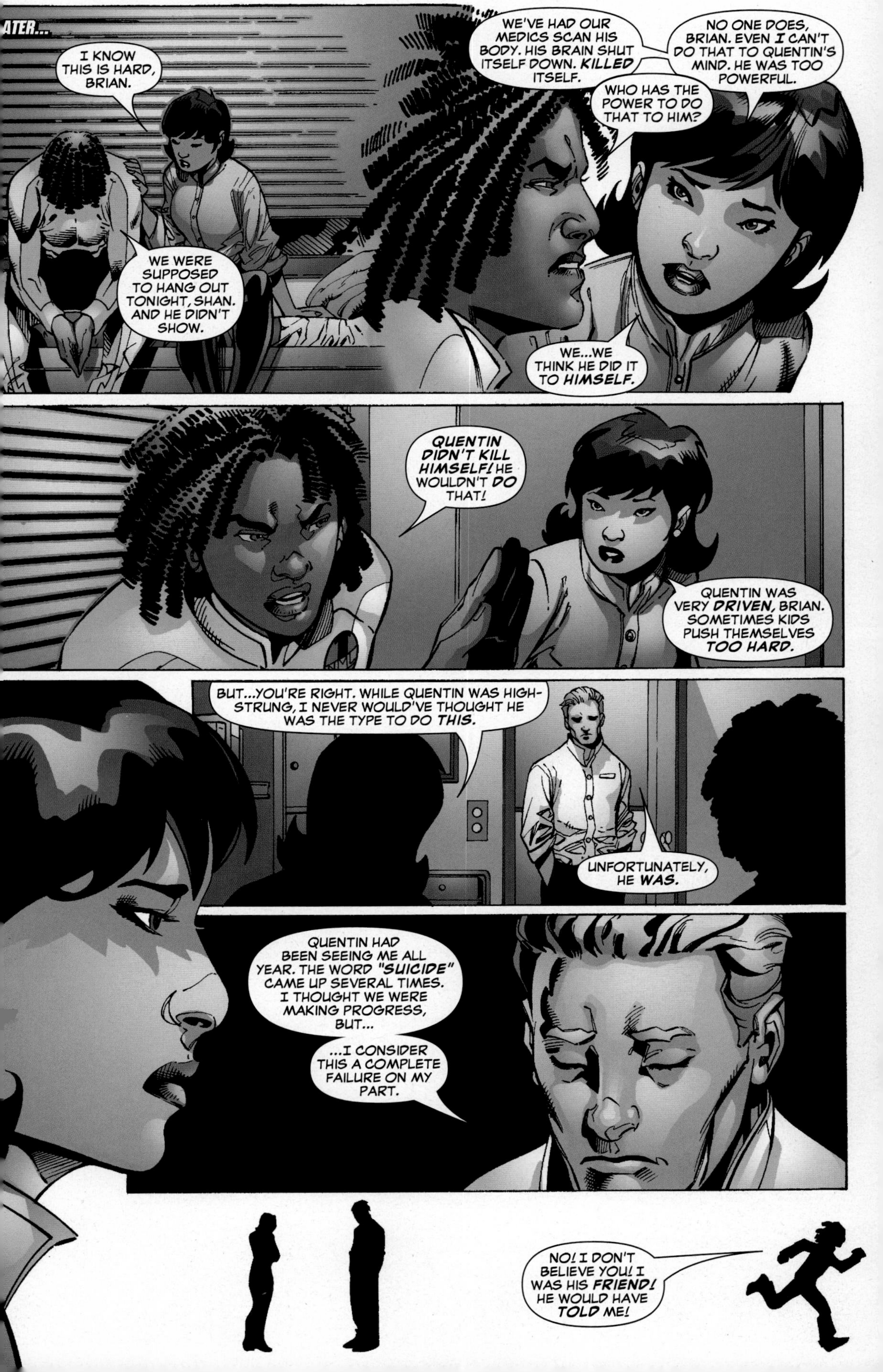
ATER...
I KNOW THIS IS HARD, BRIAN.
WE WERE SUPPOSED TO HANG OUT TONIGHT, SHAN. AND HE DIDN'T SHOW.
WE'VE HAD OUR MEDICS SCAN HIS BODY. HIS BRAIN SHUT ITSELF DOWN. KILLED ITSELF.
WHO HAS THE POWER TO DO THAT TO HIM?
NO ONE DOES, BRIAN. EVEN I CAN'T DO THAT TO QUENTIN'S MIND. HE WAS TOO POWERFUL.
WE...WE THINK HE DID IT TO HIMSELF.
QUENTIN DIDN'T KILL HIMSELF! HE WOULDN'T DO THAT!
QUENTIN WAS VERY DRIVEN, BRIAN. SOMETIMES KIDS PUSH THEMSELVES TOO HARD.
BUT...YOU'RE RIGHT. WHILE QUENTIN WAS HIGH-STRUNG, I NEVER WOULD'VE THOUGHT HE WAS THE TYPE TO DO THIS.
UNFORTUNATELY, HE WAS.
QUENTIN HAD BEEN SEEING ME ALL YEAR. THE WORD "SUICIDE" CAME UP SEVERAL TIMES. I THOUGHT WE WERE MAKING PROGRESS, BUT...
...I CONSIDER THIS A COMPLETE FAILURE ON MY PART.
NO! I DON'T BELIEVE YOU! I WAS HIS FRIEND! HE WOULD HAVE TOLD ME!

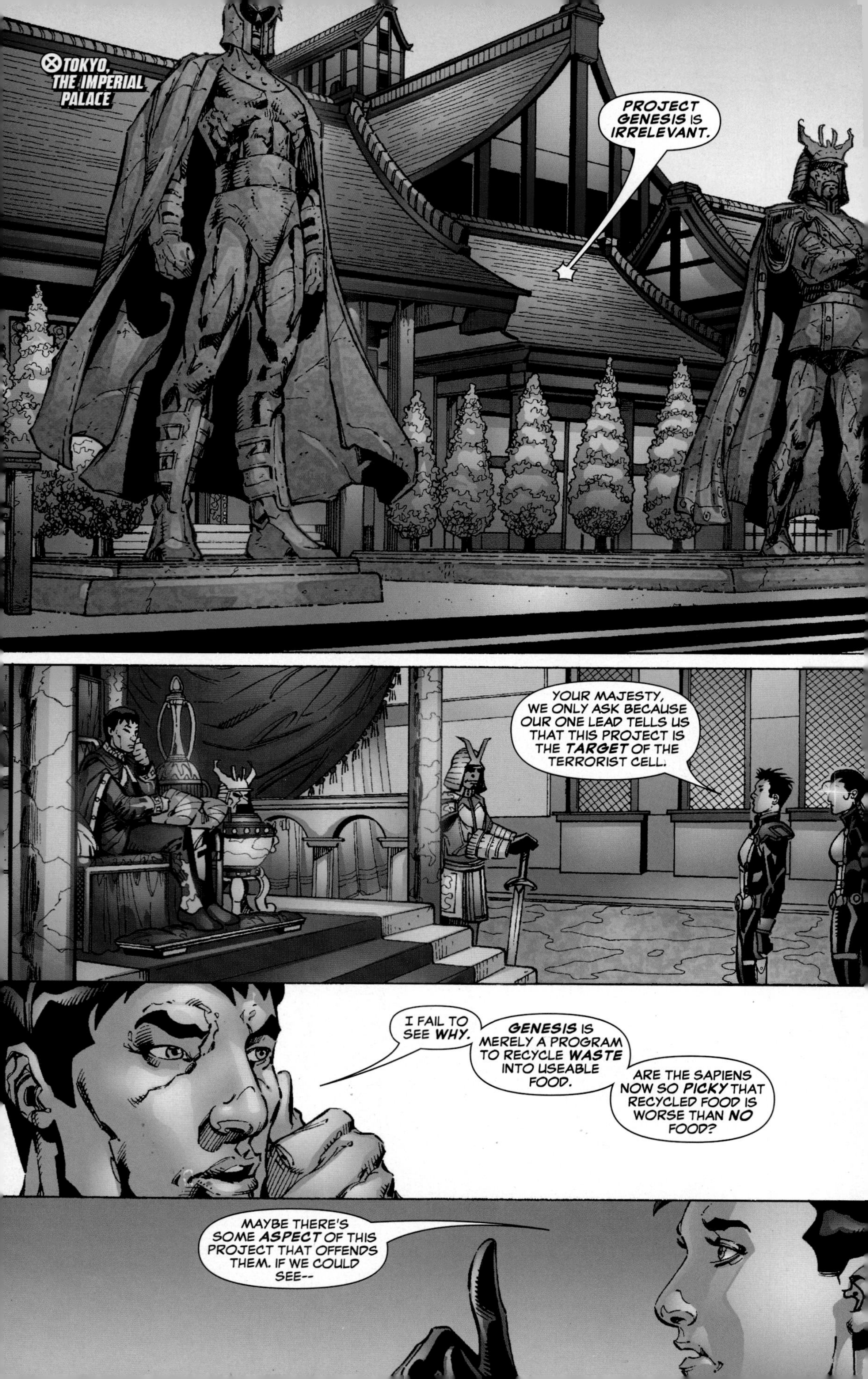
TOKYO, THE IMPERIAL PALACE
PROJECT GENESIS IS IRRELEVANT.
YOUR MAJESTY, WE ONLY ASK BECAUSE OUR ONE LEAD TELLS US THAT THIS PROJECT IS THE TARGET OF THE TERRORIST CELL.
I FAIL TO SEE WHY.
GENESIS IS MERELY A PROGRAM TO RECYCLE WASTE INTO USEABLE FOOD.
ARE THE SAPIENS NOW SO PICKY THAT RECYCLED FOOD IS WORSE THAN NO FOOD?
MAYBE THERE'S SOME ASPECT OF THIS PROJECT THAT OFFENDS THEM. IF WE COULD SEE--

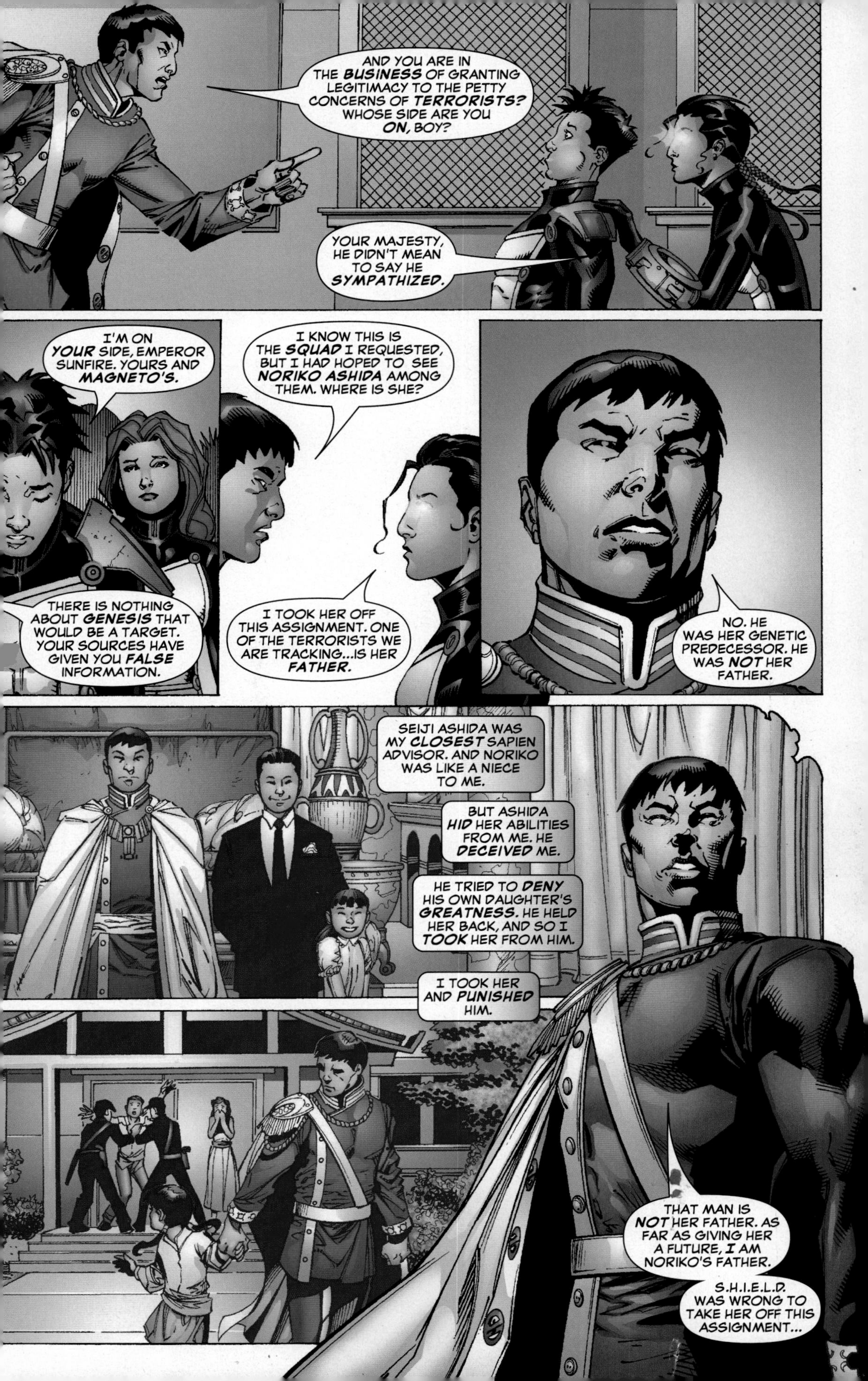

AND YOU ARE IN THE BUSINESS OF GRANTING LEGITIMACY TO THE PETTY CONCERNS OF TERRORISTS? WHOSE SIDE ARE YOU ON, BOY?
YOUR MAJESTY, HE DIDN'T MEAN TO SAY HE SYMPATHIZED.
I'M ON YOUR SIDE, EMPEROR SUNFIRE. YOURS AND MAGNETO'S.
THERE IS NOTHING ABOUT GENESIS THAT WOULD BE A TARGET. YOUR SOURCES HAVE GIVEN YOU FALSE INFORMATION.
I KNOW THIS IS THE SQUAD I REQUESTED, BUT I HAD HOPED TO SEE NORIKO ASHIDA AMONG THEM. WHERE IS SHE?
I TOOK HER OFF THIS ASSIGNMENT. ONE OF THE TERRORISTS WE ARE TRACKING...IS HER FATHER.
NO. HE WAS HER GENETIC PREDECESSOR. HE WAS NOT HER FATHER.
SEIJI ASHIDA WAS MY CLOSEST SAPIEN ADVISOR. AND NORIKO WAS LIKE A NIECE TO ME.
BUT ASHIDA HID HER ABILITIES FROM ME. HE DECEIVED ME.
HE TRIED TO DENY HIS OWN DAUGHTER'S GREATNESS. HE HELD HER BACK, AND SO I TOOK HER FROM HIM.
I TOOK HER AND PUNISHED HIM.
THAT MAN IS NOT HER FATHER. AS FAR AS GIVING HER A FUTURE, I AM NORIKO'S FATHER.
S.H.I.E.L.D. WAS WRONG TO TAKE HER OFF THIS ASSIGNMENT...

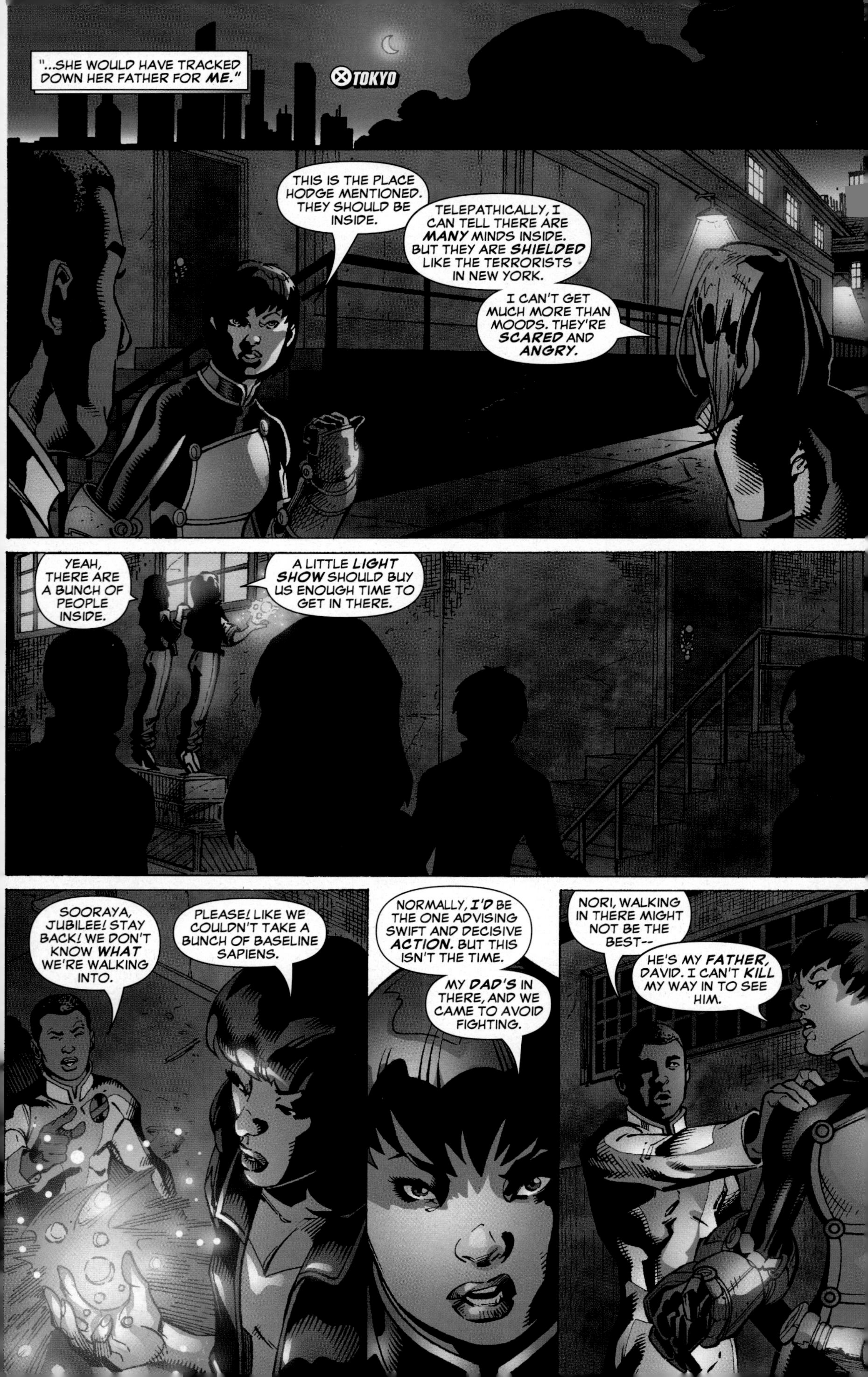
"...SHE WOULD HAVE TRACKED DOWN HER FATHER FOR ME."
TOKYO
THIS IS THE PLACE HODGE MENTIONED. THEY SHOULD BE INSIDE.
TELEPATHICALLY, I CAN TELL THERE ARE MANY MINDS INSIDE. BUT THEY ARE SHIELDED LIKE THE TERRORISTS IN NEW YORK.
I CAN'T GET MUCH MORE THAN MOODS. THEY'RE SCARED AND ANGRY.
YEAH, THERE ARE A BUNCH OF PEOPLE INSIDE.
A LITTLE LIGHT SHOW SHOULD BUY US ENOUGH TIME TO GET IN THERE.
SOORAYA, JUBILEE! STAY BACK! WE DON'T KNOW WHAT WE'RE WALKING INTO.
PLEASE! LIKE WE COULDN'T TAKE A BUNCH OF BASELINE SAPIENS.
NORMALLY, I'D BE THE ONE ADVISING SWIFT AND DECISIVE ACTION. BUT THIS ISN'T THE TIME.
MY DAD'S IN THERE, AND WE CAME TO AVOID FIGHTING.
NORI, WALKING IN THERE MIGHT NOT BE THE BEST--
HE'S MY FATHER, DAVID. I CAN'T KILL MY WAY IN TO SEE HIM.

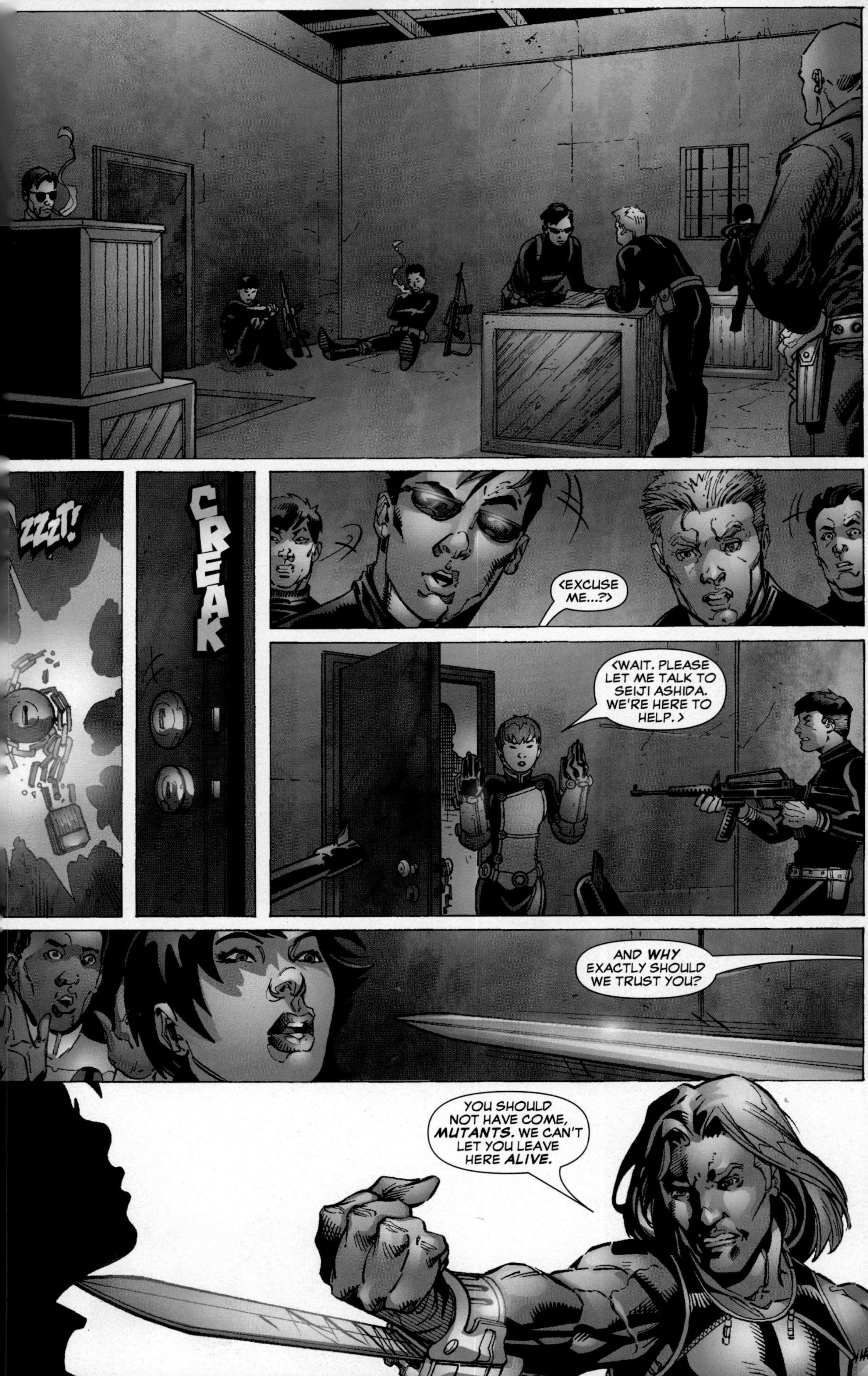
ZZzT!
CREAK
<EXCUSE ME...?>
<WAIT. PLEASE LET ME TALK TO SEIJI ASHIDA. WE'RE HERE TO HELP.>
AND WHY EXACTLY SHOULD WE TRUST YOU?
YOU SHOULD NOT HAVE COME, MUTANTS. WE CAN'T LET YOU LEAVE HERE ALIVE.

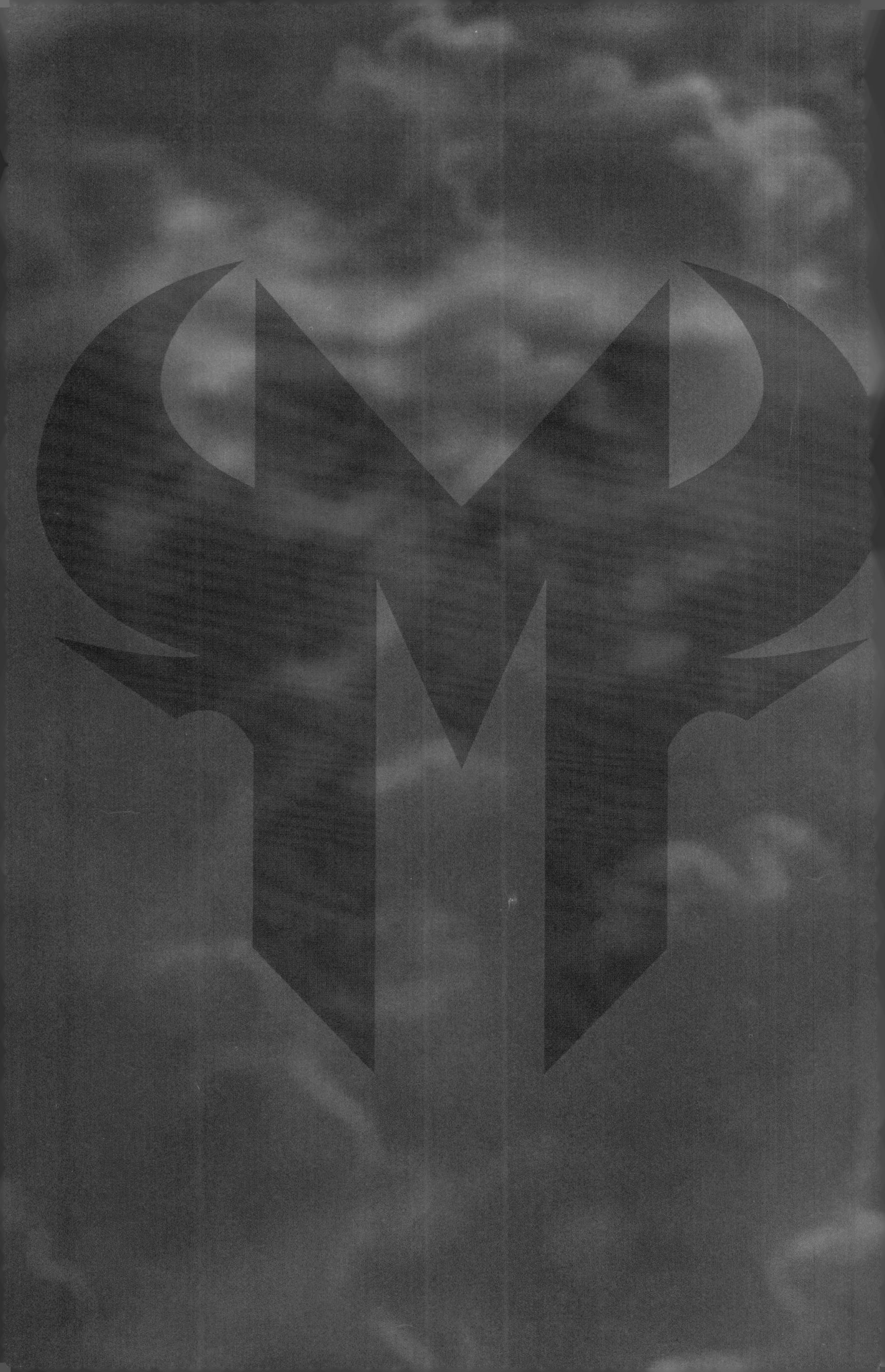

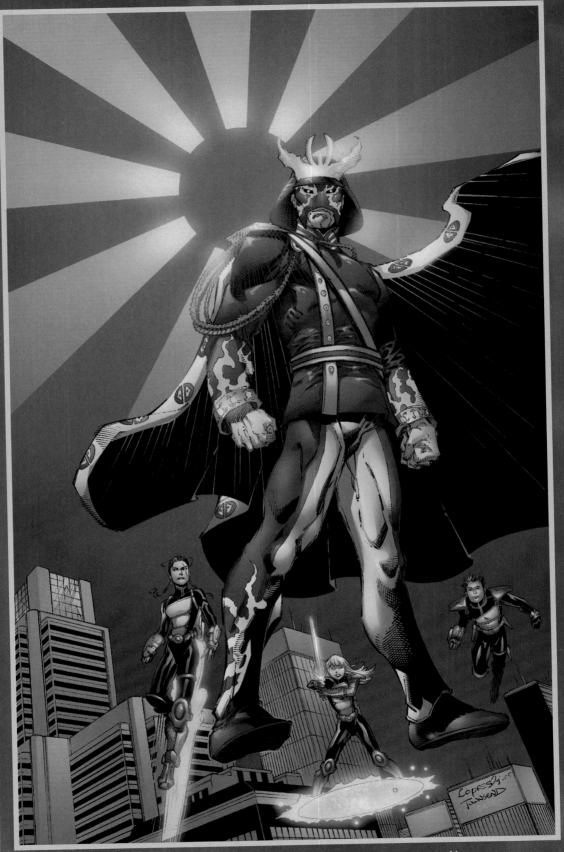

NEW X-MEN: ACADEMY X #18

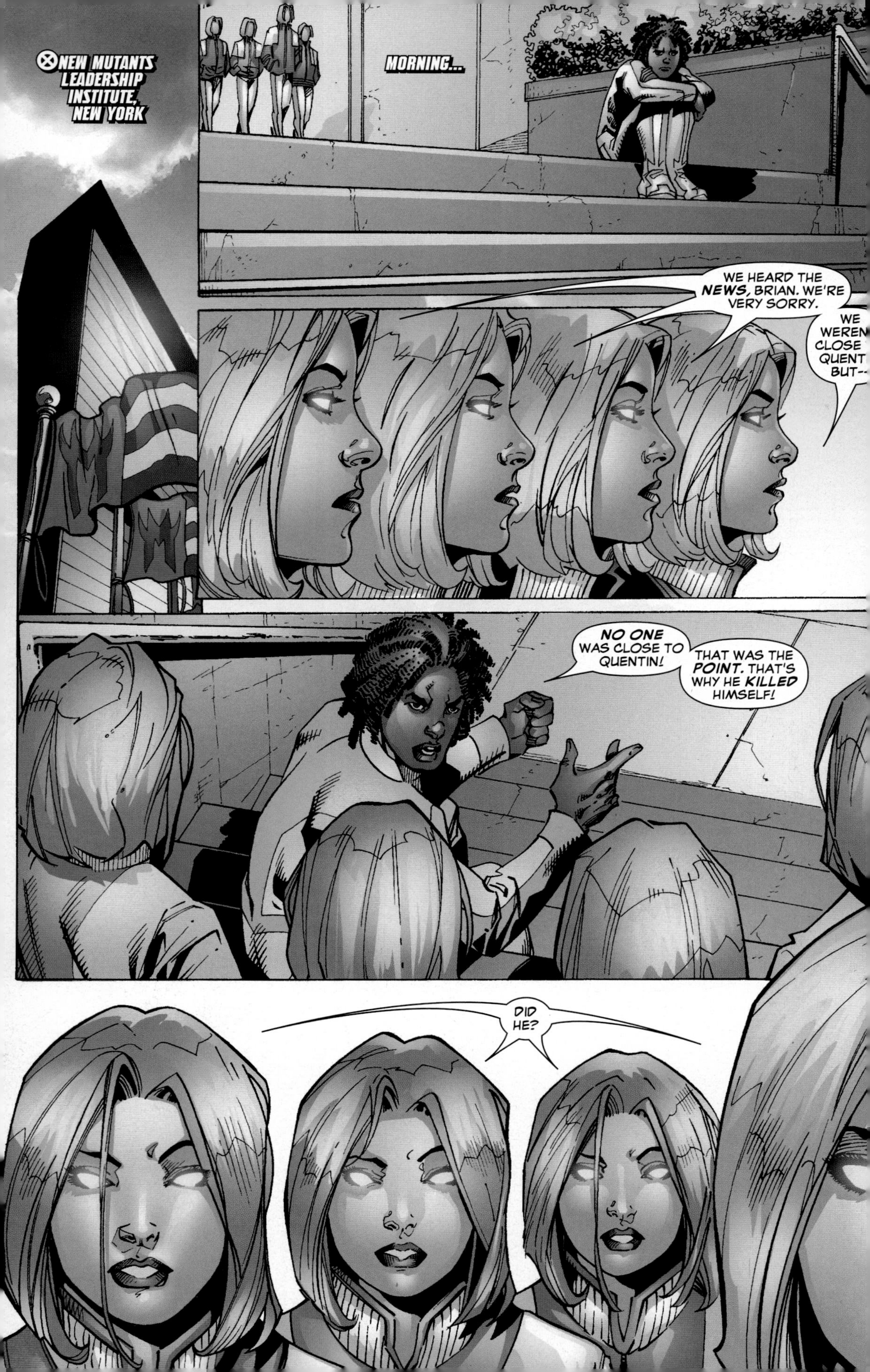
NEW MUTANTS LEADERSHIP INSTITUTE, NEW YORK
MORNING...
WE HEARD THE NEWS, BRIAN. WE'RE VERY SORRY.
WE WEREN CLOSE QUENT BUT--
NO ONE WAS CLOSE TO QUENTIN!
THAT WAS THE POINT. THAT'S WHY HE KILLED HIMSELF!
DID HE?

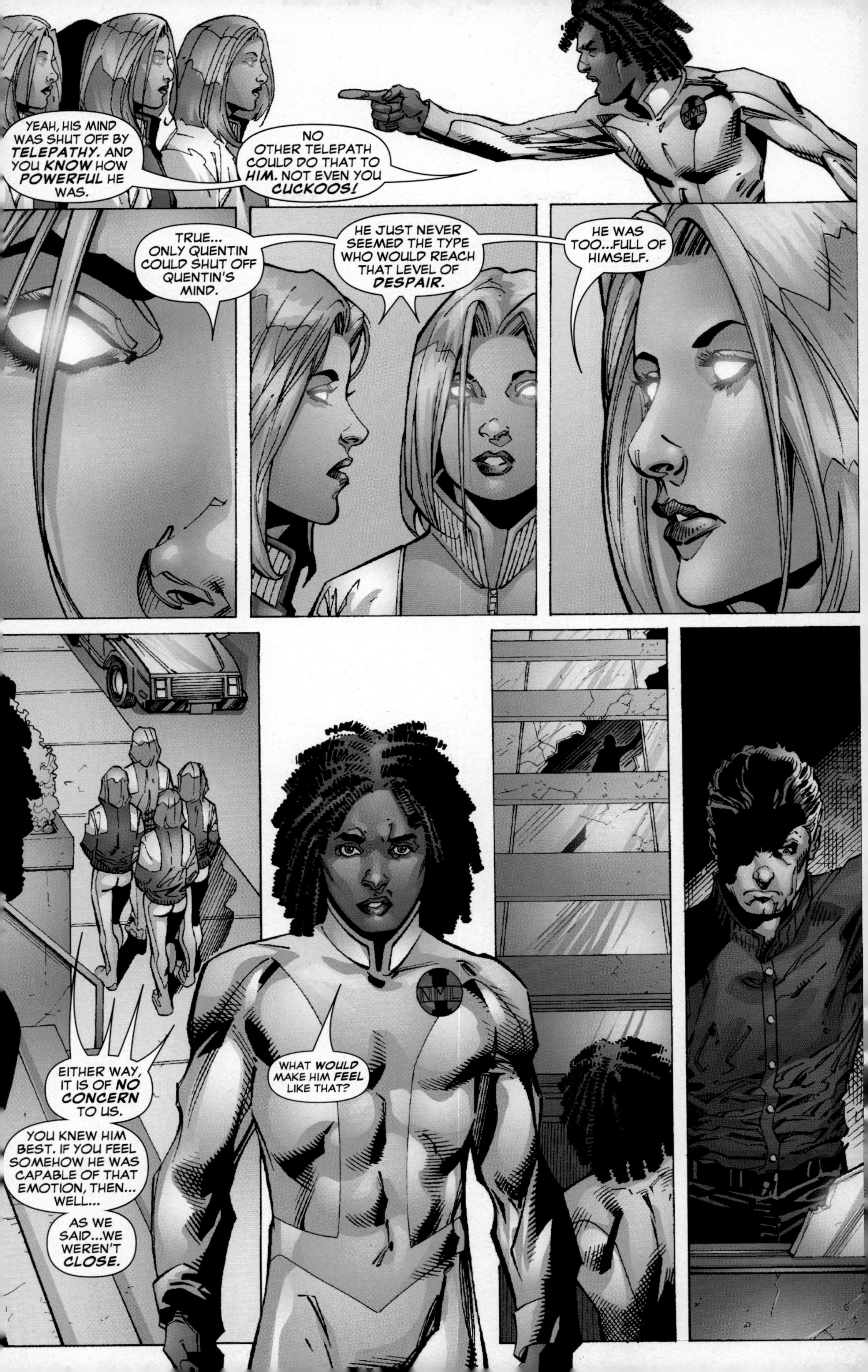
YEAH, HIS MIND WAS SHUT OFF BY TELEPATHY. AND YOU KNOW HOW POWERFUL HE WAS.
NO OTHER TELEPATH COULD DO THAT TO HIM. NOT EVEN YOU CUCKOOS!
TRUE... ONLY QUENTIN COULD SHUT OFF QUENTIN'S MIND.
HE JUST NEVER SEEMED THE TYPE WHO WOULD REACH THAT LEVEL OF DESPAIR.
HE WAS TOO...FULL OF HIMSELF.
EITHER WAY, IT IS OF NO CONCERN TO US.
YOU KNEW HIM BEST. IF YOU FEEL SOMEHOW HE WAS CAPABLE OF THAT EMOTION, THEN... WELL...
AS WE SAID...WE WEREN'T CLOSE.
WHAT WOULD MAKE HIM FEEL LIKE THAT?

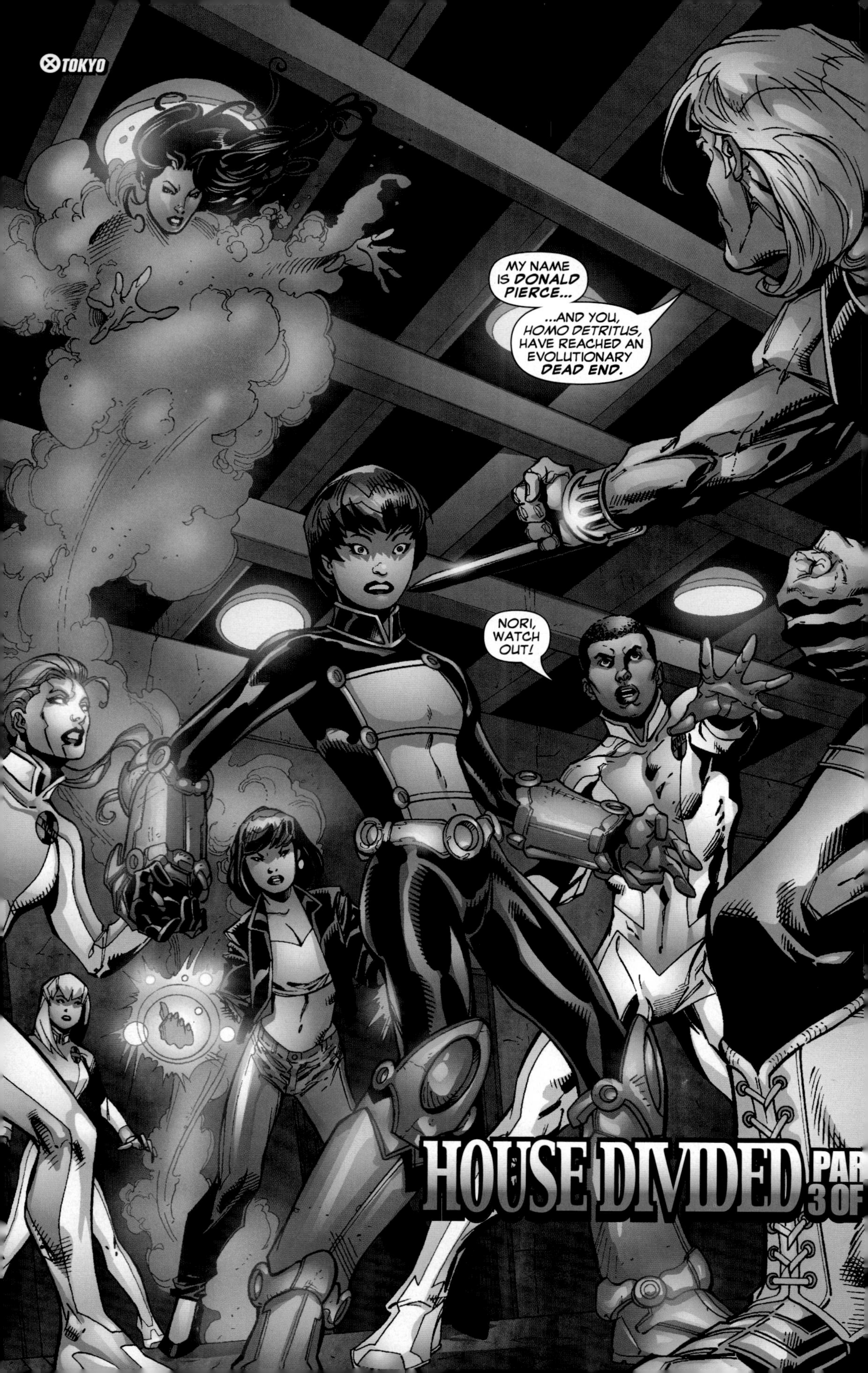
TOKYO
MY NAME IS DONALD PIERCE...
...AND YOU, HOMO DETRITUS, HAVE REACHED AN EVOLUTIONARY DEAD END.
NORI, WATCH OUT!
HOUSE DIVIDED PAR
3 OF

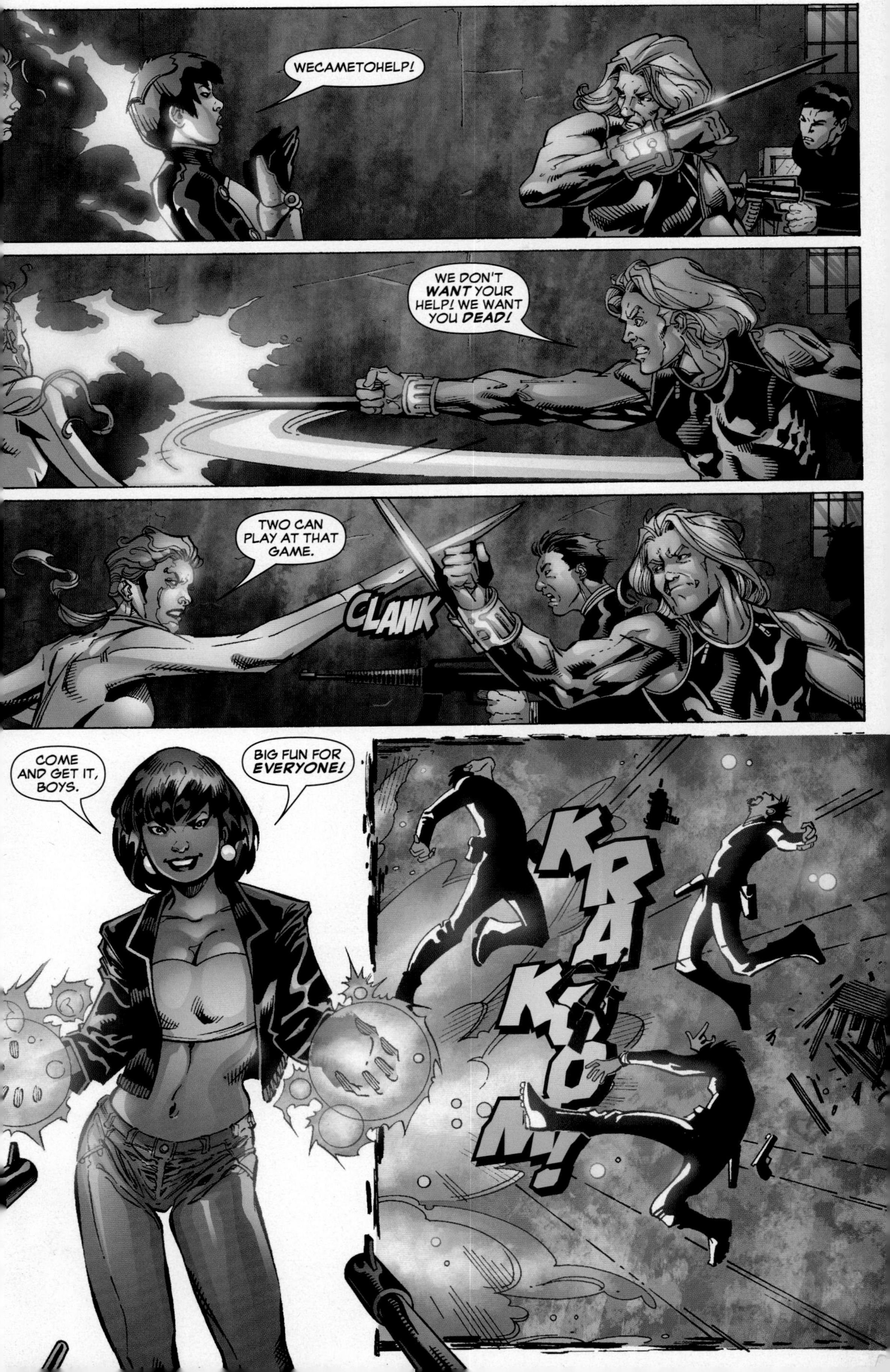
WECAMETOHELP!
WE DON'T WANT YOUR HELP! WE WANT YOU DEAD!
TWO CAN PLAY AT THAT GAME.
CLANK
COME AND GET IT, BOYS.
BIG FUN FOR EVERYONE!
KRAKOOM!

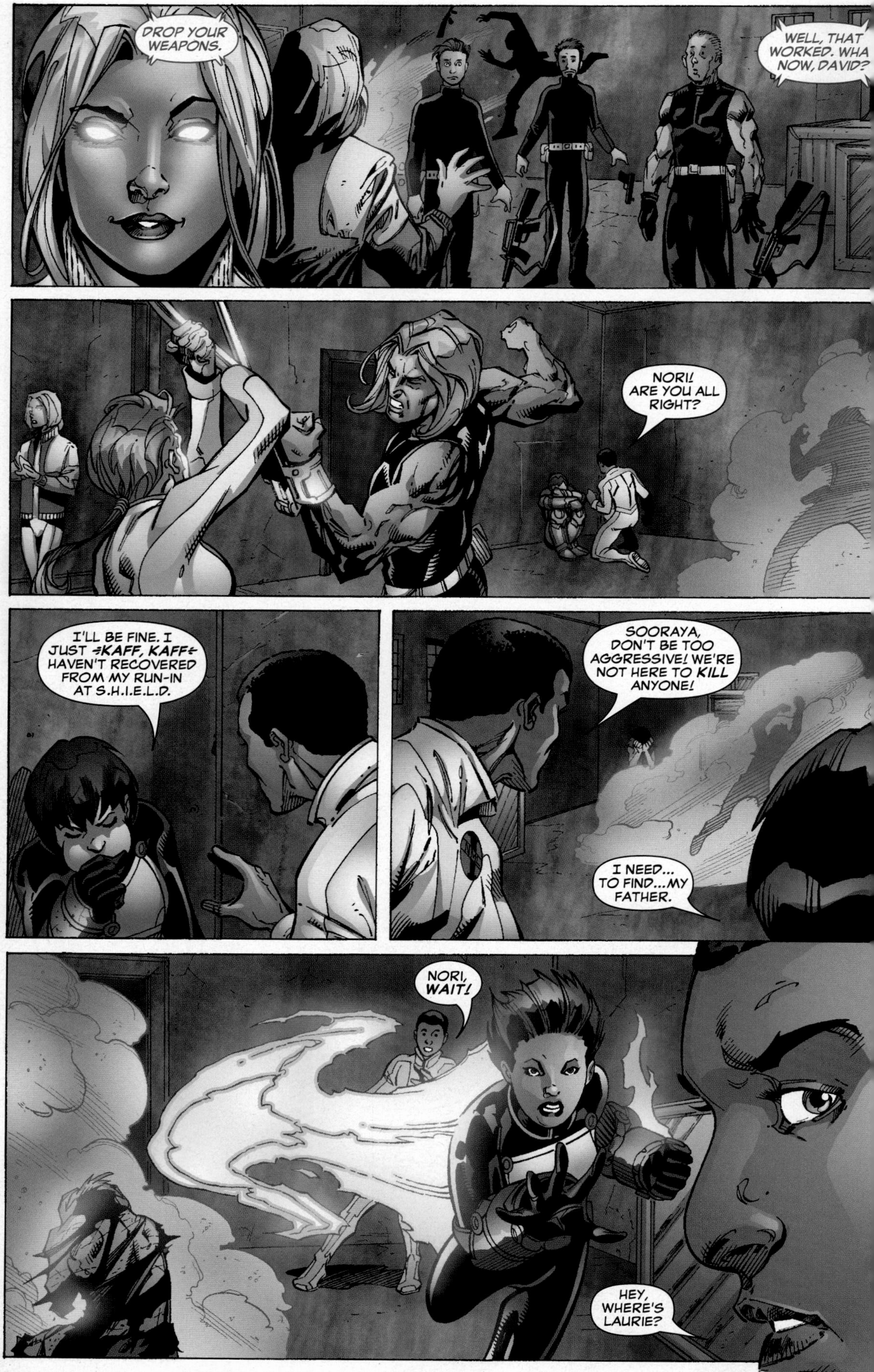
DROP YOUR WEAPONS.
WELL, THAT WORKED. WHA NOW, DAVID?
NORI! ARE YOU ALL RIGHT?
I'LL BE FINE. I JUST ≠KAFF, KAFF≠ HAVEN'T RECOVERED FROM MY RUN-IN AT S.H.I.E.L.D.
SOORAYA, DON'T BE TOO AGGRESSIVE! WE'RE NOT HERE TO KILL ANYONE!
I NEED... TO FIND... MY FATHER.
NORI, WAIT!
HEY, WHERE'S LAURIE?

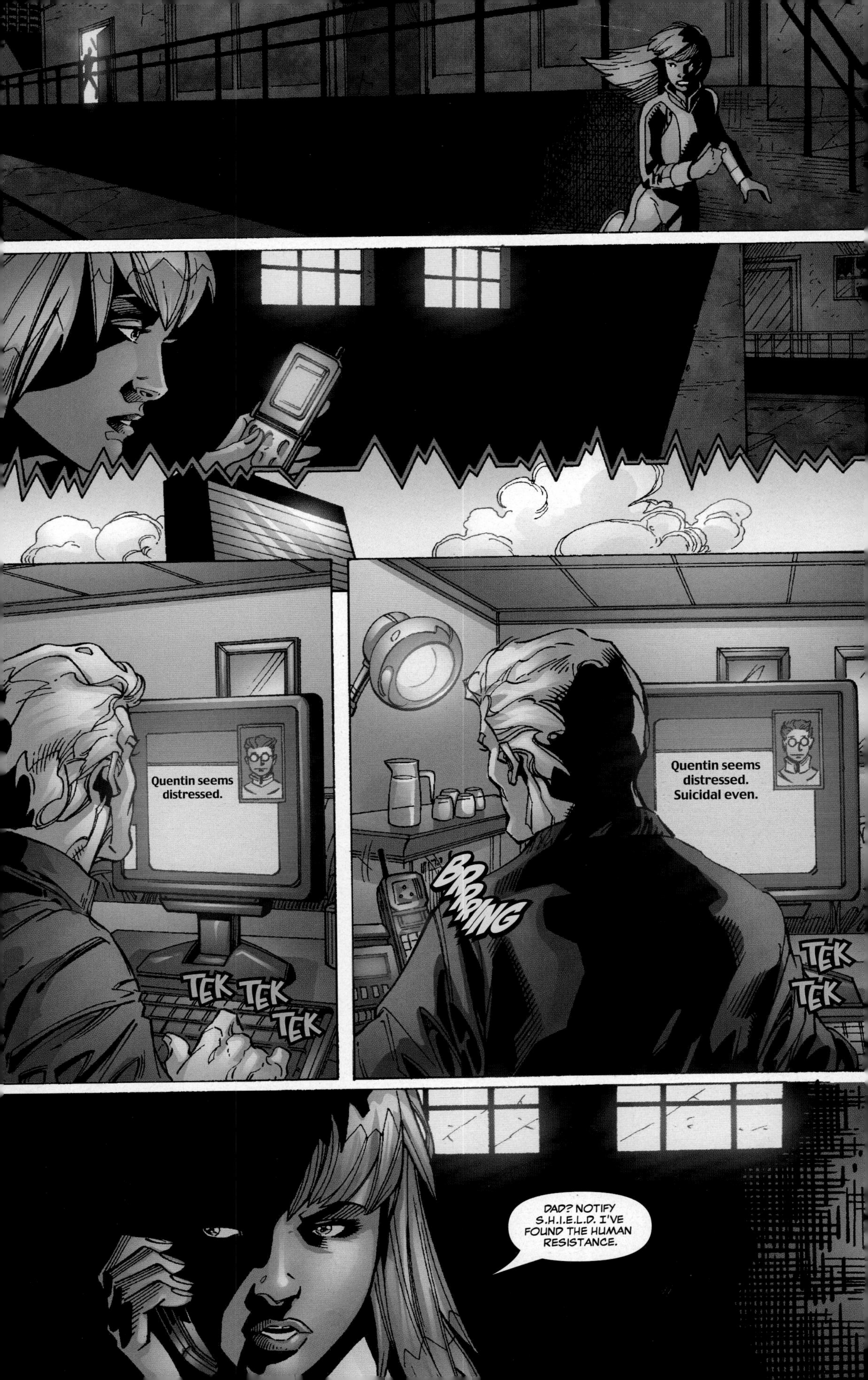
Quentin seems distressed.
TEK TEK TEK
Quentin seems distressed. Suicidal even.
BRRRING
TEK TEK
DAD? NOTIFY S.H.I.E.L.D. I'VE FOUND THE HUMAN RESISTANCE.

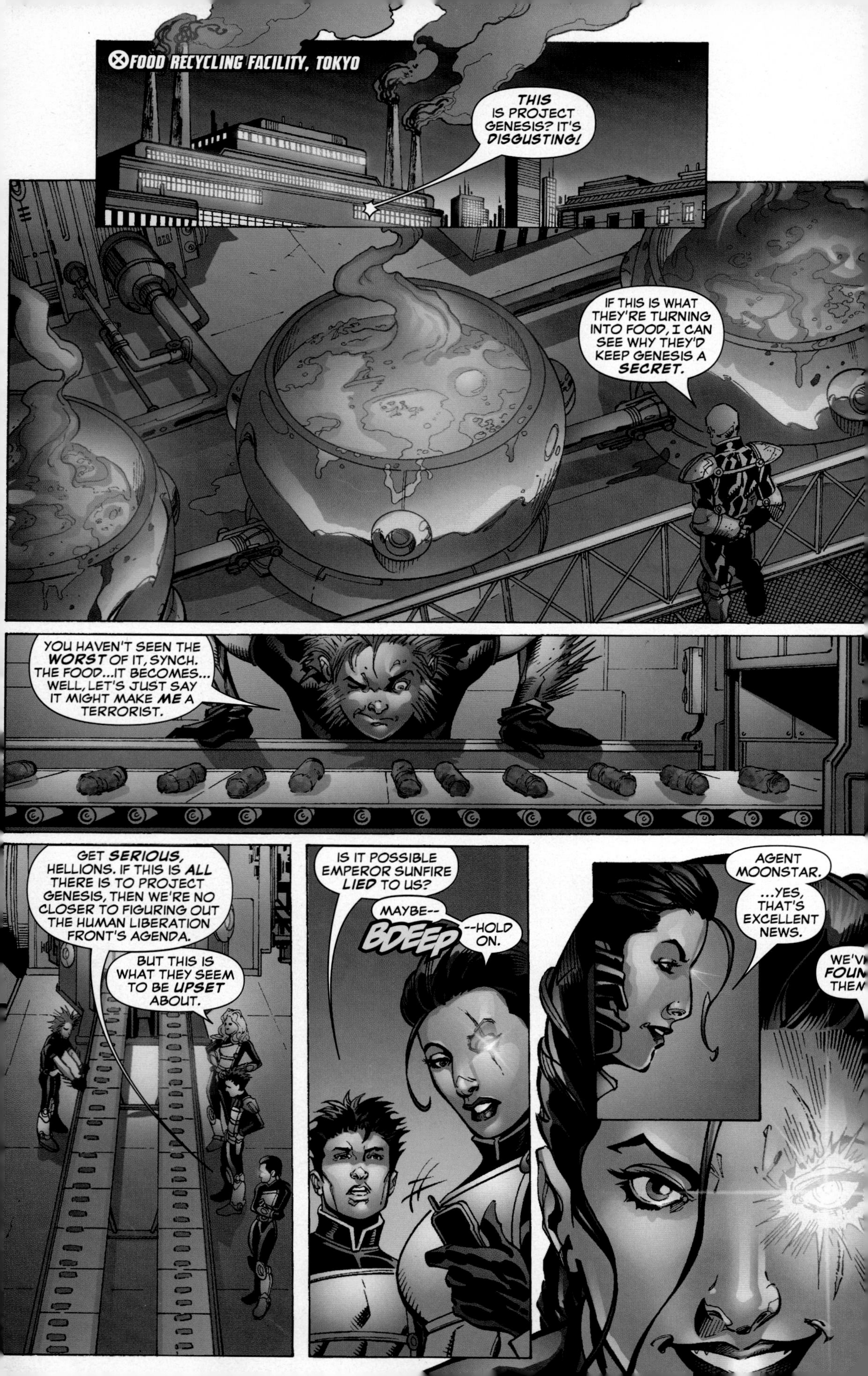
FOOD RECYCLING FACILITY, TOKYO
THIS IS PROJECT GENESIS? IT'S DISGUSTING!
IF THIS IS WHAT THEY'RE TURNING INTO FOOD, I CAN SEE WHY THEY'D KEEP GENESIS A SECRET.
YOU HAVEN'T SEEN THE WORST OF IT, SYNCH. THE FOOD...IT BECOMES... WELL, LET'S JUST SAY IT MIGHT MAKE ME A TERRORIST.
GET SERIOUS, HELLIONS. IF THIS IS ALL THERE IS TO PROJECT GENESIS, THEN WE'RE NO CLOSER TO FIGURING OUT THE HUMAN LIBERATION FRONT'S AGENDA.
BUT THIS IS WHAT THEY SEEM TO BE UPSET ABOUT.
IS IT POSSIBLE EMPEROR SUNFIRE LIED TO US?
MAYBE--
BDEEP
--HOLD ON.
AGENT MOONSTAR.
...YES, THAT'S EXCELLENT NEWS.

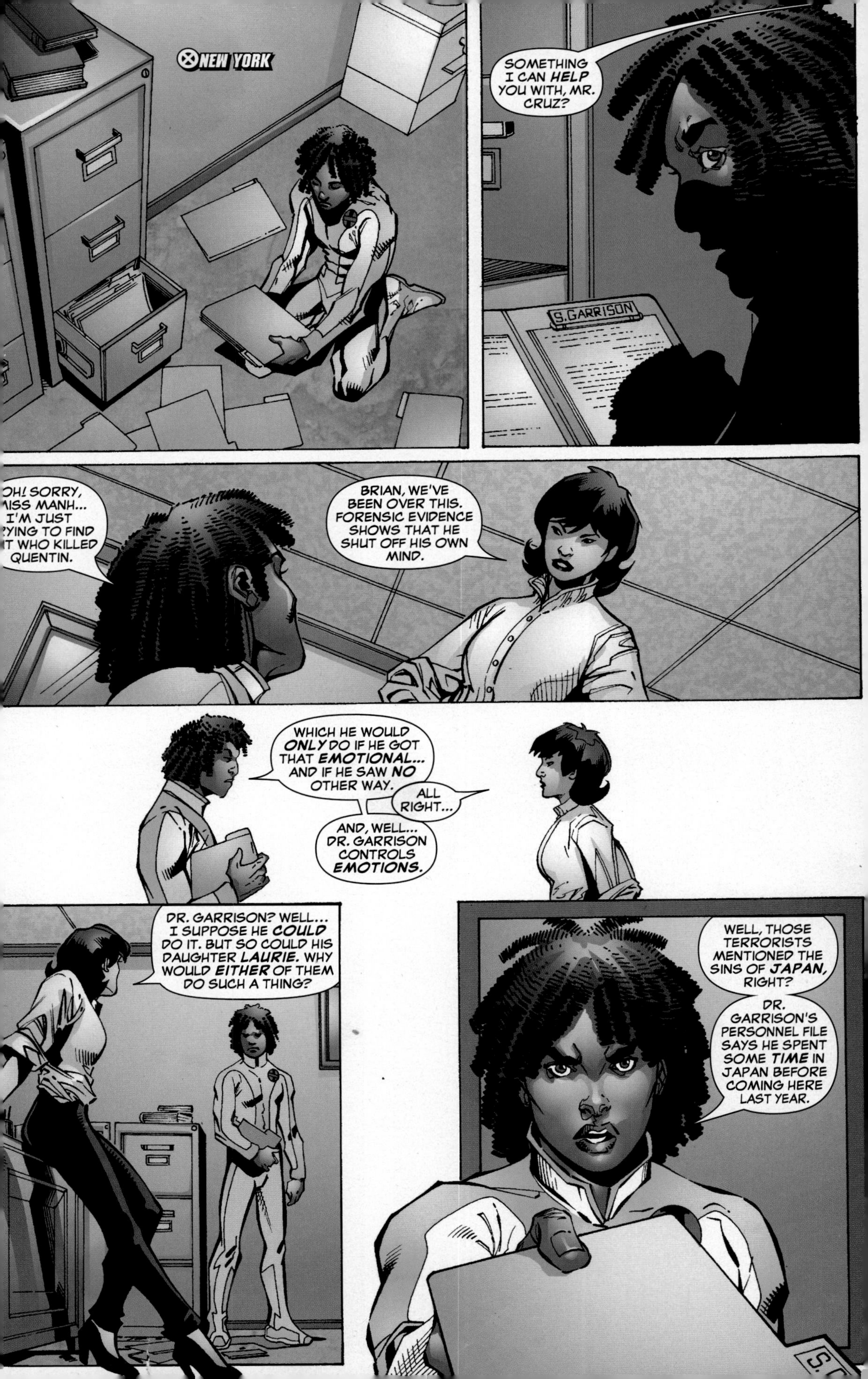
NEW YORK
SOMETHING I CAN HELP YOU WITH, MR. CRUZ?
S. GARRISON
OH! SORRY, ISS MANH... I'M JUST RYING TO FIND T WHO KILLED QUENTIN.
BRIAN, WE'VE BEEN OVER THIS. FORENSIC EVIDENCE SHOWS THAT HE SHUT OFF HIS OWN MIND.
WHICH HE WOULD ONLY DO IF HE GOT THAT EMOTIONAL... AND IF HE SAW NO OTHER WAY.
ALL RIGHT...
AND, WELL... DR. GARRISON CONTROLS EMOTIONS.
DR. GARRISON? WELL... I SUPPOSE HE COULD DO IT. BUT SO COULD HIS DAUGHTER LAURIE. WHY WOULD EITHER OF THEM DO SUCH A THING?
WELL, THOSE TERRORISTS MENTIONED THE SINS OF JAPAN, RIGHT?
DR. GARRISON'S PERSONNEL FILE SAYS HE SPENT SOME TIME IN JAPAN BEFORE COMING HERE LAST YEAR.

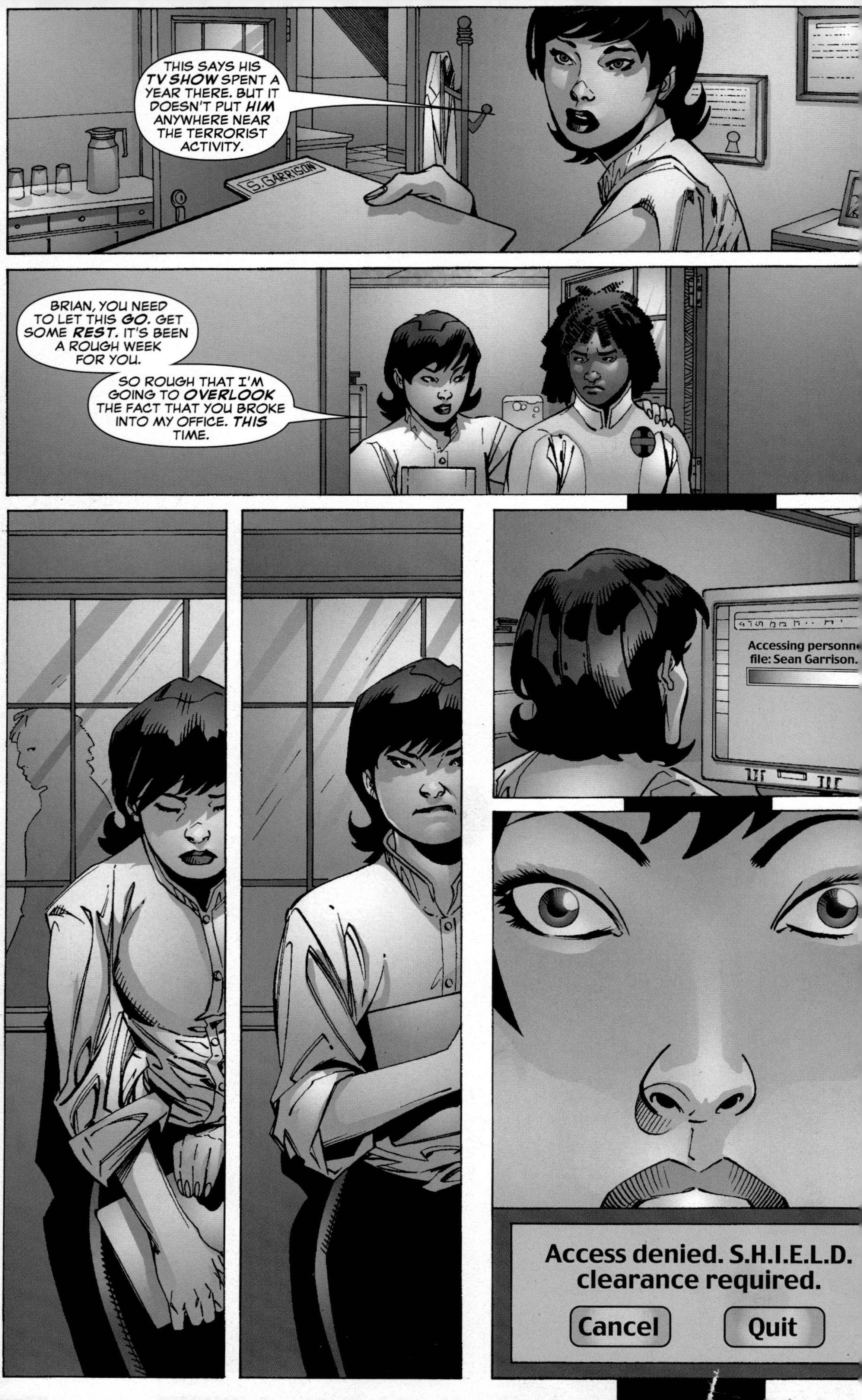
THIS SAYS HIS TV SHOW SPENT A YEAR THERE. BUT IT DOESN'T PUT HIM ANYWHERE NEAR THE TERRORIST ACTIVITY.
S.GARRISON
BRIAN, YOU NEED TO LET THIS GO. GET SOME REST. IT'S BEEN A ROUGH WEEK FOR YOU.
SO ROUGH THAT I'M GOING TO OVERLOOK THE FACT THAT YOU BROKE INTO MY OFFICE. THIS TIME.
Accessing personne
file: Sean Garrison.
Access denied. S.H.I.E.L.D. clearance required.
Cancel
Quit

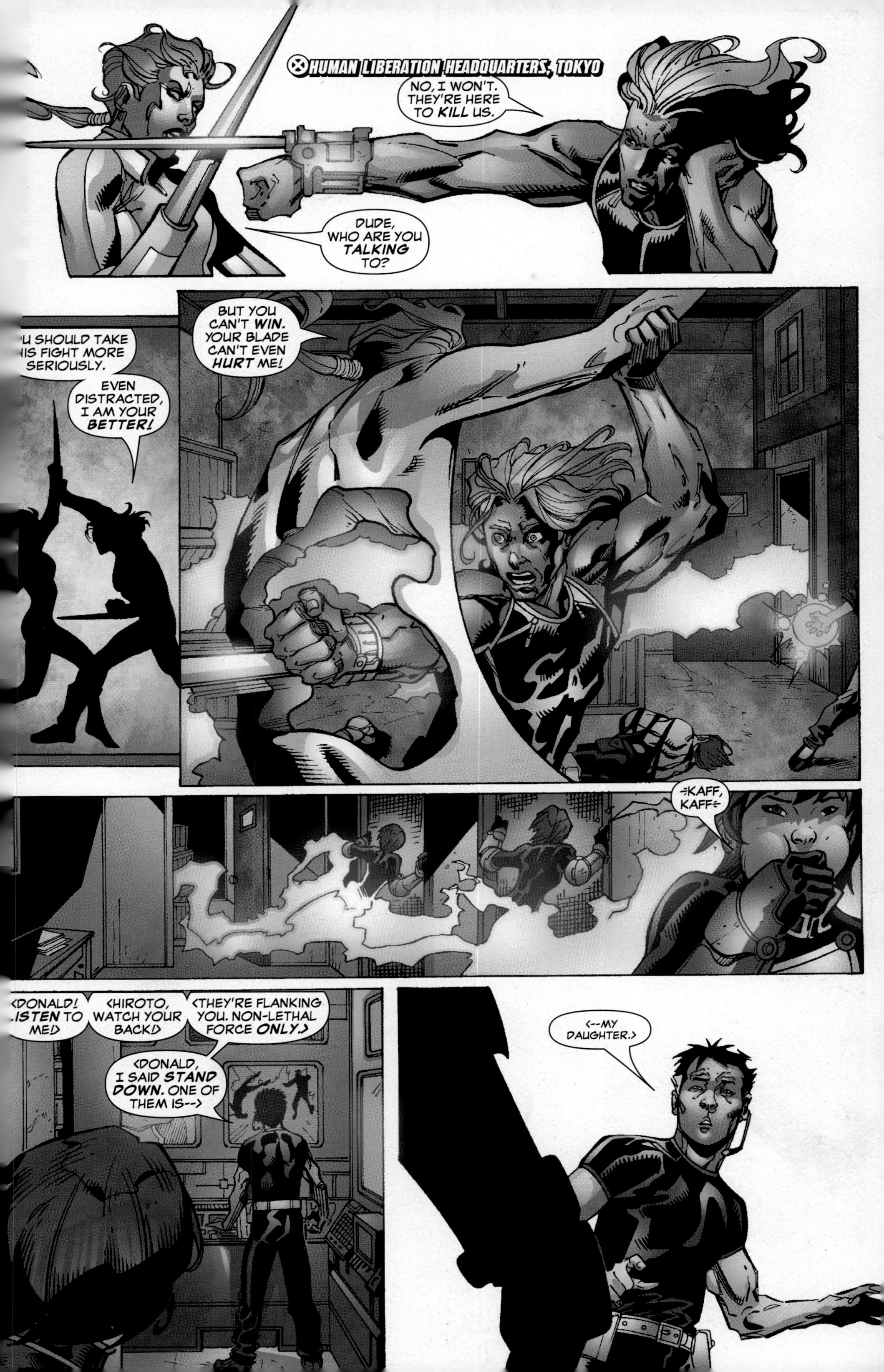
HUMAN LIBERATION HEADQUARTERS, TOKYO
NO, I WON'T. THEY'RE HERE TO KILL US.
DUDE, WHO ARE YOU TALKING TO?
U SHOULD TAKE HIS FIGHT MORE SERIOUSLY.
EVEN DISTRACTED, I AM YOUR BETTER!
BUT YOU CAN'T WIN. YOUR BLADE CAN'T EVEN HURT ME!
KAFF, KAFF
<DONALD! ISTEN TO ME!>
<HIROTO, WATCH YOUR BACK!>
<THEY'RE FLANKING YOU. NON-LETHAL FORCE ONLY.>
<DONALD, I SAID STAND DOWN. ONE OF THEM IS-->
<--MY DAUGHTER.>

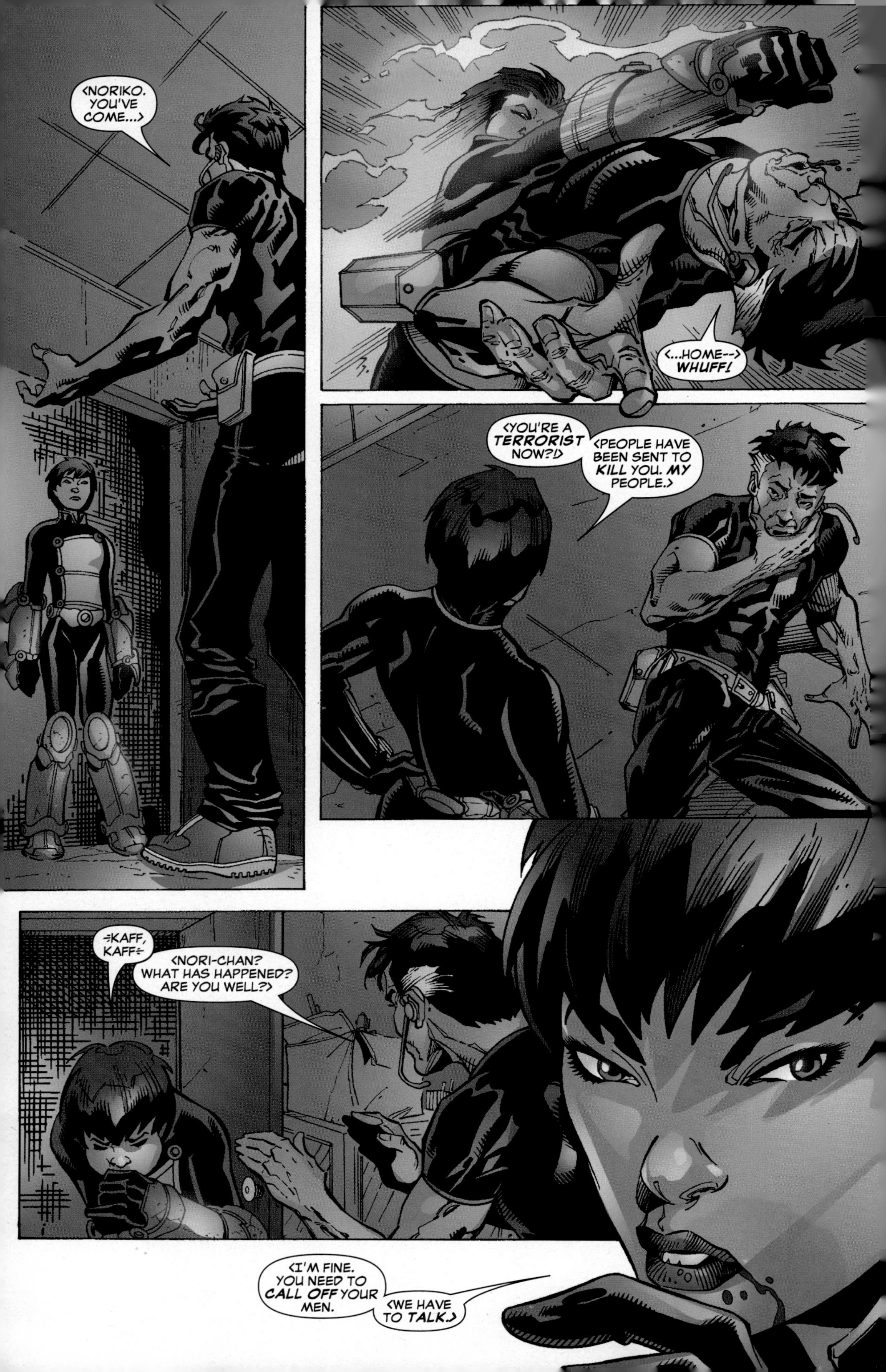

<NORIKO. YOU'VE COME...>
<...HOME--> WHUFF!
<YOU'RE A TERRORIST NOW?!>
<PEOPLE HAVE BEEN SENT TO KILL YOU. MY PEOPLE.>
=KAFF, KAFF=
<NORI-CHAN? WHAT HAS HAPPENED? ARE YOU WELL?>
<I'M FINE. YOU NEED TO CALL OFF YOUR MEN.
<WE HAVE TO TALK.>

WE KNOW ABOUT *PROJECT GENESIS.*

THEN YOU KNOW *WHY* WE HAVE NO INTEREST IN TALKING WITH YOU.

QUIET, DONALD.

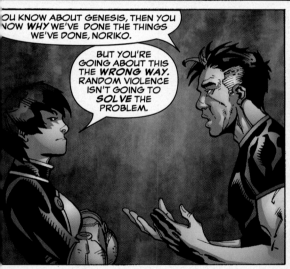

OU KNOW ABOUT GENESIS, THEN YOU NOW *WHY* WE'VE DONE THE THINGS WE'VE DONE, NORIKO.

BUT YOU'RE GOING ABOUT THIS THE *WRONG WAY.* RANDOM VIOLENCE ISN'T GOING TO *SOLVE* THE PROBLEM.

WE DO WHAT WE MUST TO MAKE PEOPLE *AWARE.* WHAT OTHER *CHOICE* DID WE HAVE? THERE AREN'T A LOT OF OPTIONS FOR *BASELINES* LIKE US.

BESIDES, IT WASN'T *RANDOM* VIOLENCE--

WHY DON'T YOU JUST ATTACK GENESIS *DIRECTLY?*

ILLIANT. *GREAT* IDEA. DO YOU HONESTLY NK A BUNCH OF CHILDREN HAVE THOUGHT OF SOMETHING *WE* HAVEN'T? WE KNOW *WHERE* GENESIS IS. WE JUST DON'T HAVE A WAY INSIDE.

YET.

THEN LET US *HELP* YOU. WE CAN GET YOU INSIDE.

SEE, NOW THAT'S A REALLY *BAD PLAN...*

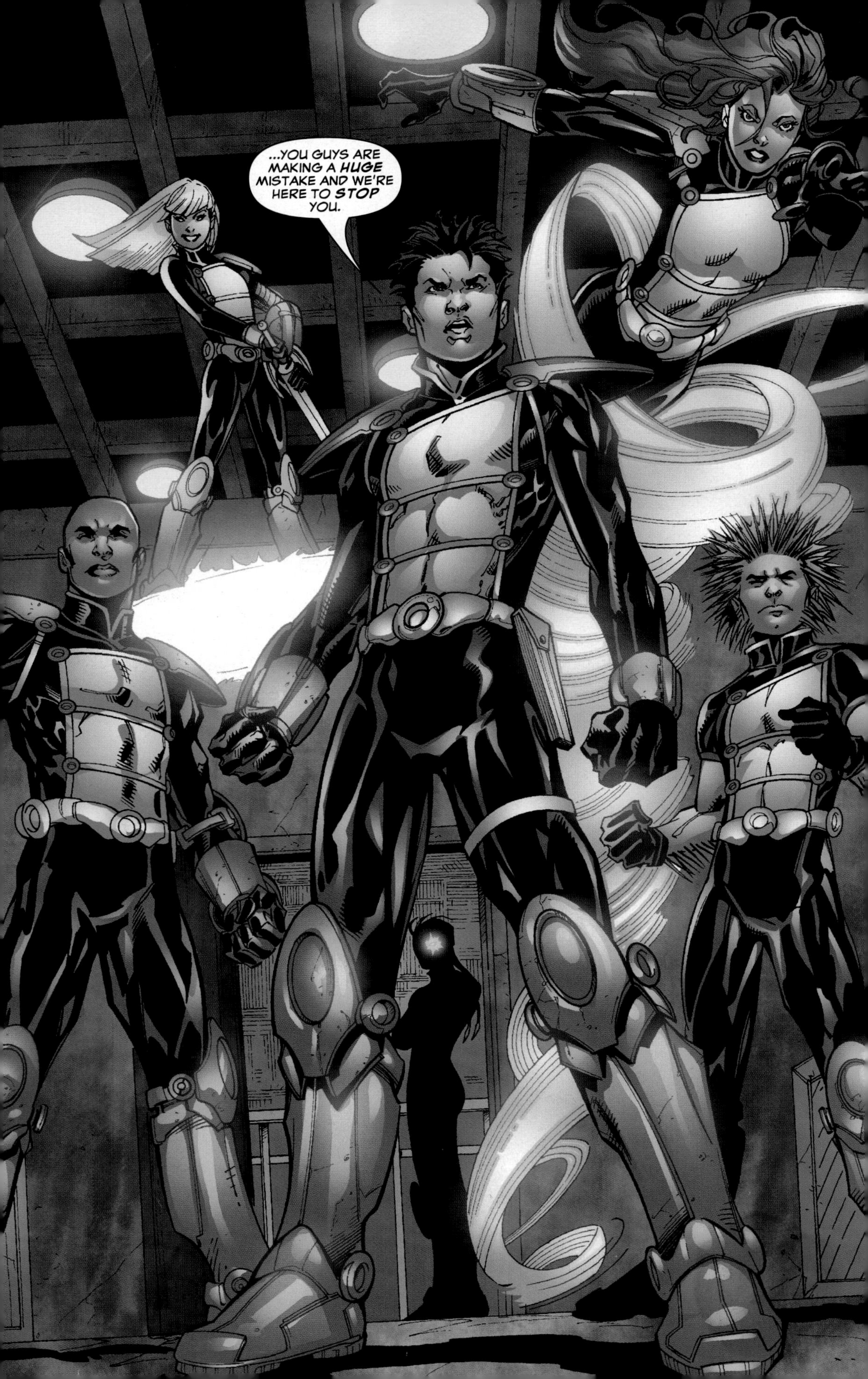
...YOU GUYS ARE MAKING A HUGE MISTAKE AND WE'RE HERE TO STOP YOU.

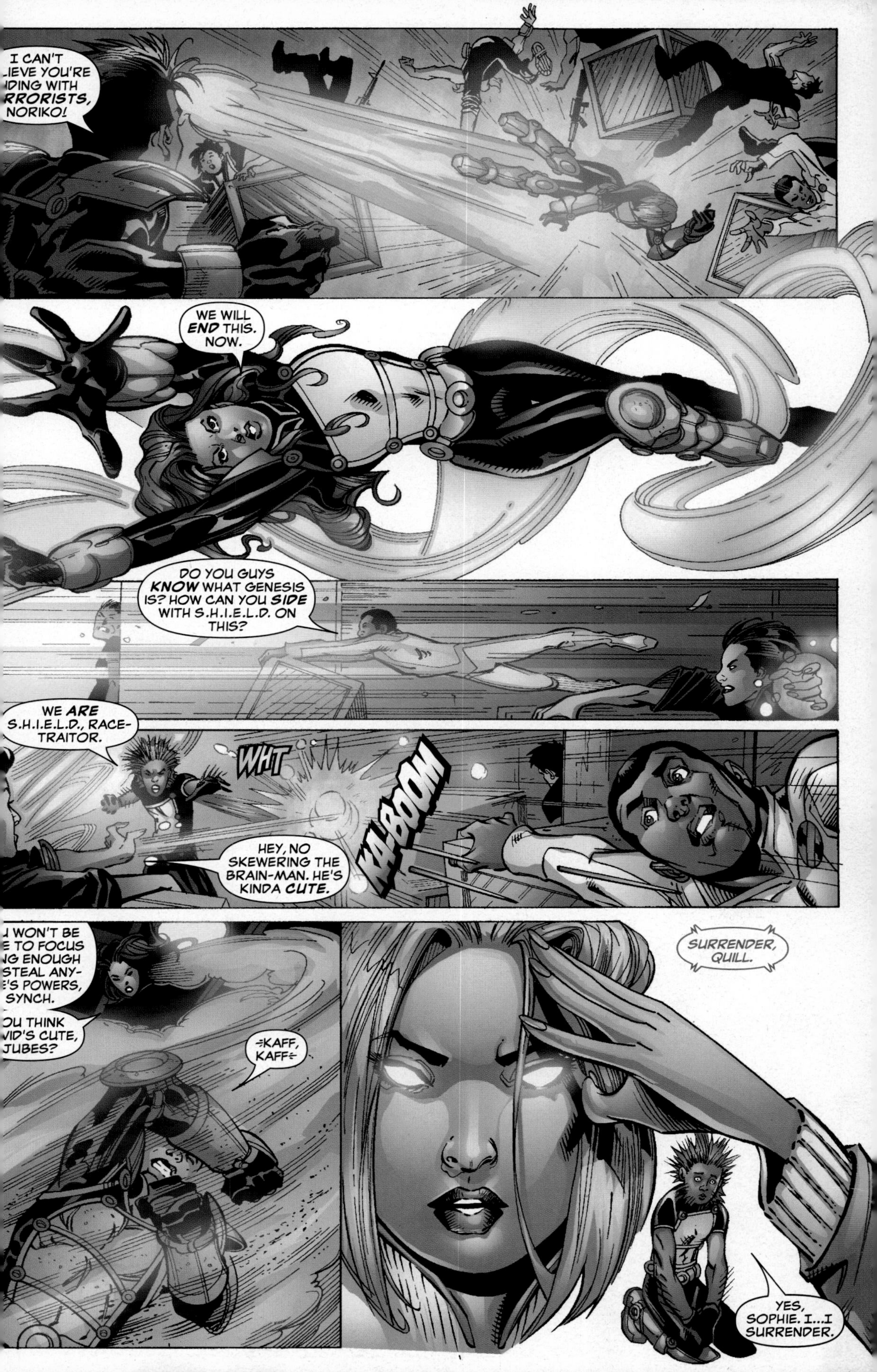
I CAN'T
LIEVE YOU'RE
IDING WITH
RRORISTS,
NORIKO!
WE WILL
END THIS.
NOW.
DO YOU GUYS
KNOW WHAT GENESIS
IS? HOW CAN YOU SIDE
WITH S.H.I.E.L.D. ON
THIS?
WE ARE
S.H.I.E.L.D., RACE-TRAITOR.
WHT
KA-BOOM
HEY, NO
SKEWERING THE
BRAIN-MAN. HE'S
KINDA CUTE.
U WON'T BE
E TO FOCUS
NG ENOUGH
STEAL ANY-
E'S POWERS,
SYNCH.
OU THINK
VID'S CUTE,
JUBES?
KAFF,
KAFF
SURRENDER,
QUILL.
YES,
SOPHIE. I...I
SURRENDER.

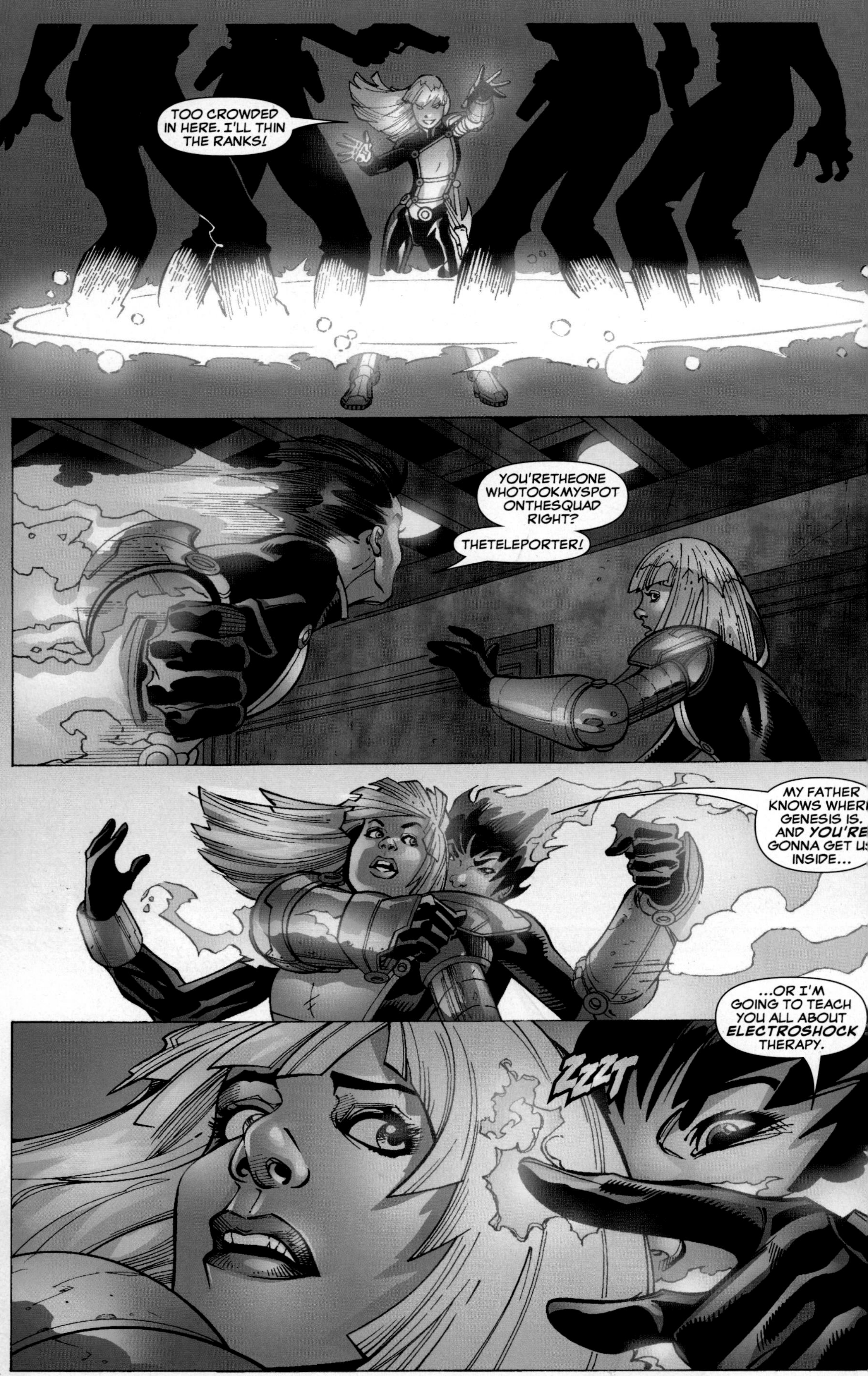
TOO CROWDED IN HERE. I'LL THIN THE RANKS!
YOU'RETHEONE WHOTOOKMYSPOT ONTHESQUAD RIGHT?
THETELEPORTER!
MY FATHER KNOWS WHER GENESIS IS. AND *YOU'RE* GONNA GET US INSIDE...
...OR I'M GOING TO TEACH YOU ALL ABOUT ***ELECTROSHOCK*** THERAPY.
ZZZT

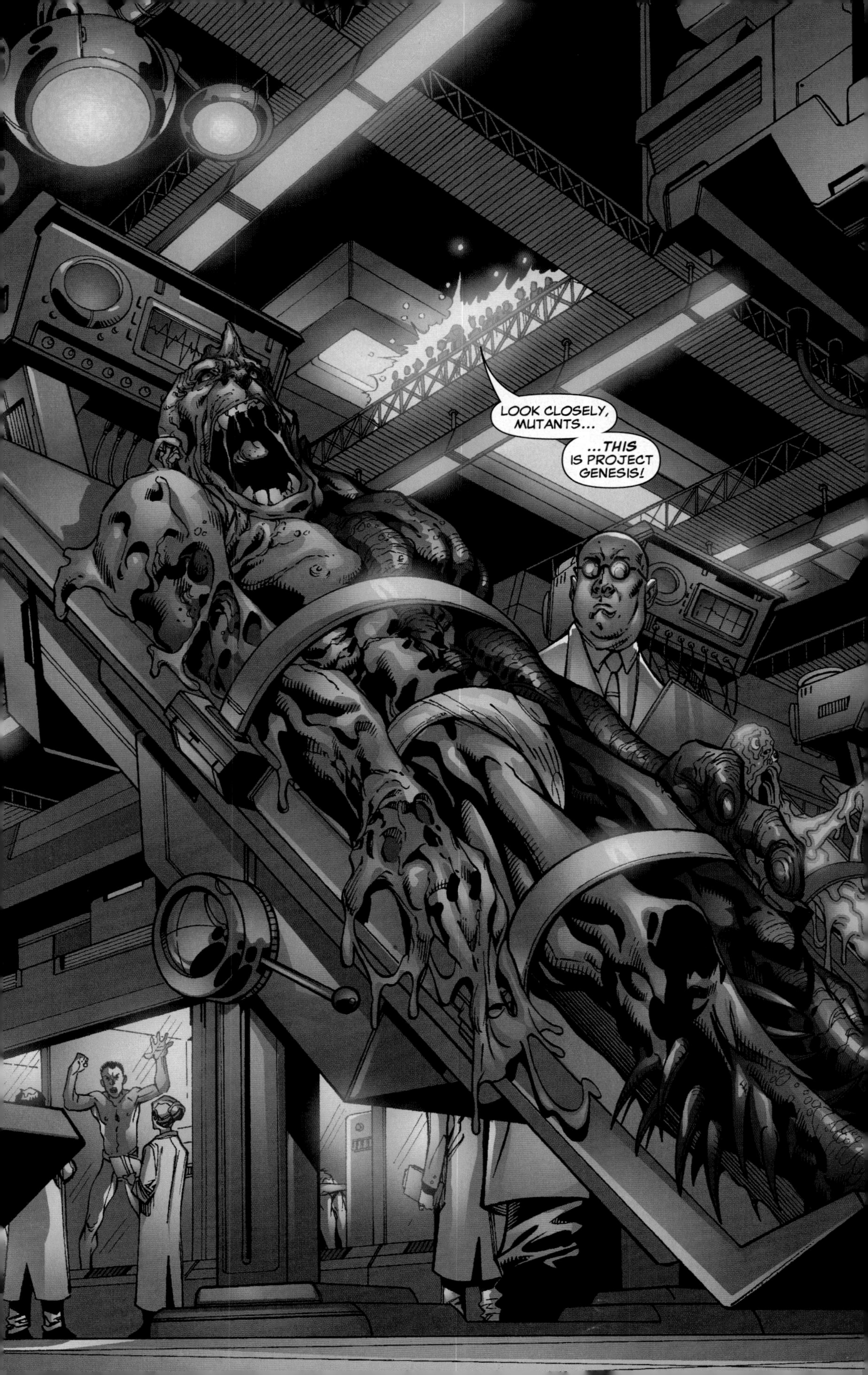

LOOK CLOSELY, MUTANTS...
...THIS IS PROJECT GENESIS!

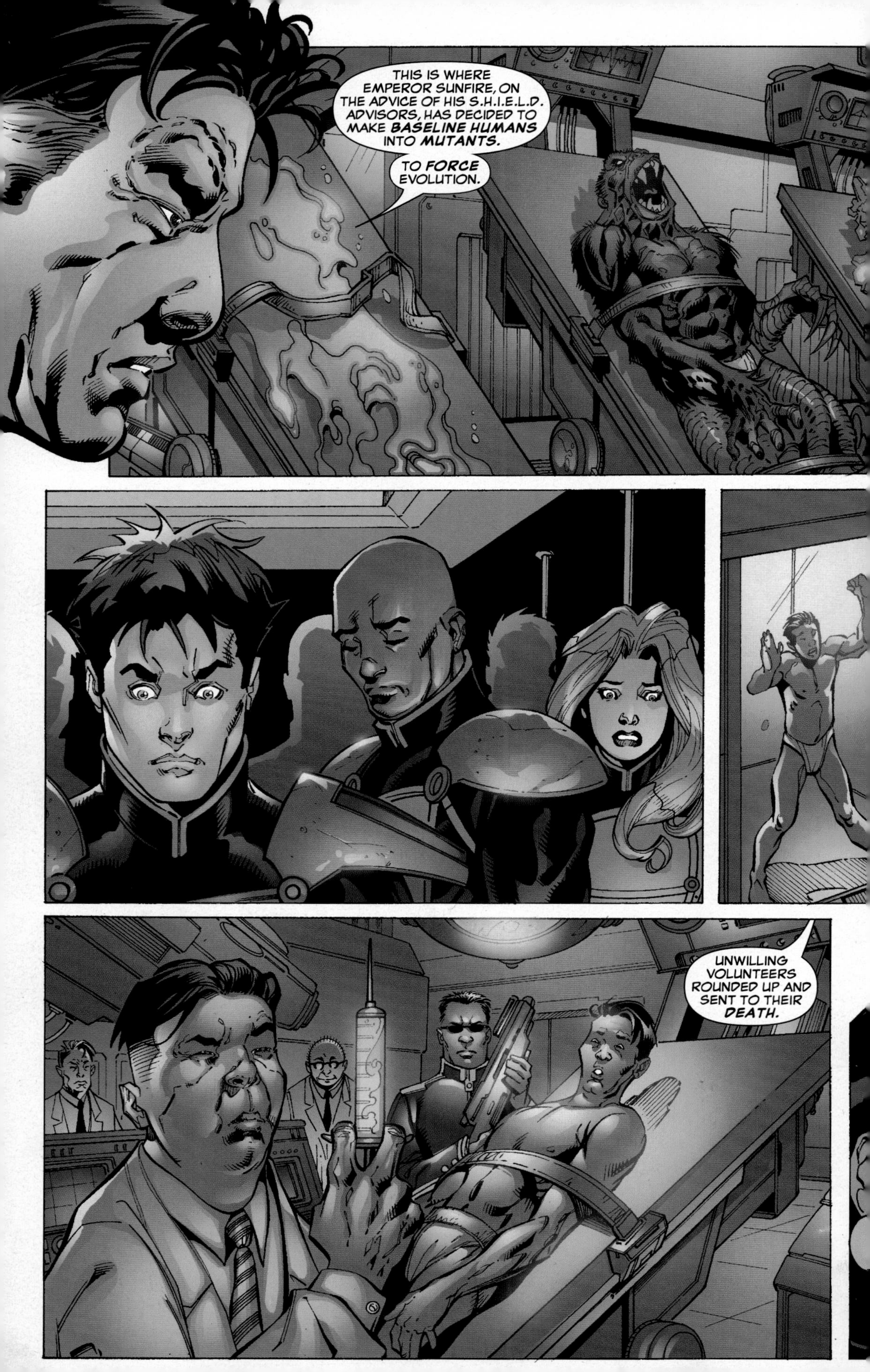
THIS IS WHERE EMPEROR SUNFIRE, ON THE ADVICE OF HIS S.H.I.E.L.D. ADVISORS, HAS DECIDED TO MAKE BASELINE HUMANS INTO MUTANTS.
TO FORCE EVOLUTION.
UNWILLING VOLUNTEERS ROUNDED UP AND SENT TO THEIR DEATH.

IT DOES NOT MATTER *HOW MANY* MUTATIONS THEY PUT IN ONE BODY.

IT DOESN'T MATTER IF THEIR BODIES CANNOT *HANDLE* IT...IF THEY *DIE* IN THE PROCESS.

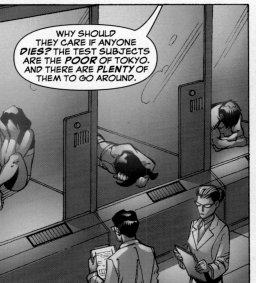

WHY SHOULD THEY CARE IF ANYONE *DIES?* THE TEST SUBJECTS ARE THE *POOR* OF TOKYO. AND THERE ARE *PLENTY* OF THEM TO GO AROUND.

WAKE UP AND SEE *REALITY* FOR WHAT IT IS, MUTANTS.

SEE WHAT YOUR *HOUSE OF M* HAS WROUGHT.

THIS CHANGES *EVERYTHING.*

DOES IT?

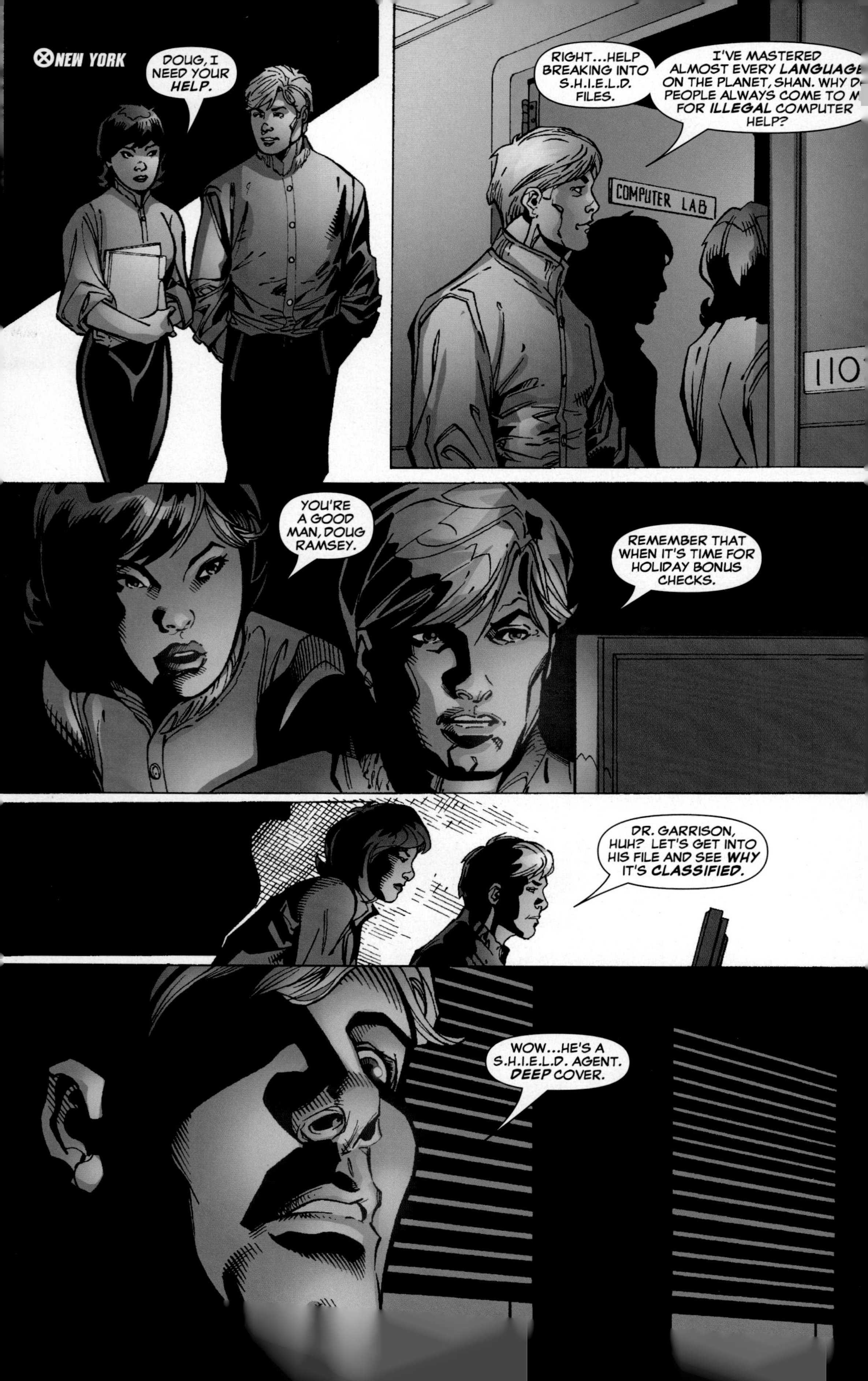
NEW YORK
DOUG, I NEED YOUR HELP.
RIGHT...HELP BREAKING INTO S.H.I.E.L.D. FILES.
I'VE MASTERED ALMOST EVERY LANGUAG ON THE PLANET, SHAN. WHY D PEOPLE ALWAYS COME TO M FOR ILLEGAL COMPUTER HELP?
COMPUTER LAB
110
YOU'RE A GOOD MAN, DOUG RAMSEY.
REMEMBER THAT WHEN IT'S TIME FOR HOLIDAY BONUS CHECKS.
DR. GARRISON, HUH? LET'S GET INTO HIS FILE AND SEE WHY IT'S CLASSIFIED.
WOW...HE'S A S.H.I.E.L.D. AGENT. DEEP COVER.

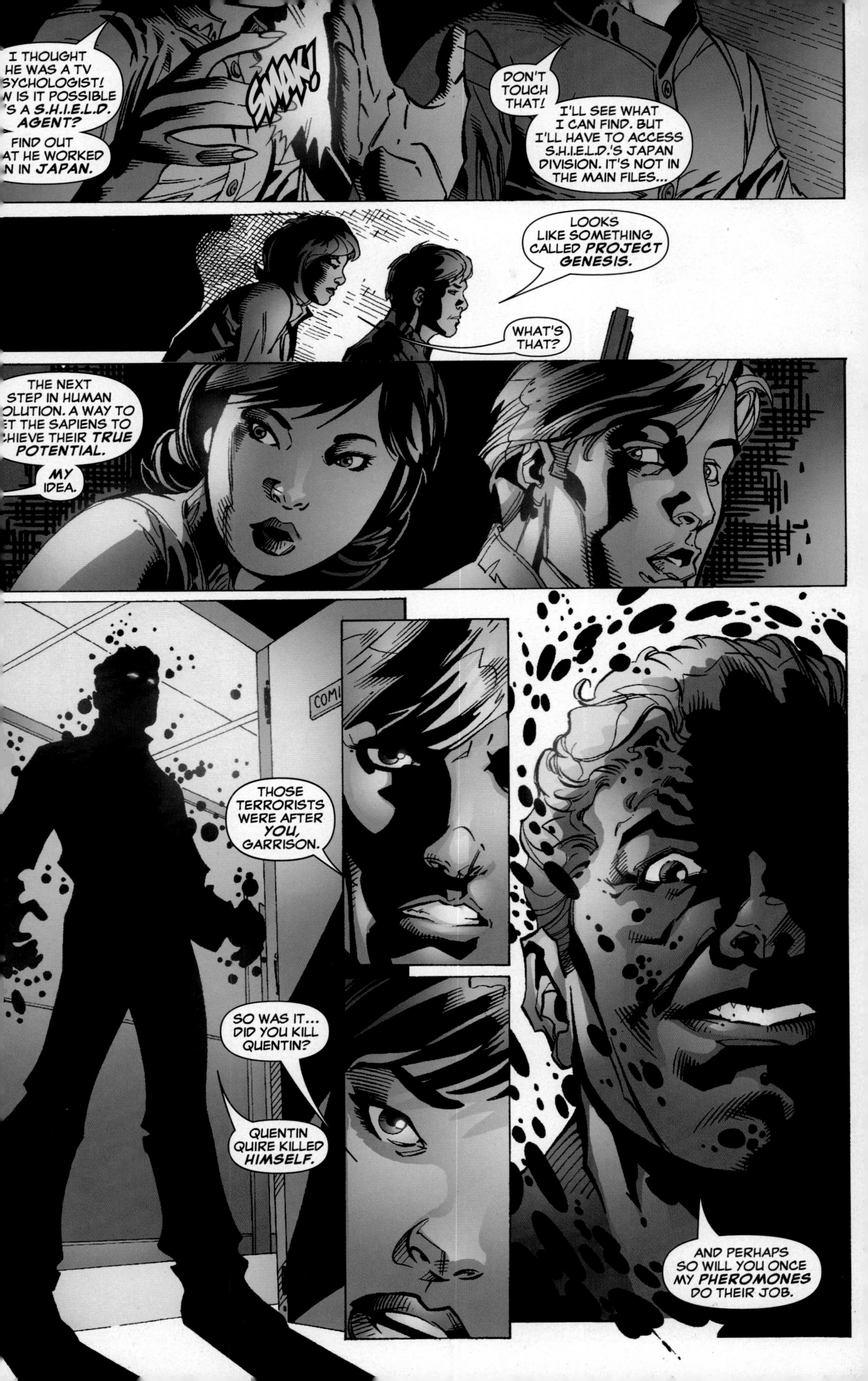

I THOUGHT HE WAS A TV SYCHOLOGIST! W IS IT POSSIBLE 'S A S.H.I.E.L.D. AGENT?
FIND OUT AT HE WORKED N IN JAPAN.
SMAK!
DON'T TOUCH THAT!
I'LL SEE WHAT I CAN FIND. BUT I'LL HAVE TO ACCESS S.H.I.E.L.D.'S JAPAN DIVISION. IT'S NOT IN THE MAIN FILES...
LOOKS LIKE SOMETHING CALLED PROJECT GENESIS.
WHAT'S THAT?
THE NEXT STEP IN HUMAN OLUTION. A WAY TO ET THE SAPIENS TO CHIEVE THEIR TRUE POTENTIAL.
MY IDEA.
COMI
THOSE TERRORISTS WERE AFTER YOU, GARRISON.
SO WAS IT... DID YOU KILL QUENTIN?
QUENTIN QUIRE KILLED HIMSELF.
AND PERHAPS SO WILL YOU ONCE MY PHEROMONES DO THEIR JOB.

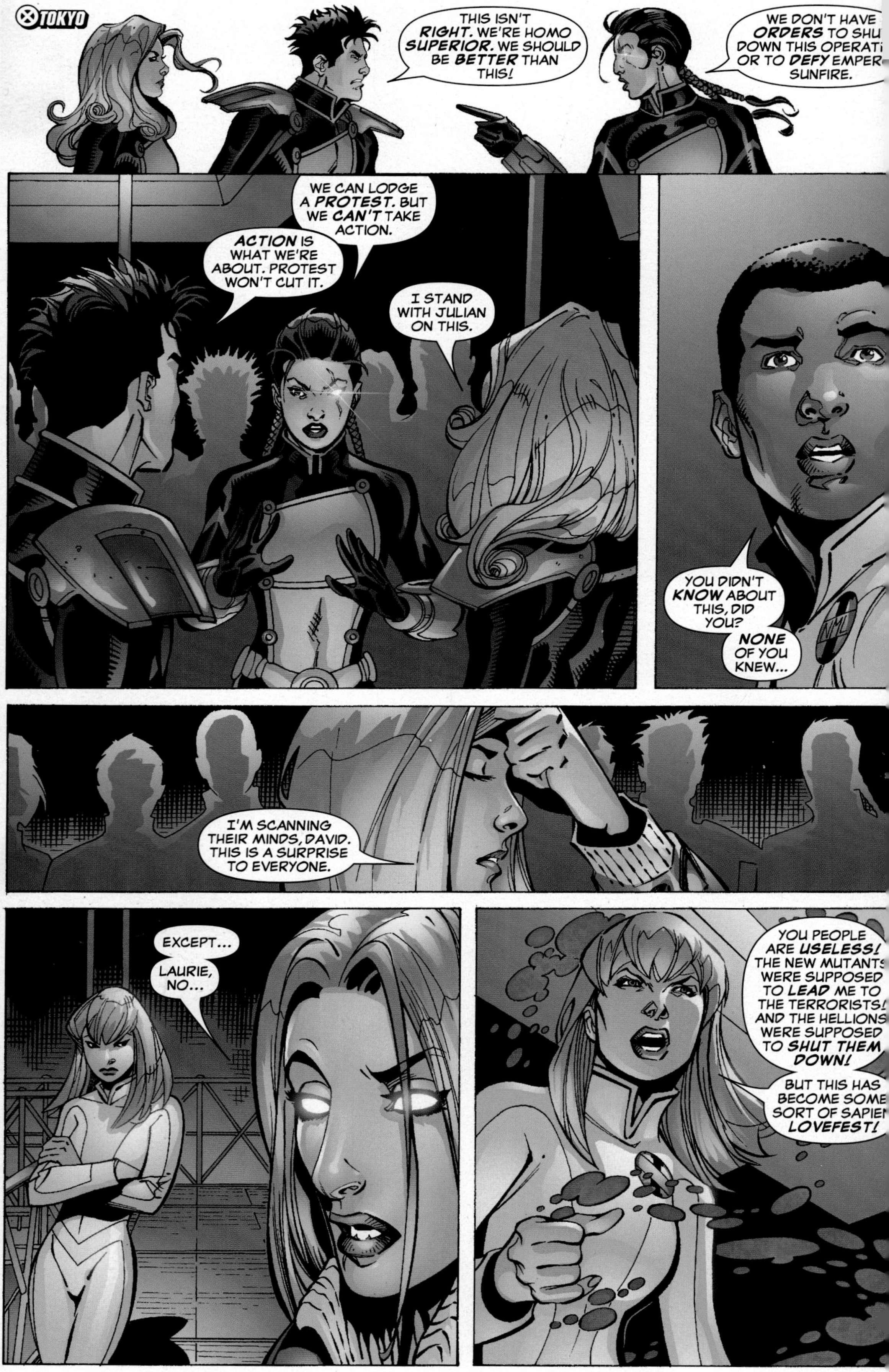
TOKYO
THIS ISN'T RIGHT. WE'RE HOMO SUPERIOR. WE SHOULD BE BETTER THAN THIS!
WE DON'T HAVE ORDERS TO SHU DOWN THIS OPERATI OR TO DEFY EMPER SUNFIRE.
WE CAN LODGE A PROTEST. BUT WE CAN'T TAKE ACTION.
ACTION IS WHAT WE'RE ABOUT. PROTEST WON'T CUT IT.
I STAND WITH JULIAN ON THIS.
YOU DIDN'T KNOW ABOUT THIS, DID YOU?
NONE OF YOU KNEW...
I'M SCANNING THEIR MINDS, DAVID. THIS IS A SURPRISE TO EVERYONE.
EXCEPT...
LAURIE, NO...
YOU PEOPLE ARE USELESS! THE NEW MUTANTS WERE SUPPOSED TO LEAD ME TO THE TERRORISTS! AND THE HELLIONS WERE SUPPOSED TO SHUT THEM DOWN!
BUT THIS HAS BECOME SOME SORT OF SAPIEN LOVEFEST!

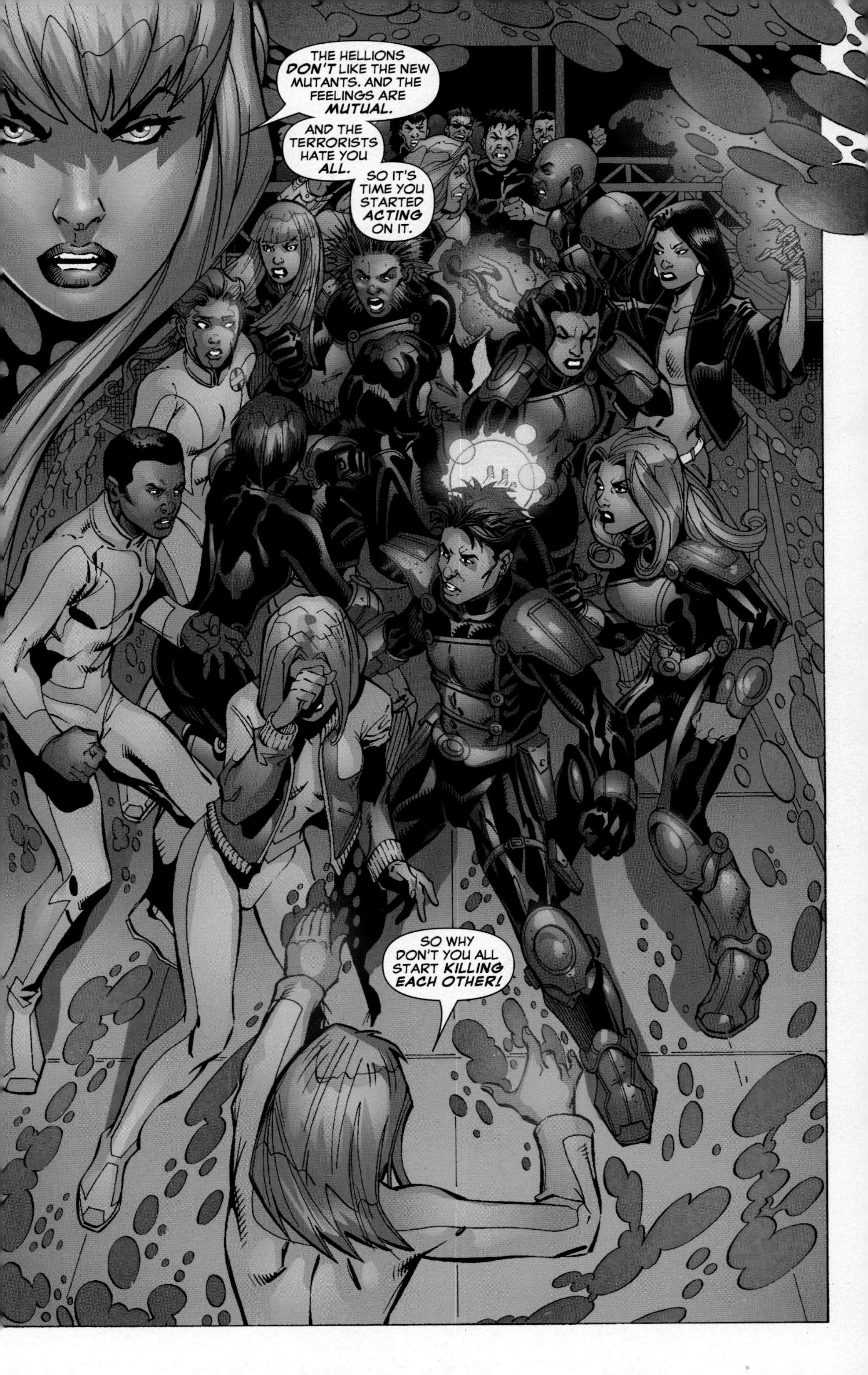
THE HELLIONS DON'T LIKE THE NEW MUTANTS. AND THE FEELINGS ARE MUTUAL.
AND THE TERRORISTS HATE YOU ALL.
SO IT'S TIME YOU STARTED ACTING ON IT.
SO WHY DON'T YOU ALL START KILLING EACH OTHER!

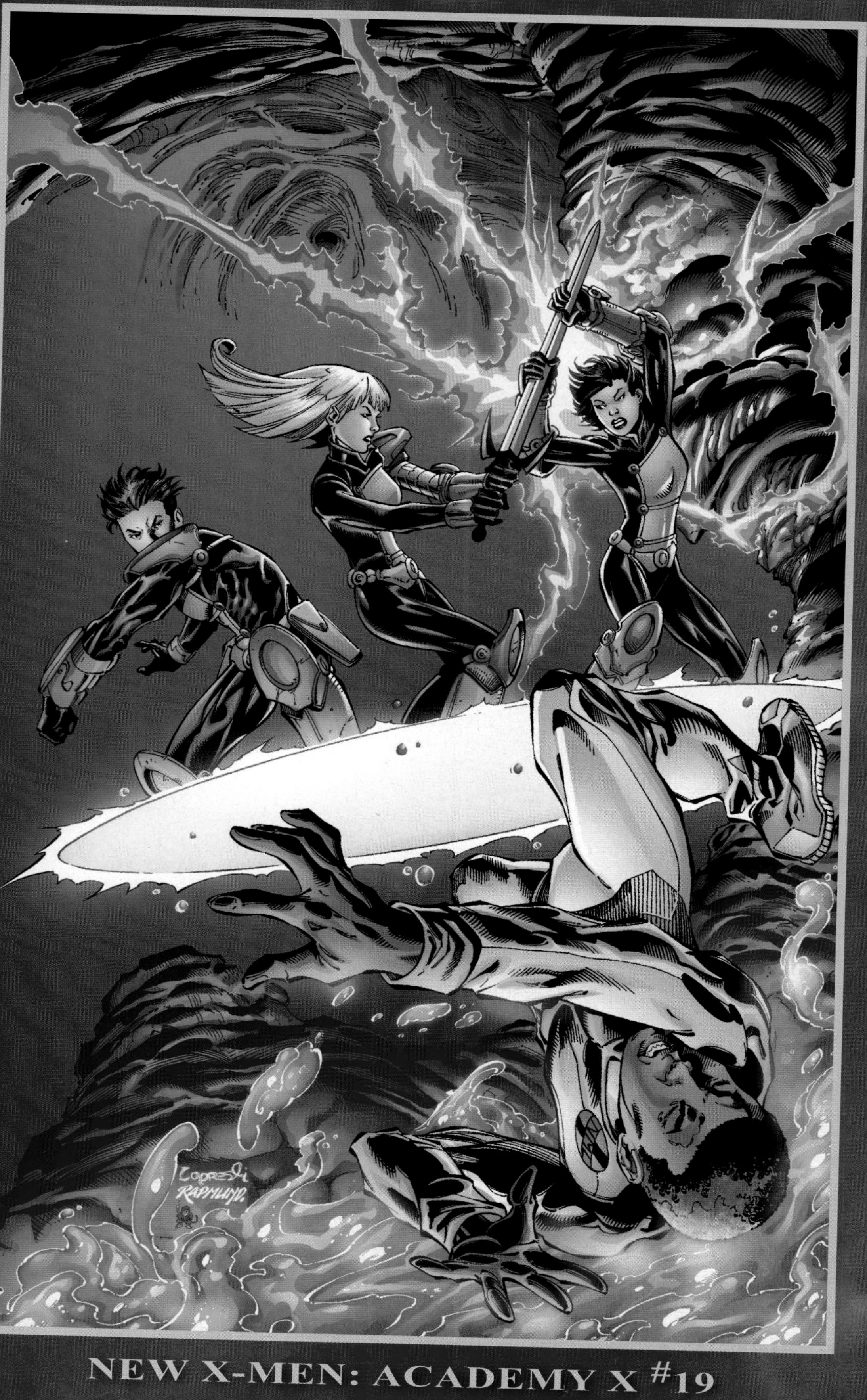

NEW X-MEN: ACADEMY X #19

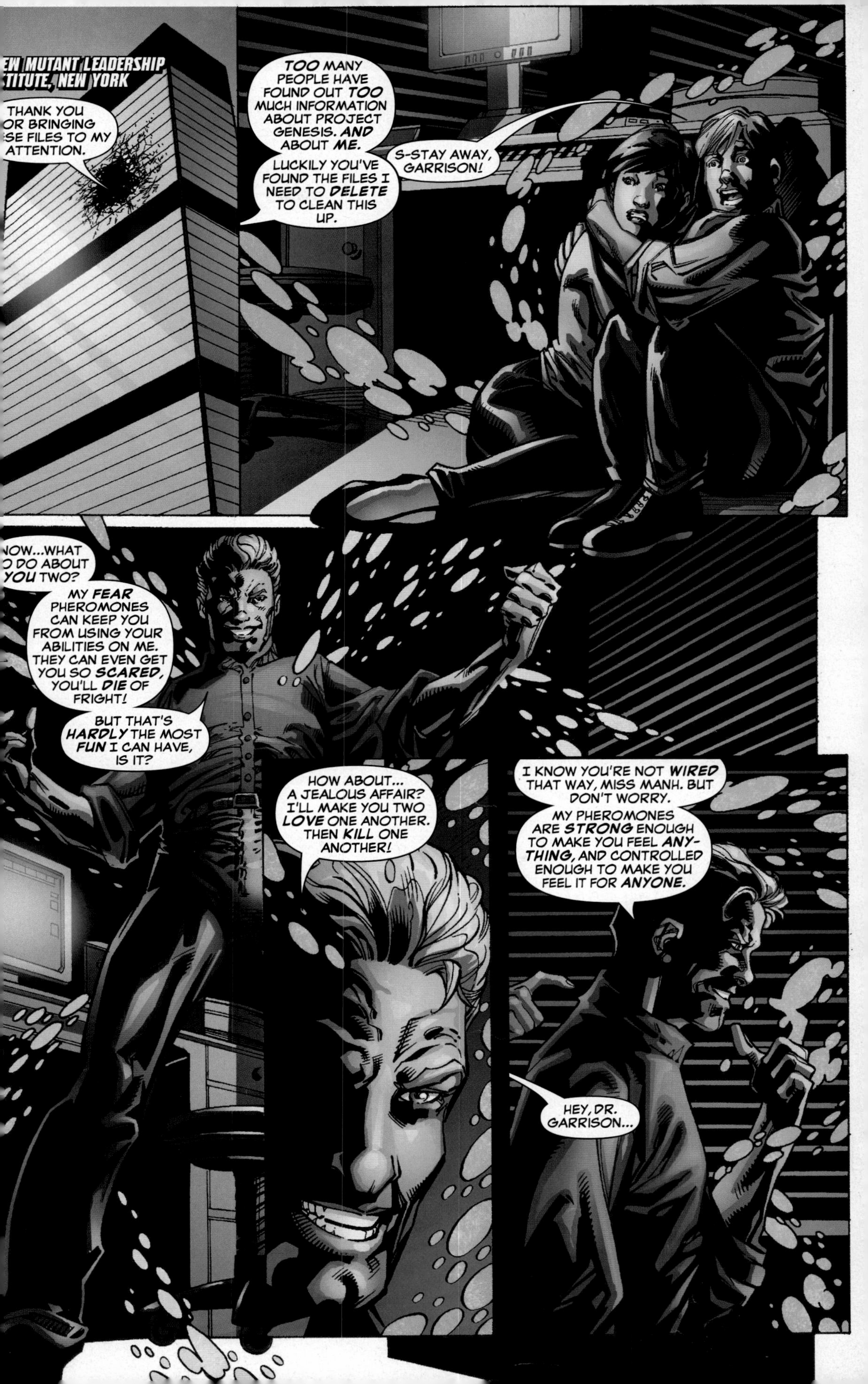
EW MUTANT LEADERSHIP
STITUTE, NEW YORK
THANK YOU
OR BRINGING
SE FILES TO MY
ATTENTION.
TOO MANY PEOPLE HAVE FOUND OUT TOO MUCH INFORMATION ABOUT PROJECT GENESIS. AND ABOUT ME.
LUCKILY YOU'VE FOUND THE FILES I NEED TO DELETE TO CLEAN THIS UP.
S-STAY AWAY, GARRISON!
NOW...WHAT
O DO ABOUT
YOU TWO?
MY FEAR PHEROMONES CAN KEEP YOU FROM USING YOUR ABILITIES ON ME. THEY CAN EVEN GET YOU SO SCARED, YOU'LL DIE OF FRIGHT!
BUT THAT'S HARDLY THE MOST FUN I CAN HAVE, IS IT?
HOW ABOUT... A JEALOUS AFFAIR? I'LL MAKE YOU TWO LOVE ONE ANOTHER. THEN KILL ONE ANOTHER!
I KNOW YOU'RE NOT WIRED THAT WAY, MISS MANH. BUT DON'T WORRY.
MY PHEROMONES ARE STRONG ENOUGH TO MAKE YOU FEEL ANY-THING, AND CONTROLLED ENOUGH TO MAKE YOU FEEL IT FOR ANYONE.
HEY, DR. GARRISON...

TAG! YOU'RE IT!

MUST... GET... AWAY.

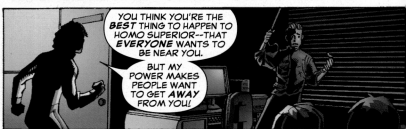

YOU THINK YOU'RE THE *BEST* THING TO HAPPEN TO HOMO SUPERIOR--THAT *EVERYONE* WANTS TO BE NEAR YOU.

BUT MY POWER MAKES PEOPLE WANT TO GET *AWAY* FROM YOU!

EXCEPT, SINCE YOU'VE ALWAYS BEE[N] YOUR OWN BIGGEST FA[N], I DECIDED TO MAKE *YOU* WHO WANTS T[O] GET AWAY.

CALL IT MY *REVENGE* FOR WHAT YOU DID TO QUENTIN.

KSSSS[H]

NO! MUST...GET... AWAY...

YOU MUST... BUT YOU *CAN'T.*

MUST... GET... AWAY.

NO... WAIT!

STOP HIM!

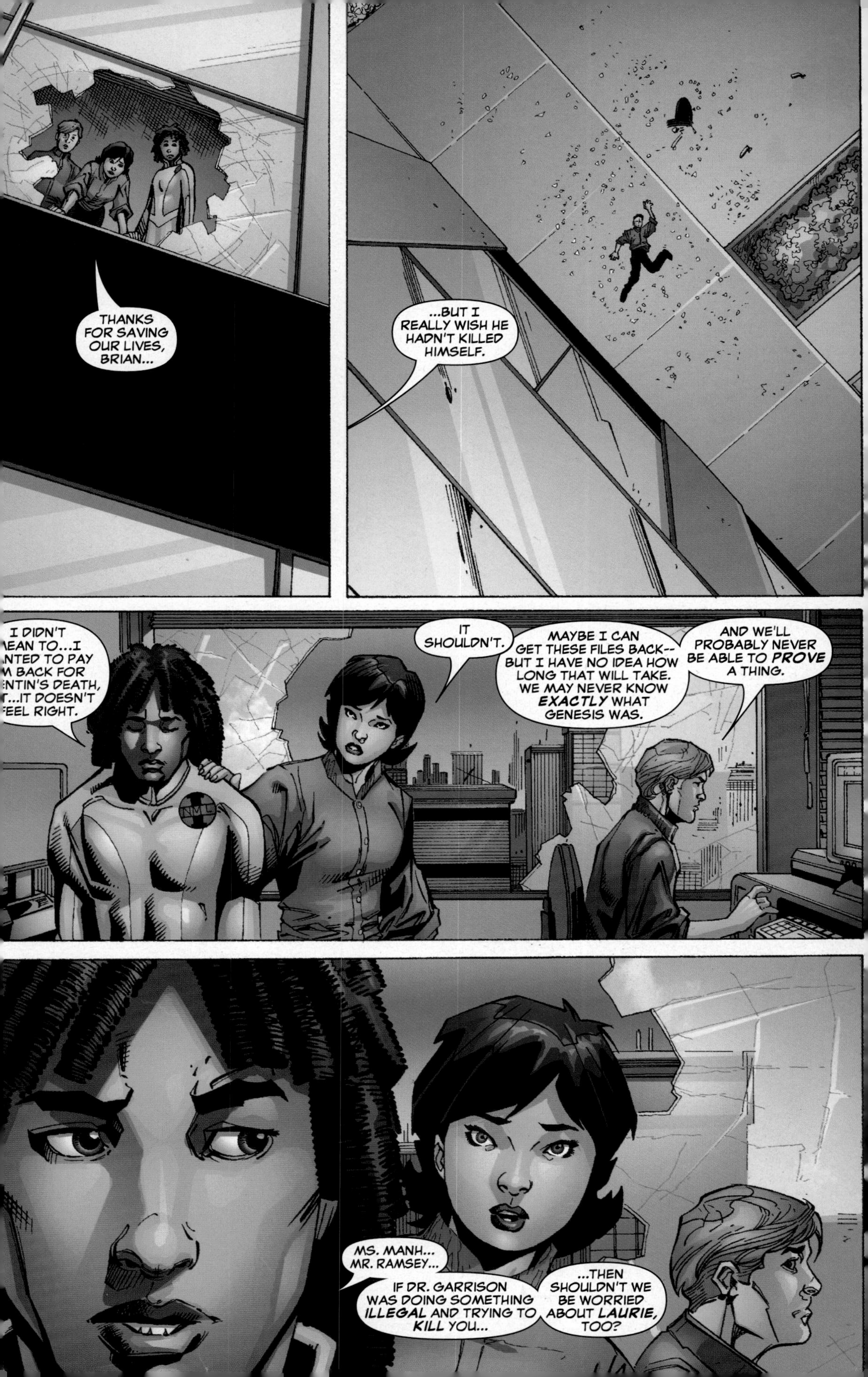

THANKS FOR SAVING OUR LIVES, BRIAN...
...BUT I REALLY WISH HE HADN'T KILLED HIMSELF.
I DIDN'T
EAN TO...I
NTED TO PAY
M BACK FOR
ENTIN'S DEATH,
T...IT DOESN'T
FEEL RIGHT.
IT SHOULDN'T.
MAYBE I CAN GET THESE FILES BACK-- BUT I HAVE NO IDEA HOW LONG THAT WILL TAKE. WE MAY NEVER KNOW EXACTLY WHAT GENESIS WAS.
AND WE'LL PROBABLY NEVER BE ABLE TO PROVE A THING.
MS. MANH... MR. RAMSEY...
IF DR. GARRISON WAS DOING SOMETHING ILLEGAL AND TRYING TO KILL YOU...
...THEN SHOULDN'T WE BE WORRIED ABOUT LAURIE, TOO?

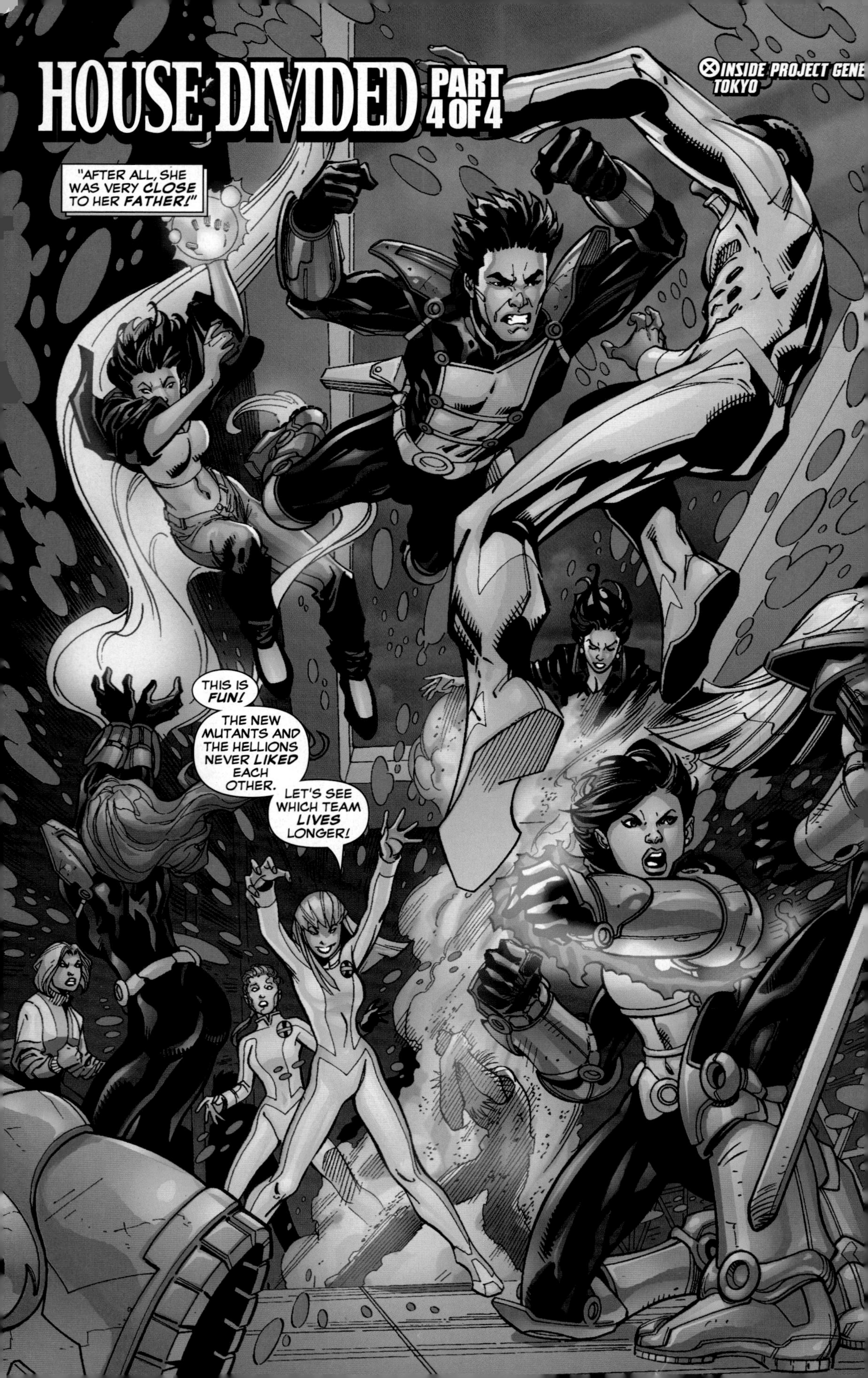
HOUSE DIVIDED PART 4 OF 4
INSIDE PROJECT GENE TOKYO
"AFTER ALL, SHE WAS VERY CLOSE TO HER FATHER!"
THIS IS FUN!
THE NEW MUTANTS AND THE HELLIONS NEVER LIKED EACH OTHER.
LET'S SEE WHICH TEAM LIVES LONGER!

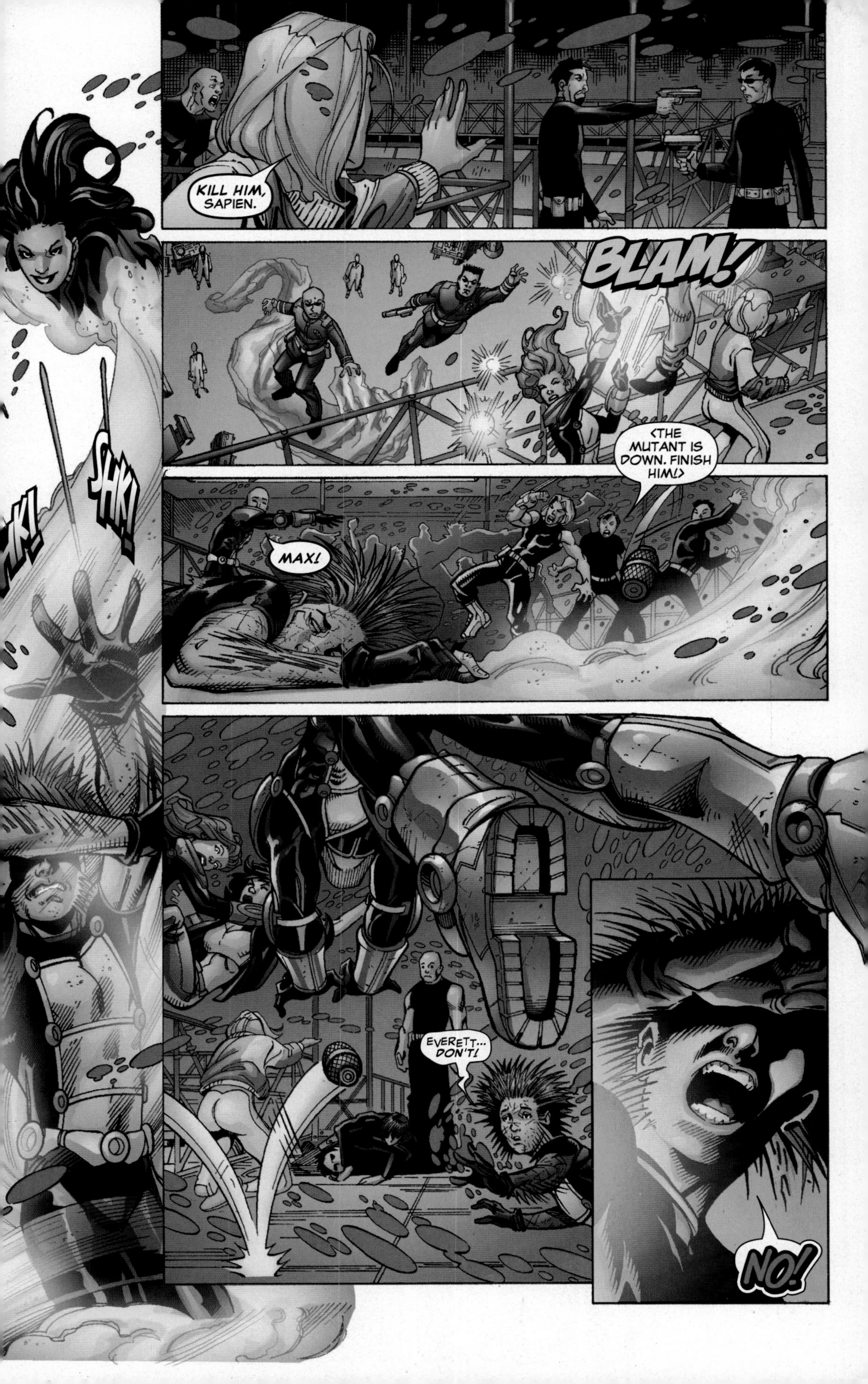

KILL HIM, SAPIEN.
BLAM!
SHK!
SHK!
<THE MUTANT IS DOWN. FINISH HIM!>
MAX!
EVERETT... DON'T!
NO!

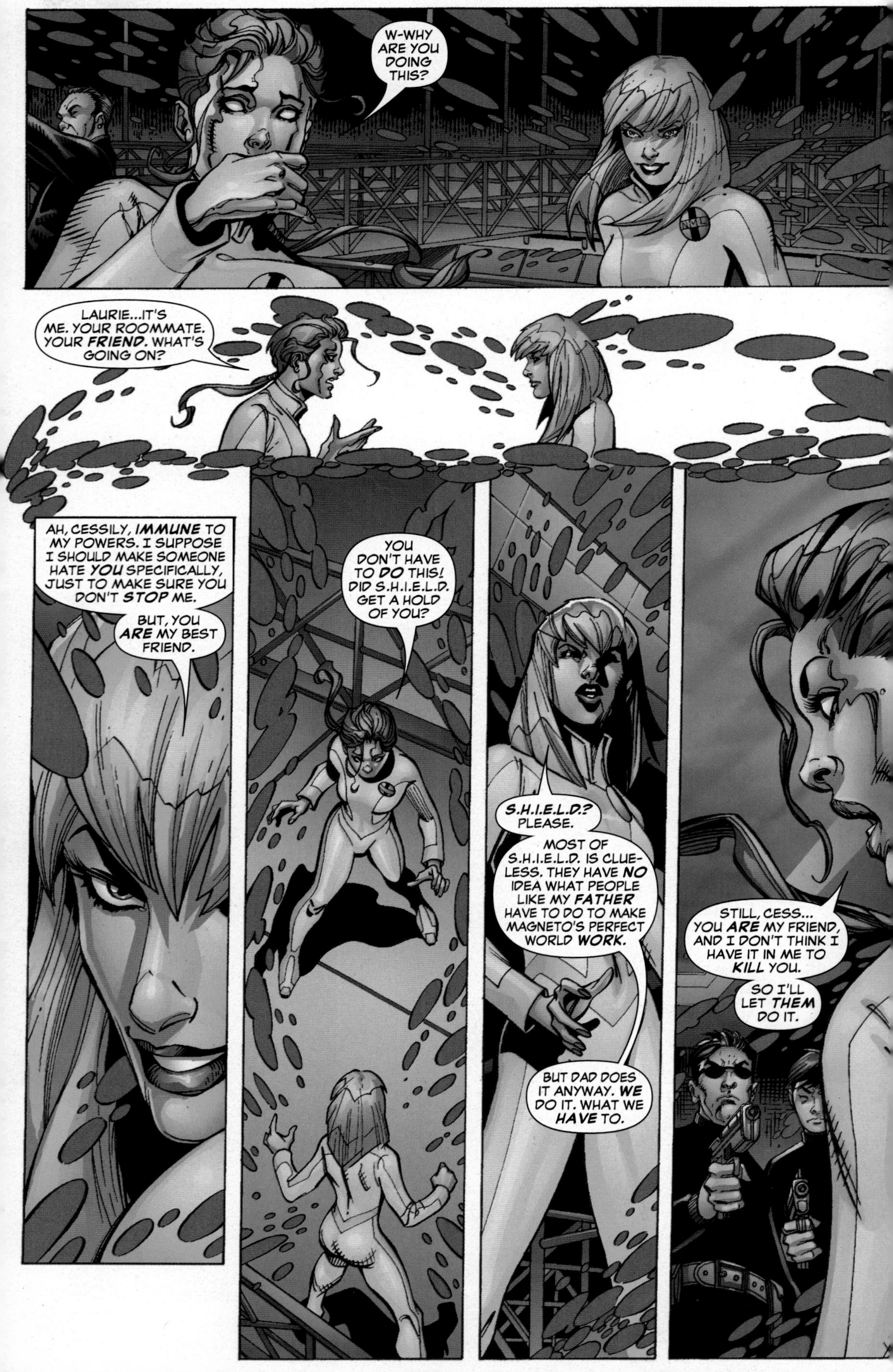
W-WHY ARE YOU DOING THIS?
LAURIE...IT'S ME. YOUR ROOMMATE. YOUR FRIEND. WHAT'S GOING ON?
AH, CESSILY, IMMUNE TO MY POWERS. I SUPPOSE I SHOULD MAKE SOMEONE HATE YOU SPECIFICALLY, JUST TO MAKE SURE YOU DON'T STOP ME.
BUT, YOU ARE MY BEST FRIEND.
YOU DON'T HAVE TO DO THIS! DID S.H.I.E.L.D. GET A HOLD OF YOU?
S.H.I.E.L.D.? PLEASE.
MOST OF S.H.I.E.L.D. IS CLUELESS. THEY HAVE NO IDEA WHAT PEOPLE LIKE MY FATHER HAVE TO DO TO MAKE MAGNETO'S PERFECT WORLD WORK.
BUT DAD DOES IT ANYWAY. WE DO IT. WHAT WE HAVE TO.
STILL, CESS... YOU ARE MY FRIEND, AND I DON'T THINK I HAVE IT IN ME TO KILL YOU.
SO I'LL LET THEM DO IT.

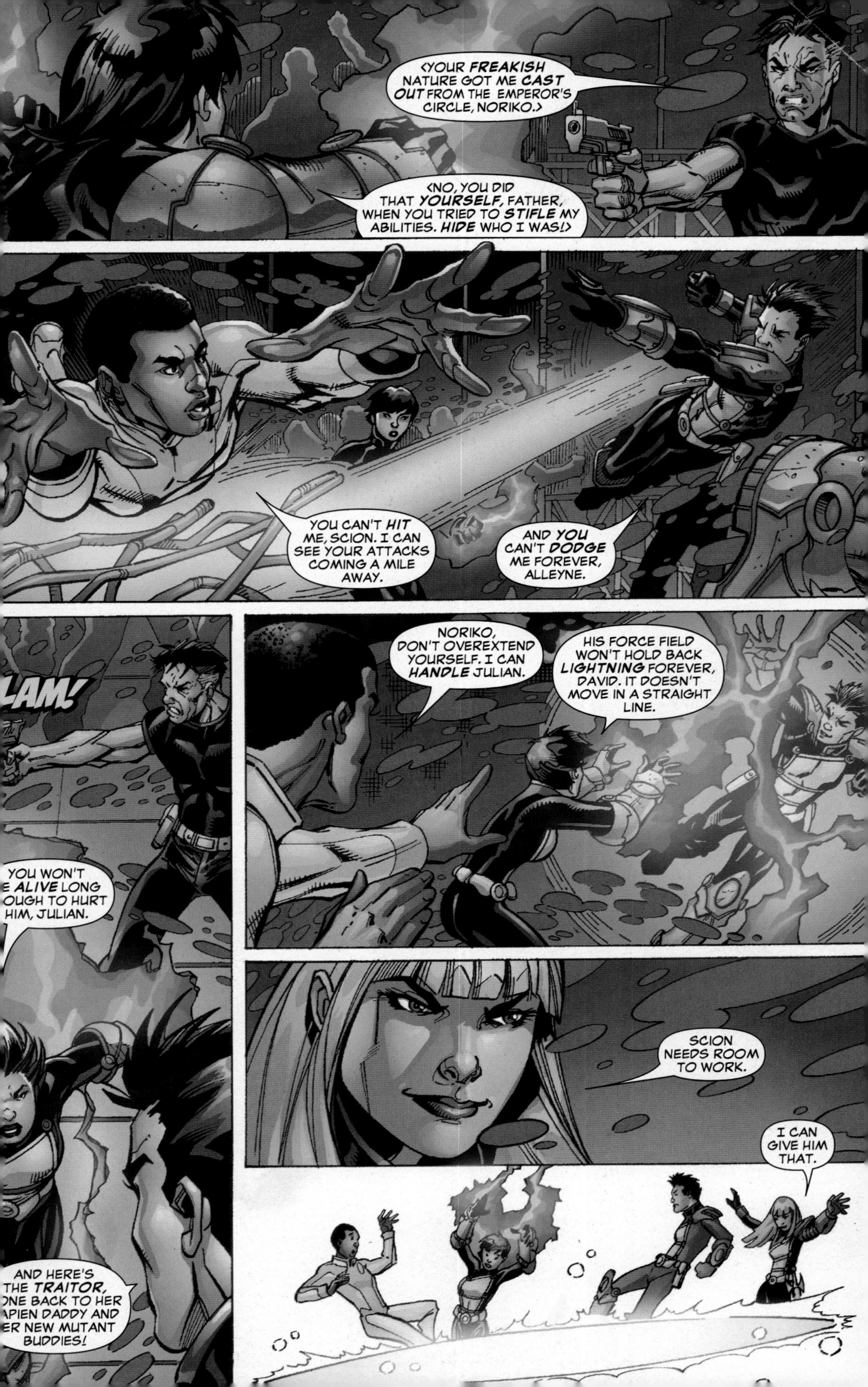
<YOUR FREAKISH NATURE GOT ME CAST OUT FROM THE EMPEROR'S CIRCLE, NORIKO.>
<NO, YOU DID THAT YOURSELF, FATHER, WHEN YOU TRIED TO STIFLE MY ABILITIES. HIDE WHO I WAS!>
YOU CAN'T HIT ME, SCION. I CAN SEE YOUR ATTACKS COMING A MILE AWAY.
AND YOU CAN'T DODGE ME FOREVER, ALLEYNE.
LAM!
YOU WON'T E ALIVE LONG OUGH TO HURT HIM, JULIAN.
AND HERE'S THE TRAITOR, ONE BACK TO HER APIEN DADDY AND ER NEW MUTANT BUDDIES!
NORIKO, DON'T OVEREXTEND YOURSELF. I CAN HANDLE JULIAN.
HIS FORCE FIELD WON'T HOLD BACK LIGHTNING FOREVER, DAVID. IT DOESN'T MOVE IN A STRAIGHT LINE.
SCION NEEDS ROOM TO WORK.
I CAN GIVE HIM THAT.

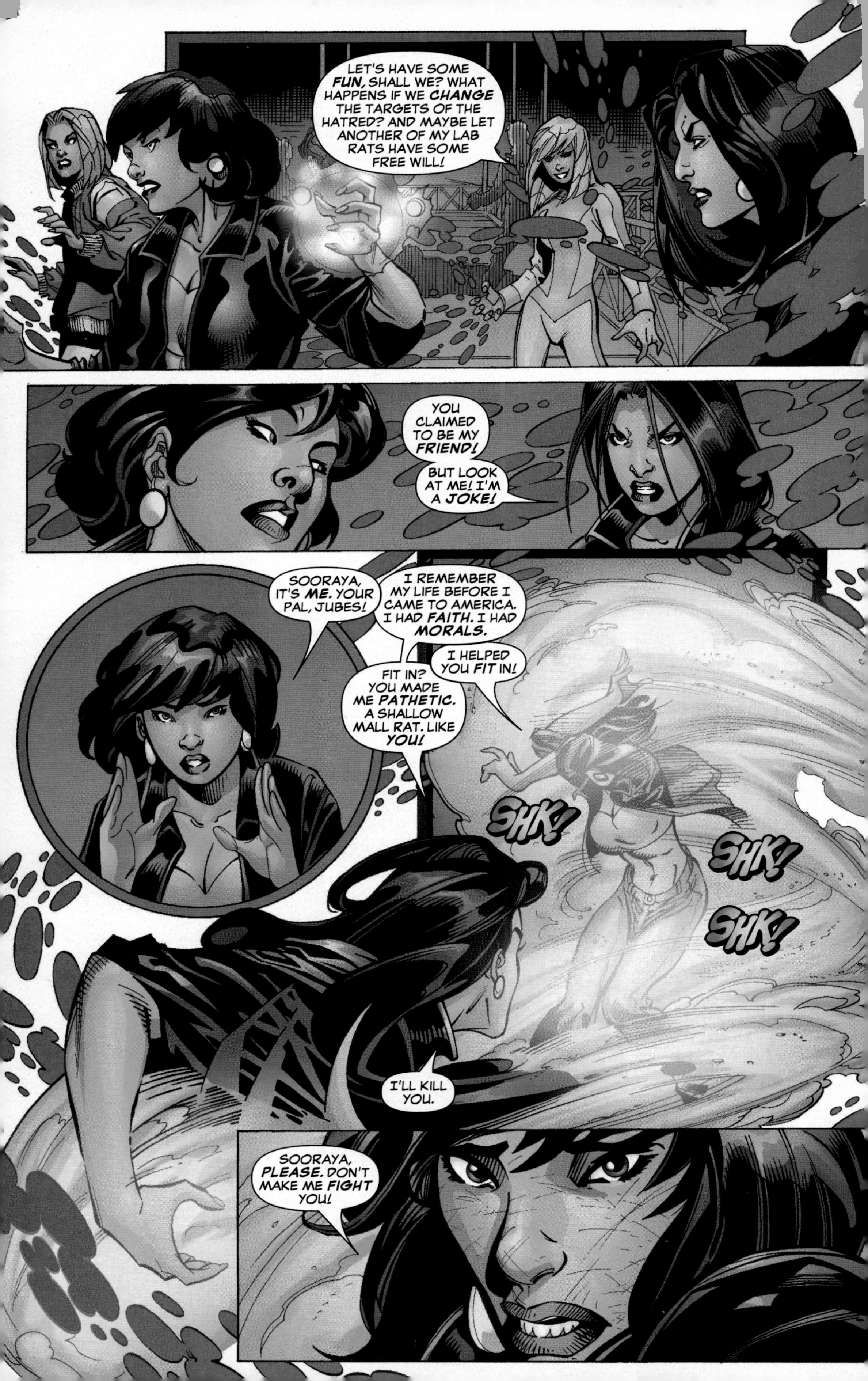
LET'S HAVE SOME FUN, SHALL WE? WHAT HAPPENS IF WE CHANGE THE TARGETS OF THE HATRED? AND MAYBE LET ANOTHER OF MY LAB RATS HAVE SOME FREE WILL!
YOU CLAIMED TO BE MY FRIEND!
BUT LOOK AT ME! I'M A JOKE!
SOORAYA, IT'S ME. YOUR PAL, JUBES!
I REMEMBER MY LIFE BEFORE I CAME TO AMERICA. I HAD FAITH. I HAD MORALS.
I HELPED YOU FIT IN!
FIT IN? YOU MADE ME PATHETIC. A SHALLOW MALL RAT. LIKE YOU!
SHK!
SHK!
SHK!
I'LL KILL YOU.
SOORAYA, PLEASE. DON'T MAKE ME FIGHT YOU!

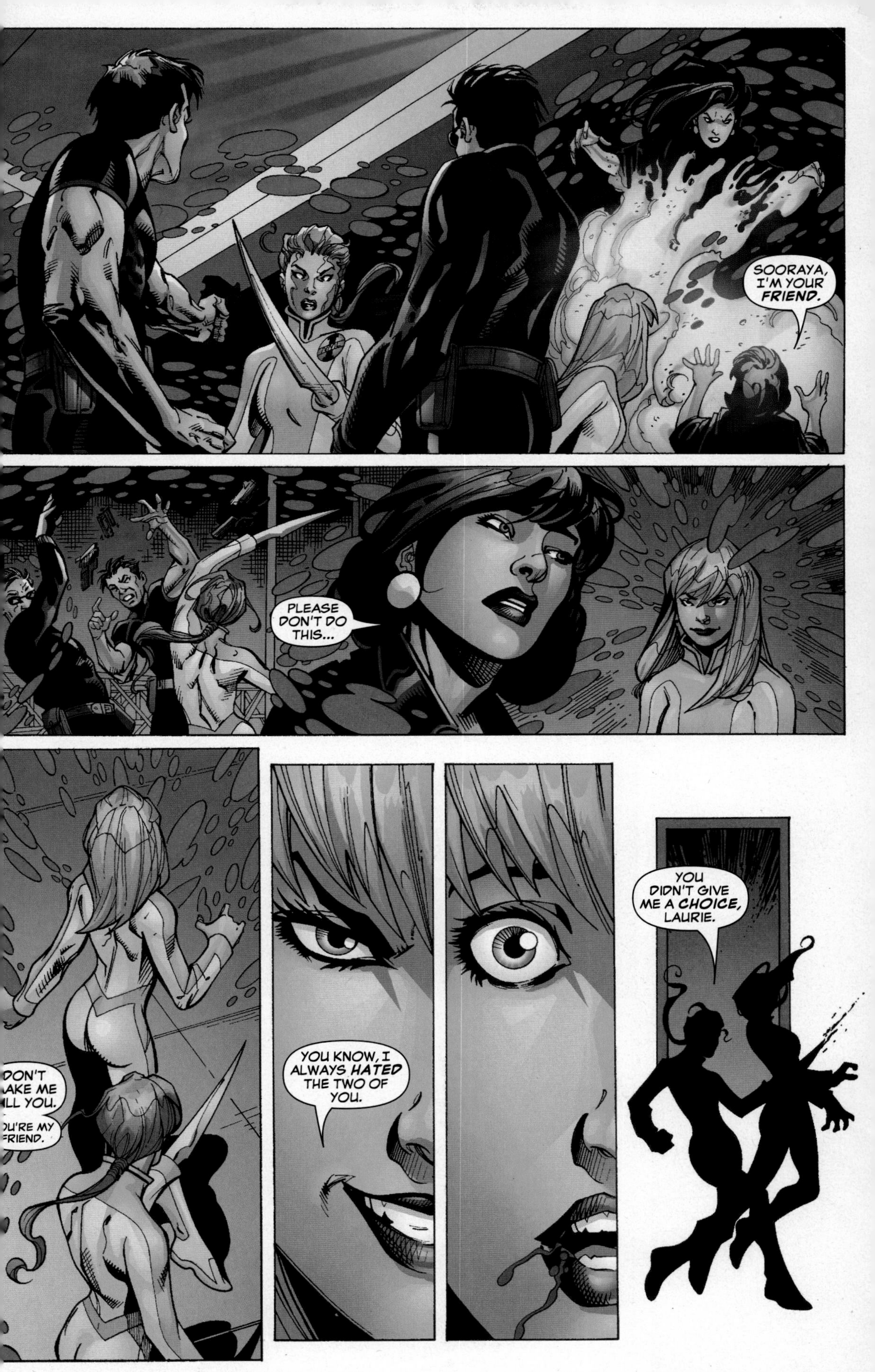
SOORAYA, I'M YOUR FRIEND.
PLEASE DON'T DO THIS...
DON'T AKE ME ILL YOU.
OU'RE MY FRIEND.
YOU KNOW, I ALWAYS HATED THE TWO OF YOU.
YOU DIDN'T GIVE ME A CHOICE, LAURIE.

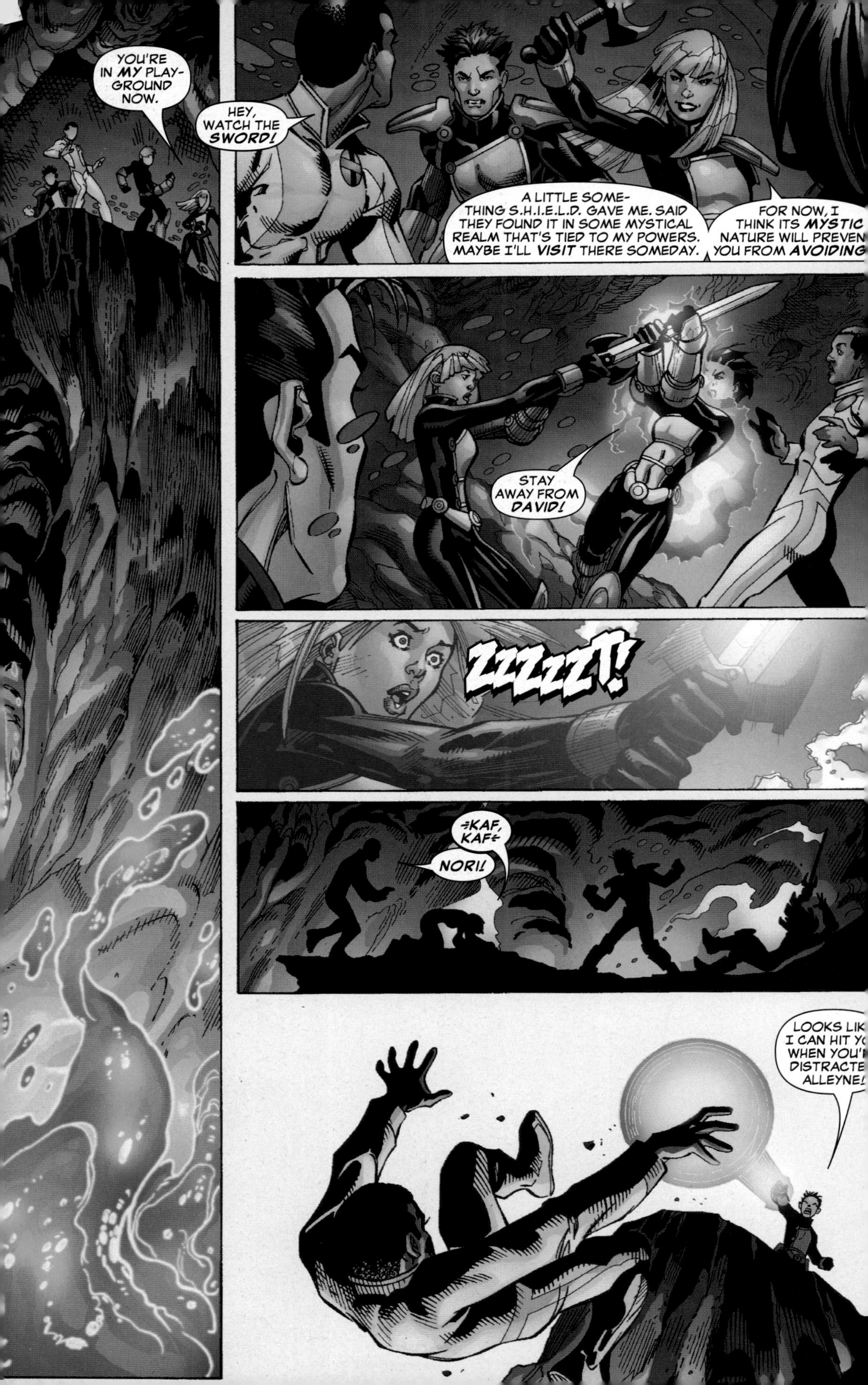
YOU'RE IN MY PLAY-GROUND NOW.
HEY, WATCH THE SWORD!
A LITTLE SOMETHING S.H.I.E.L.D. GAVE ME. SAID THEY FOUND IT IN SOME MYSTICAL REALM THAT'S TIED TO MY POWERS. MAYBE I'LL VISIT THERE SOMEDAY.
FOR NOW, I THINK ITS MYSTIC NATURE WILL PREVEN YOU FROM AVOIDING
STAY AWAY FROM DAVID!
ZZZZZT!
KAF, KAF
NORI!
LOOKS LIK I CAN HIT YO WHEN YOU'R DISTRACTE ALLEYNE!

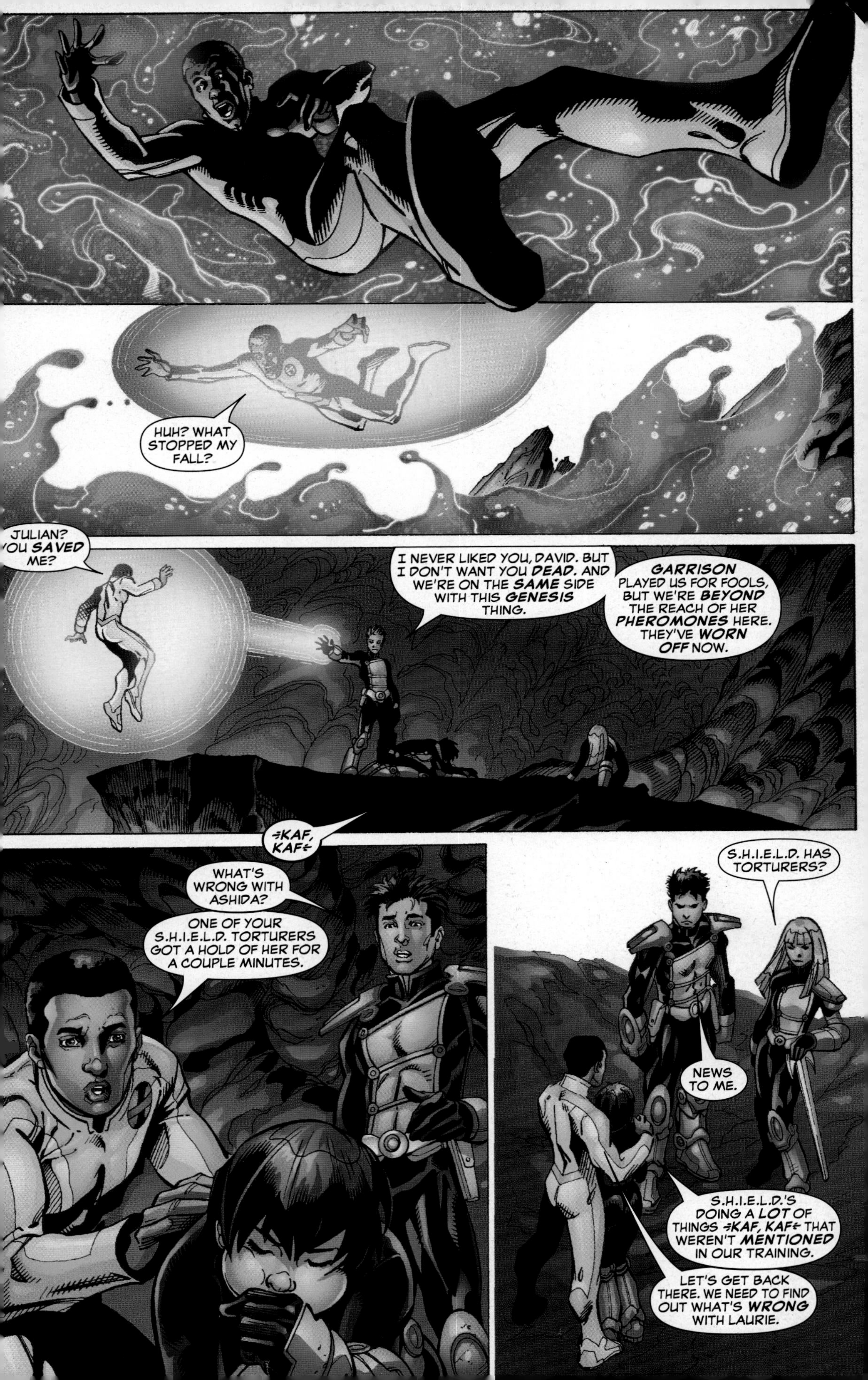
HUH? WHAT STOPPED MY FALL?
JULIAN? YOU SAVED ME?
I NEVER LIKED YOU, DAVID. BUT I DON'T WANT YOU DEAD. AND WE'RE ON THE SAME SIDE WITH THIS GENESIS THING.
GARRISON PLAYED US FOR FOOLS, BUT WE'RE BEYOND THE REACH OF HER PHEROMONES HERE. THEY'VE WORN OFF NOW.
KAF, KAF
WHAT'S WRONG WITH ASHIDA?
ONE OF YOUR S.H.I.E.L.D. TORTURERS GOT A HOLD OF HER FOR A COUPLE MINUTES.
S.H.I.E.L.D. HAS TORTURERS?
NEWS TO ME.
S.H.I.E.L.D.'S DOING A LOT OF THINGS KAF, KAF THAT WEREN'T MENTIONED IN OUR TRAINING.
LET'S GET BACK THERE. WE NEED TO FIND OUT WHAT'S WRONG WITH LAURIE.

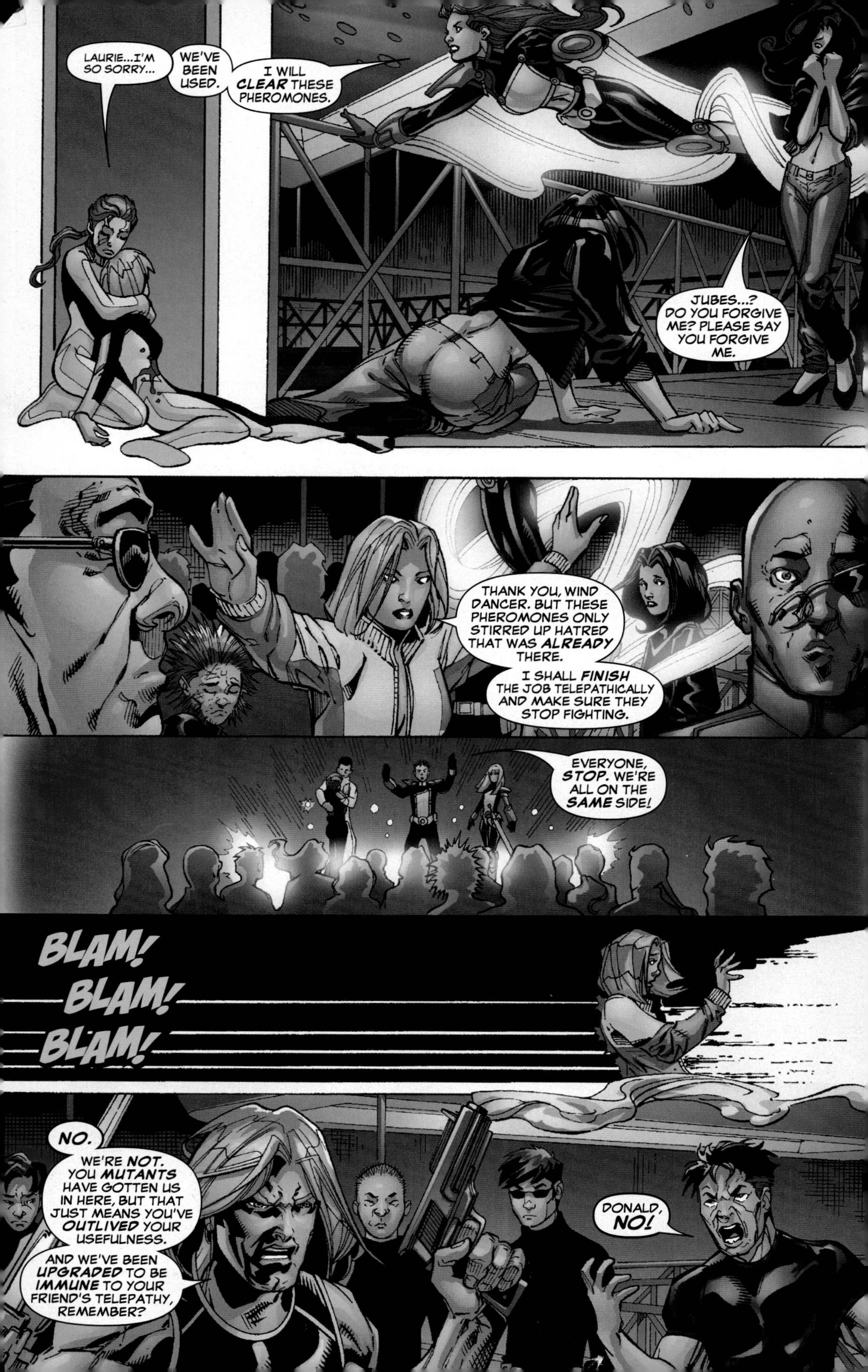
LAURIE...I'M SO SORRY...
WE'VE BEEN USED.
I WILL CLEAR THESE PHEROMONES.
JUBES...? DO YOU FORGIVE ME? PLEASE SAY YOU FORGIVE ME.
THANK YOU, WIND DANCER. BUT THESE PHEROMONES ONLY STIRRED UP HATRED THAT WAS ALREADY THERE.
I SHALL FINISH THE JOB TELEPATHICALLY AND MAKE SURE THEY STOP FIGHTING.
EVERYONE, STOP. WE'RE ALL ON THE SAME SIDE!
BLAM!
BLAM!
BLAM!
NO.
WE'RE NOT. YOU MUTANTS HAVE GOTTEN US IN HERE, BUT THAT JUST MEANS YOU'VE OUTLIVED YOUR USEFULNESS.
AND WE'VE BEEN UPGRADED TO BE IMMUNE TO YOUR FRIEND'S TELEPATHY, REMEMBER?
DONALD, NO!

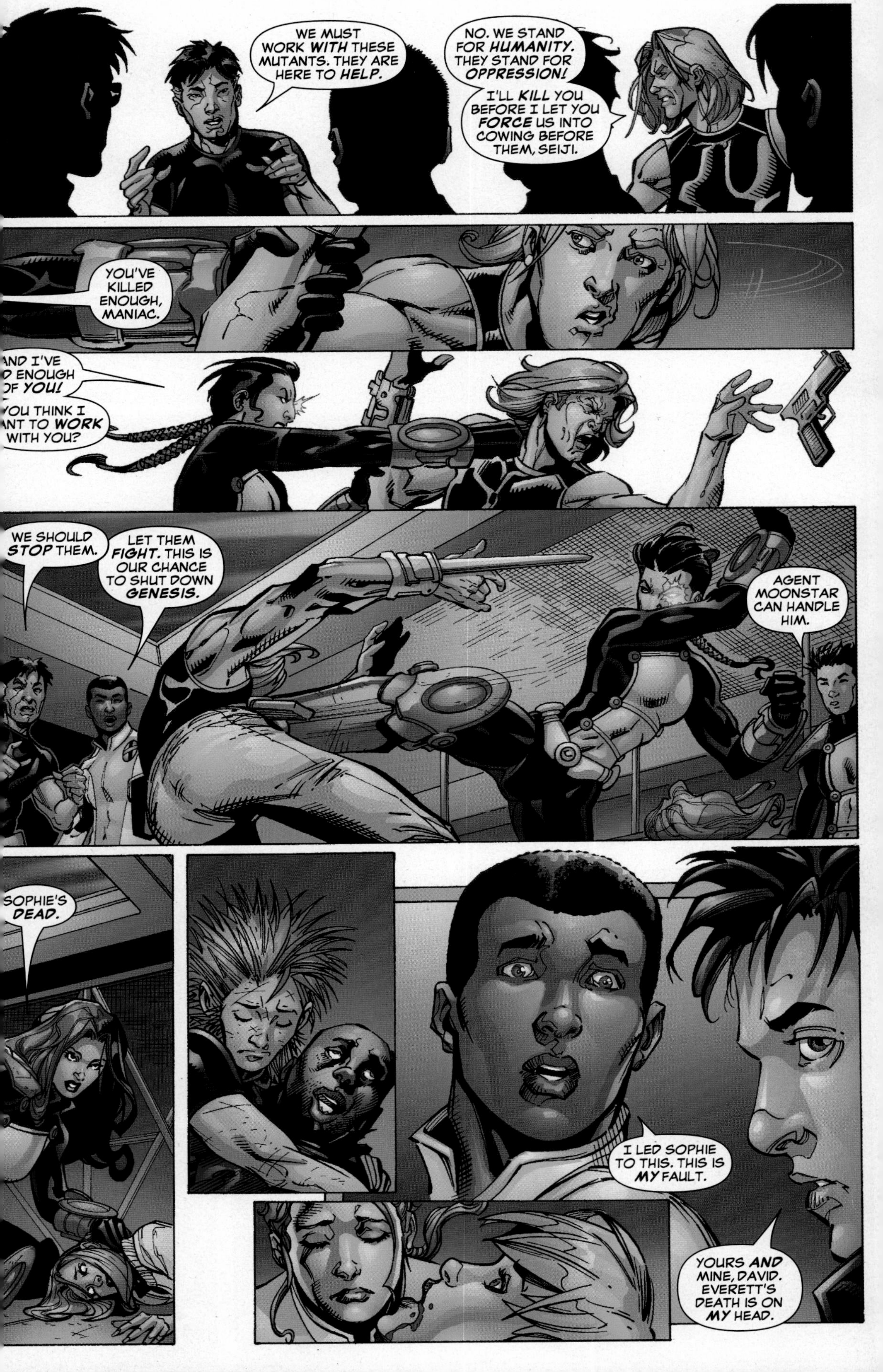
WE MUST WORK **WITH** THESE MUTANTS. THEY ARE HERE TO **HELP.**
NO. WE STAND FOR **HUMANITY.** THEY STAND FOR **OPPRESSION!**
I'LL **KILL** YOU BEFORE I LET YOU **FORCE** US INTO COWING BEFORE THEM, SEIJI.
YOU'VE KILLED ENOUGH, MANIAC.
AND I'VE D ENOUGH F **YOU!**
YOU THINK I ANT TO **WORK** WITH YOU?
WE SHOULD **STOP** THEM.
LET THEM **FIGHT.** THIS IS OUR CHANCE TO SHUT DOWN **GENESIS.**
AGENT **MOONSTAR** CAN HANDLE HIM.
SOPHIE'S **DEAD.**
I LED SOPHIE TO THIS. THIS IS **MY** FAULT.
YOURS **AND** MINE, DAVID. EVERETT'S DEATH IS ON **MY** HEAD.

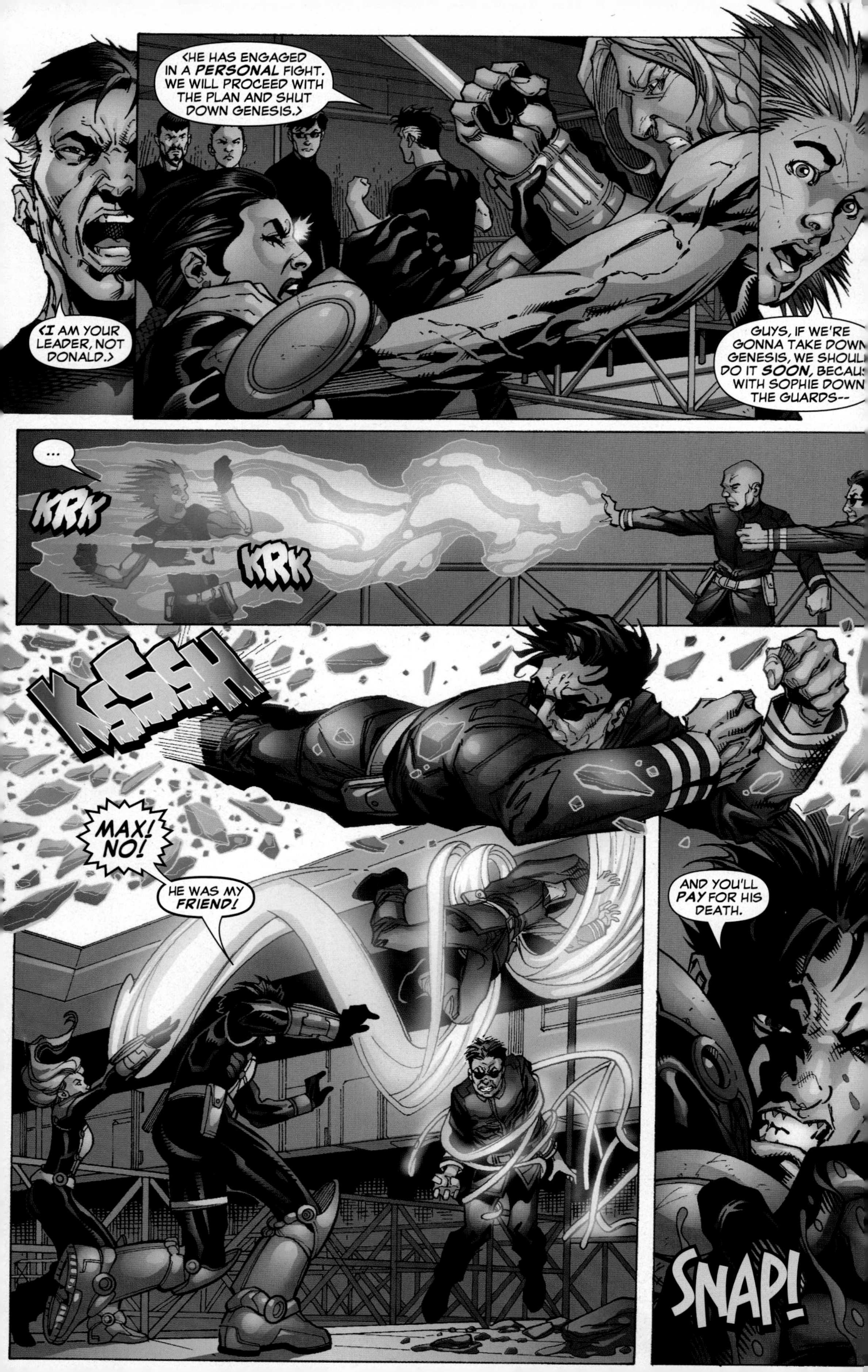
<I AM YOUR LEADER, NOT DONALD.>
<HE HAS ENGAGED IN A *PERSONAL* FIGHT. WE WILL PROCEED WITH THE PLAN AND SHUT DOWN GENESIS.>
GUYS, IF WE'RE GONNA TAKE DOWN GENESIS, WE SHOUL DO IT *SOON,* BECAUS WITH SOPHIE DOWN THE GUARDS--
...
KRK
KRK
KSSSH
MAX! NO!
HE WAS MY *FRIEND!*
AND YOU'LL *PAY* FOR HIS DEATH.
SNAP!

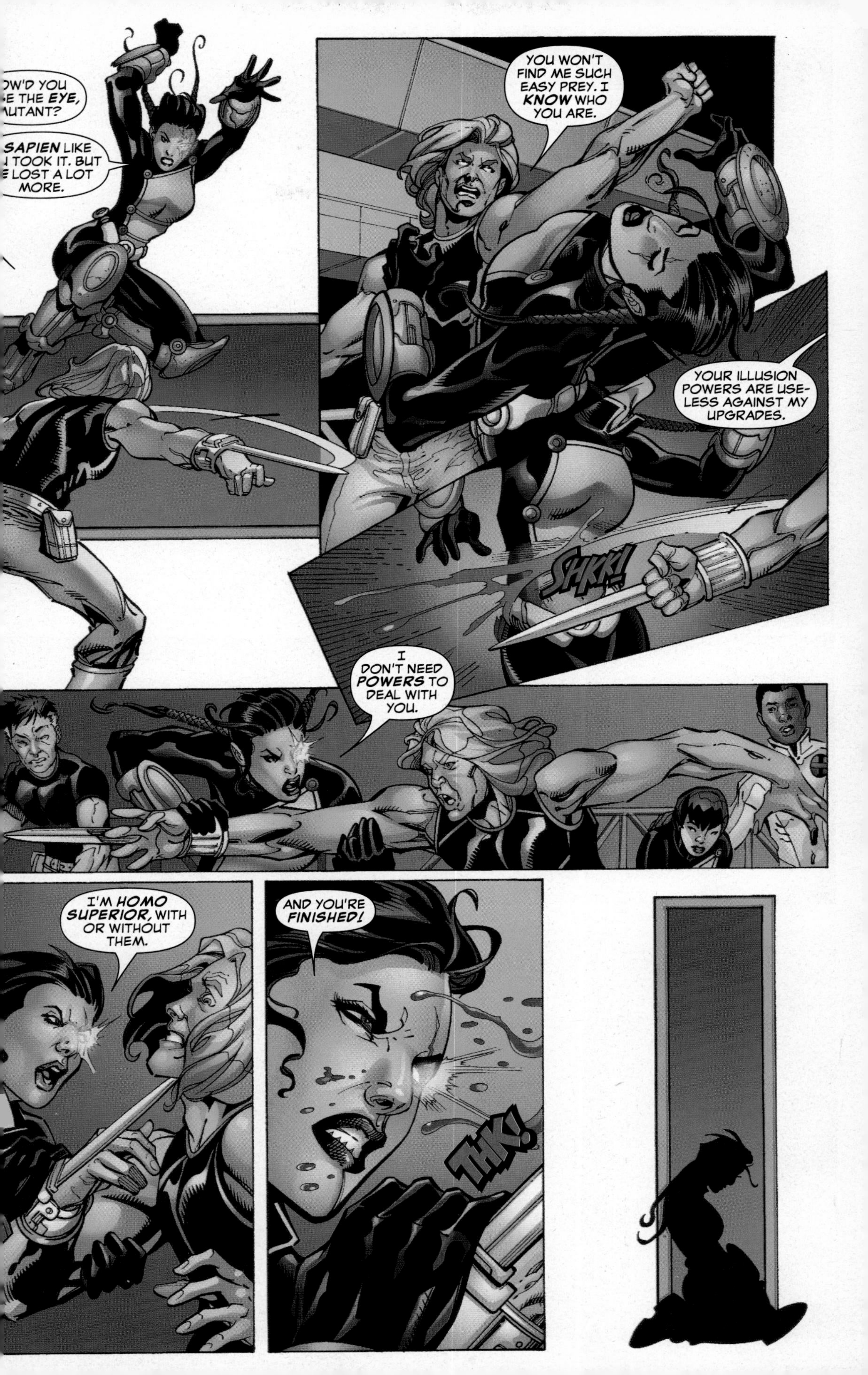
OW'D YOU
E THE EYE,
UTANT?
SAPIEN LIKE
TOOK IT. BUT
LOST A LOT
MORE.
YOU WON'T FIND ME SUCH EASY PREY. I KNOW WHO YOU ARE.
YOUR ILLUSION POWERS ARE USELESS AGAINST MY UPGRADES.
SHKK!
I DON'T NEED POWERS TO DEAL WITH YOU.
I'M HOMO SUPERIOR, WITH OR WITHOUT THEM.
AND YOU'RE FINISHED!
THK!

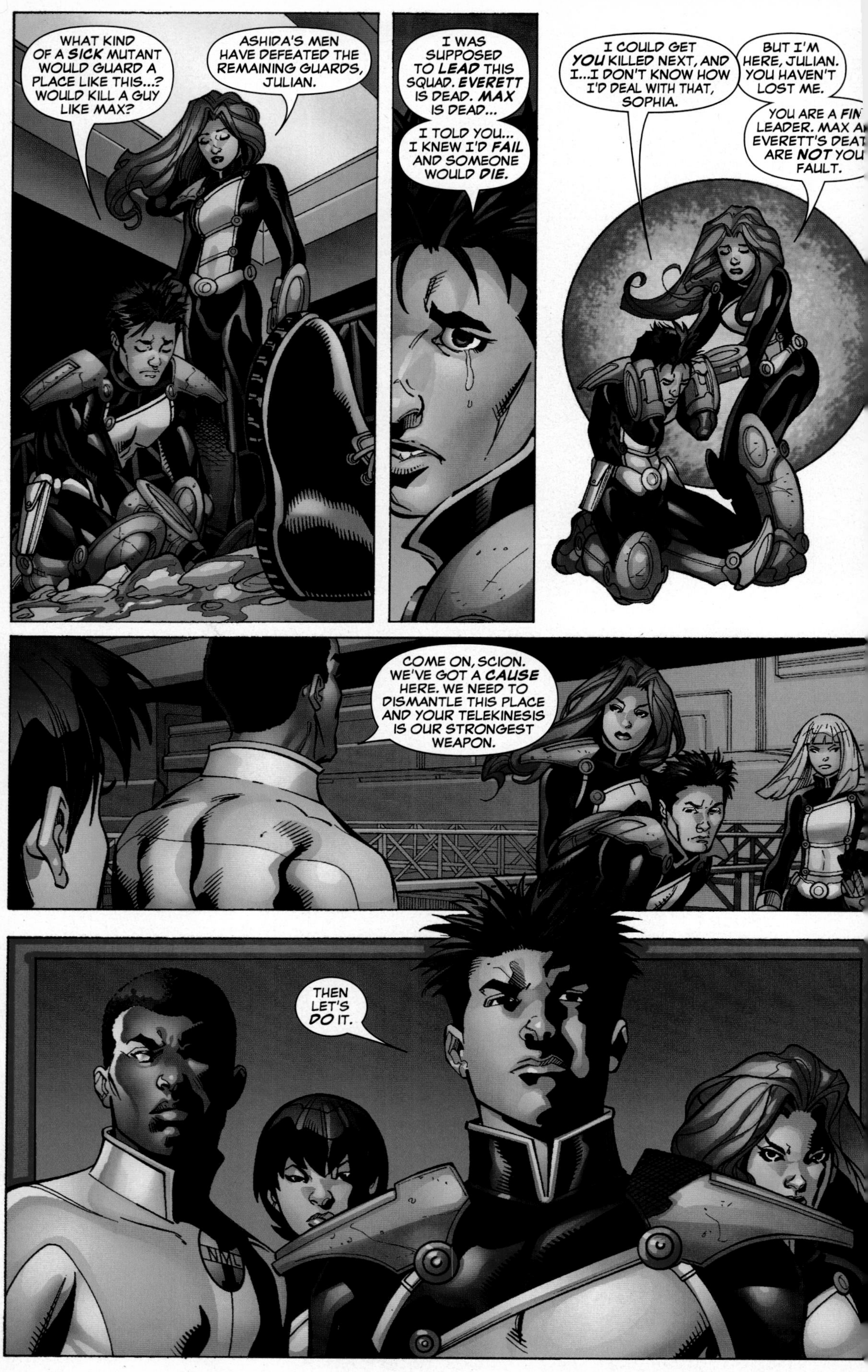

WHAT KIND OF A SICK MUTANT WOULD GUARD A PLACE LIKE THIS...? WOULD KILL A GUY LIKE MAX?
ASHIDA'S MEN HAVE DEFEATED THE REMAINING GUARDS, JULIAN.
I WAS SUPPOSED TO LEAD THIS SQUAD. EVERETT IS DEAD. MAX IS DEAD...
I TOLD YOU... I KNEW I'D FAIL AND SOMEONE WOULD DIE.
I COULD GET YOU KILLED NEXT, AND I...I DON'T KNOW HOW I'D DEAL WITH THAT, SOPHIA.
BUT I'M HERE, JULIAN. YOU HAVEN'T LOST ME.
YOU ARE A FIN LEADER. MAX A EVERETT'S DEAT ARE NOT YOU FAULT.
COME ON, SCION. WE'VE GOT A CAUSE HERE. WE NEED TO DISMANTLE THIS PLACE AND YOUR TELEKINESIS IS OUR STRONGEST WEAPON.
THEN LET'S DO IT.

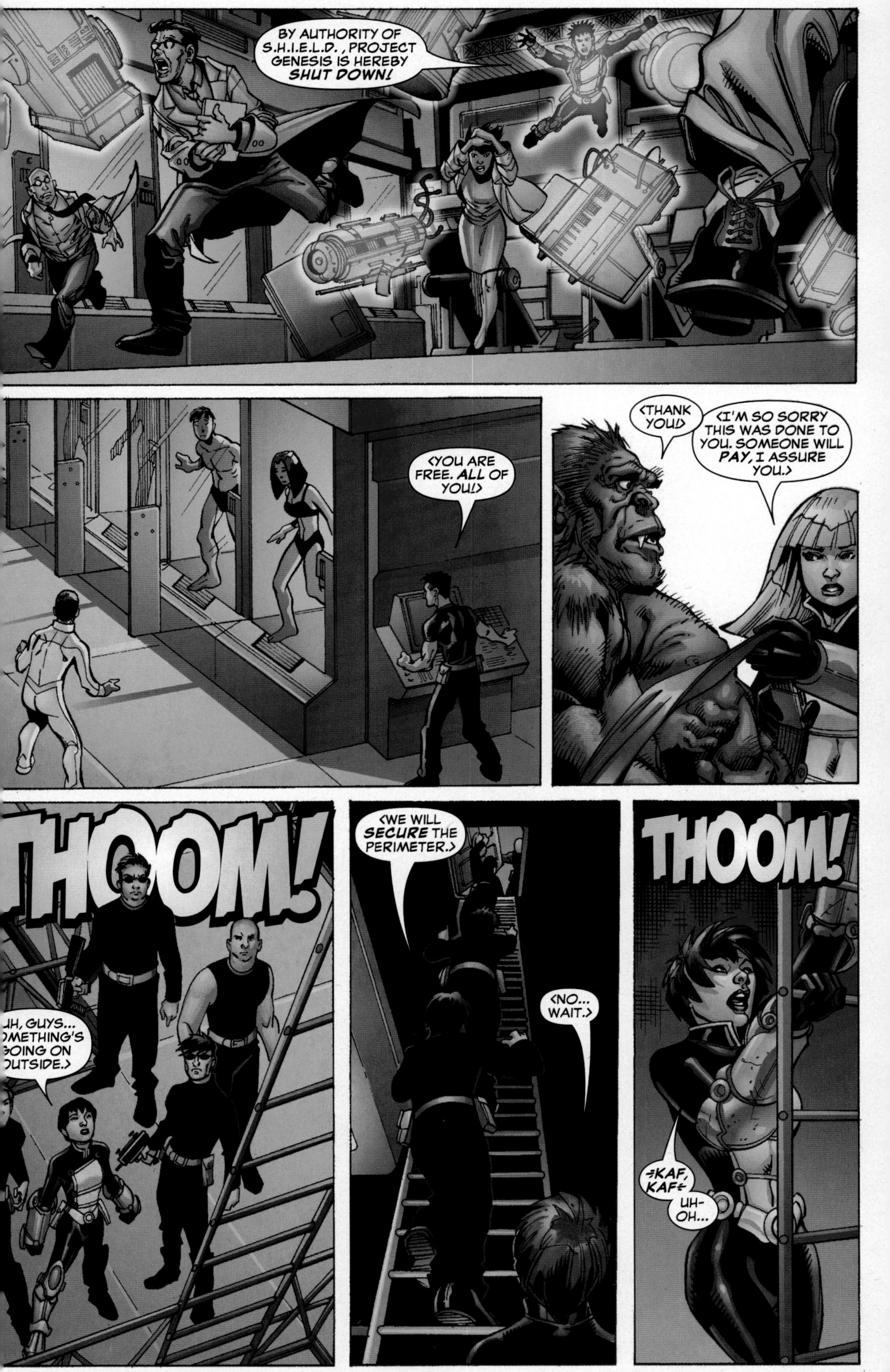
BY AUTHORITY OF S.H.I.E.L.D., PROJECT GENESIS IS HEREBY SHUT DOWN!
<YOU ARE FREE. ALL OF YOU!>
<THANK YOU!>
<I'M SO SORRY THIS WAS DONE TO YOU. SOMEONE WILL PAY, I ASSURE YOU.>
THOOM!
UH, GUYS... SOMETHING'S GOING ON OUTSIDE.>
<WE WILL SECURE THE PERIMETER.>
<NO... WAIT.>
THOOM!
=KAF, KAF=
UH-OH...

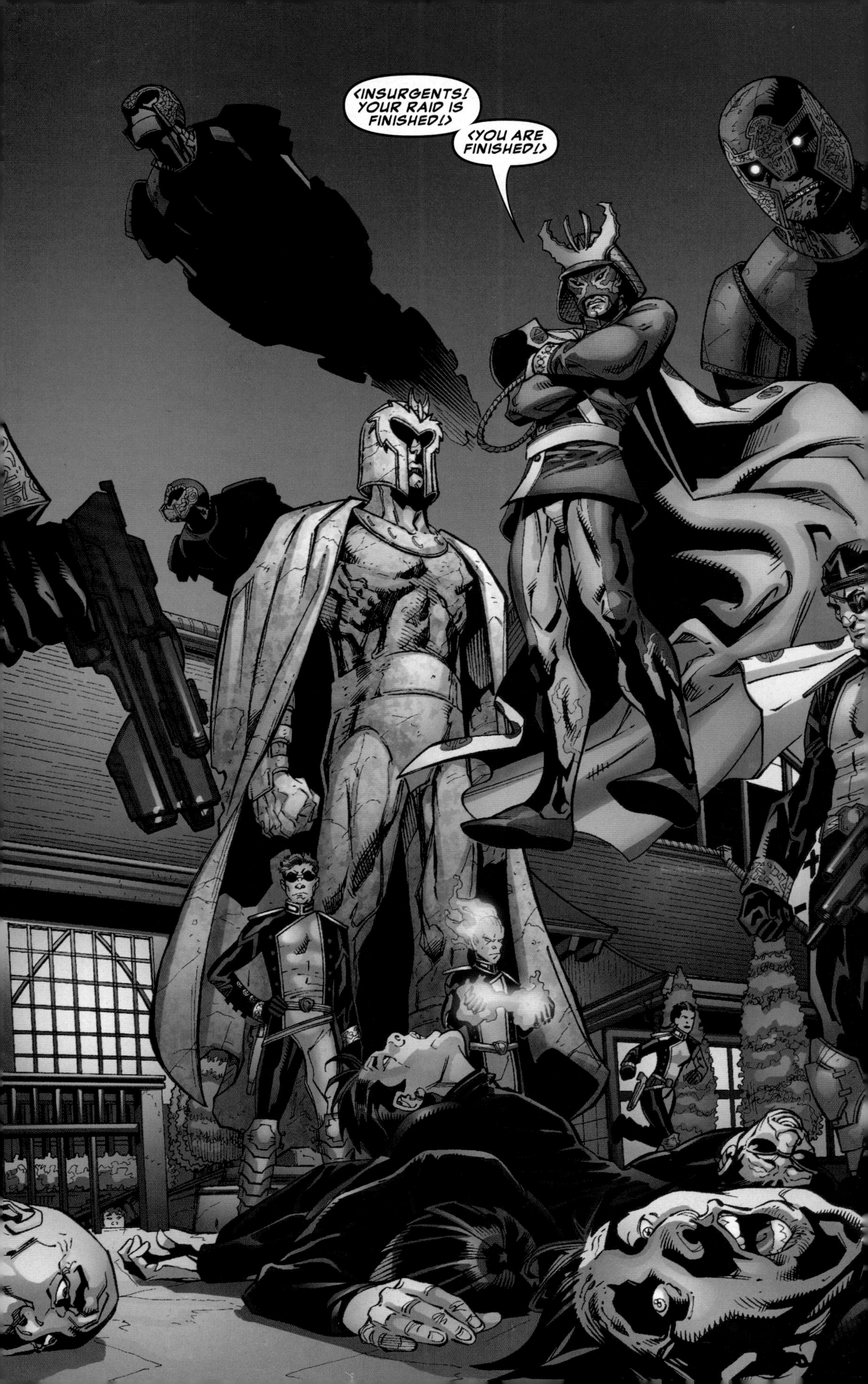
<INSURGENTS! YOUR RAID IS FINISHED!>
<YOU ARE FINISHED!>

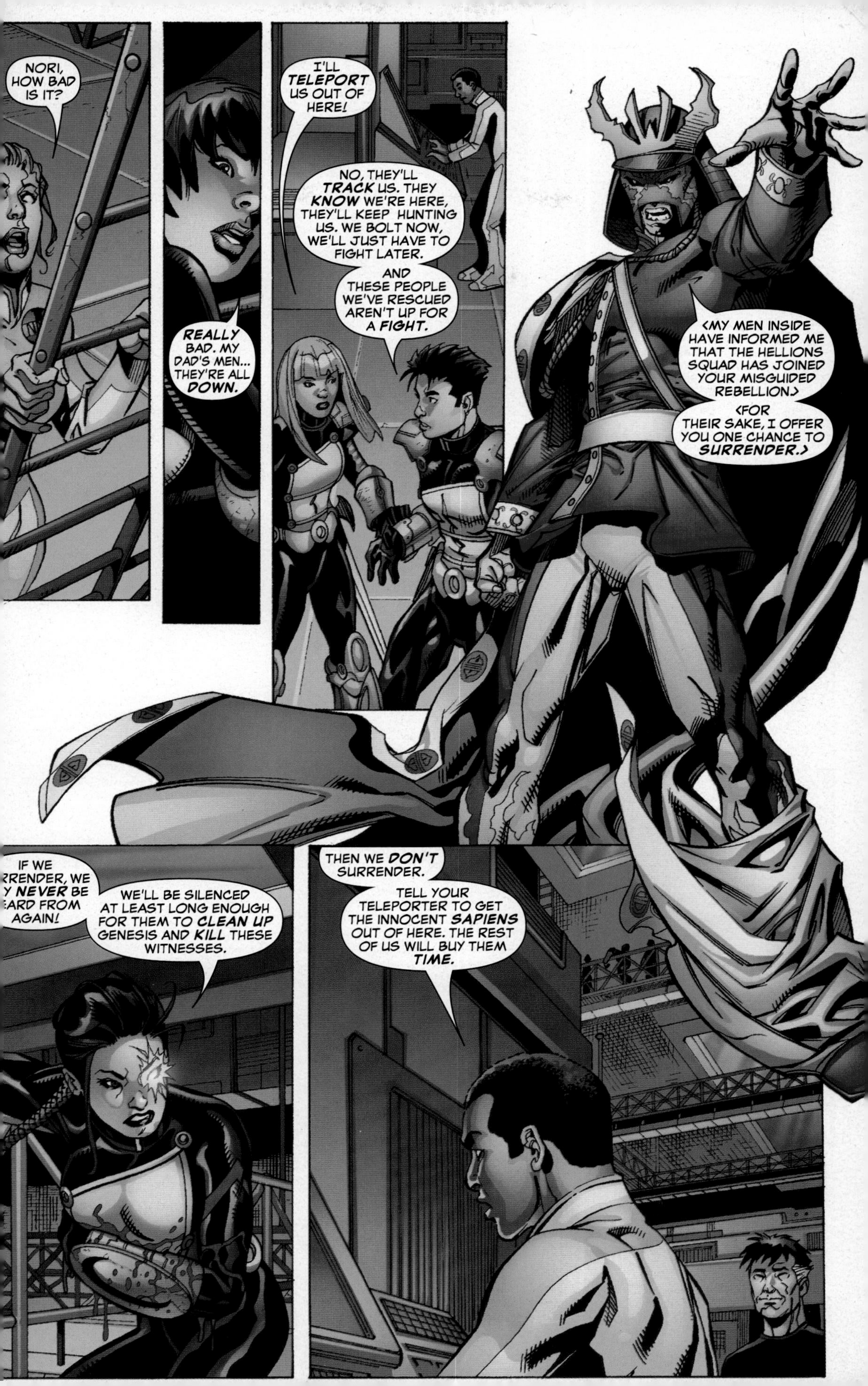
NORI, HOW BAD IS IT?
REALLY BAD. MY DAD'S MEN... THEY'RE ALL DOWN.
I'LL TELEPORT US OUT OF HERE!
NO, THEY'LL TRACK US. THEY KNOW WE'RE HERE, THEY'LL KEEP HUNTING US. WE BOLT NOW, WE'LL JUST HAVE TO FIGHT LATER.
AND THESE PEOPLE WE'VE RESCUED AREN'T UP FOR A FIGHT.
<MY MEN INSIDE HAVE INFORMED ME THAT THE HELLIONS SQUAD HAS JOINED YOUR MISGUIDED REBELLION.>
<FOR THEIR SAKE, I OFFER YOU ONE CHANCE TO SURRENDER.>
IF WE RRENDER, WE Y NEVER BE EARD FROM AGAIN!
WE'LL BE SILENCED AT LEAST LONG ENOUGH FOR THEM TO CLEAN UP GENESIS AND KILL THESE WITNESSES.
THEN WE DON'T SURRENDER.
TELL YOUR TELEPORTER TO GET THE INNOCENT SAPIENS OUT OF HERE. THE REST OF US WILL BUY THEM TIME.

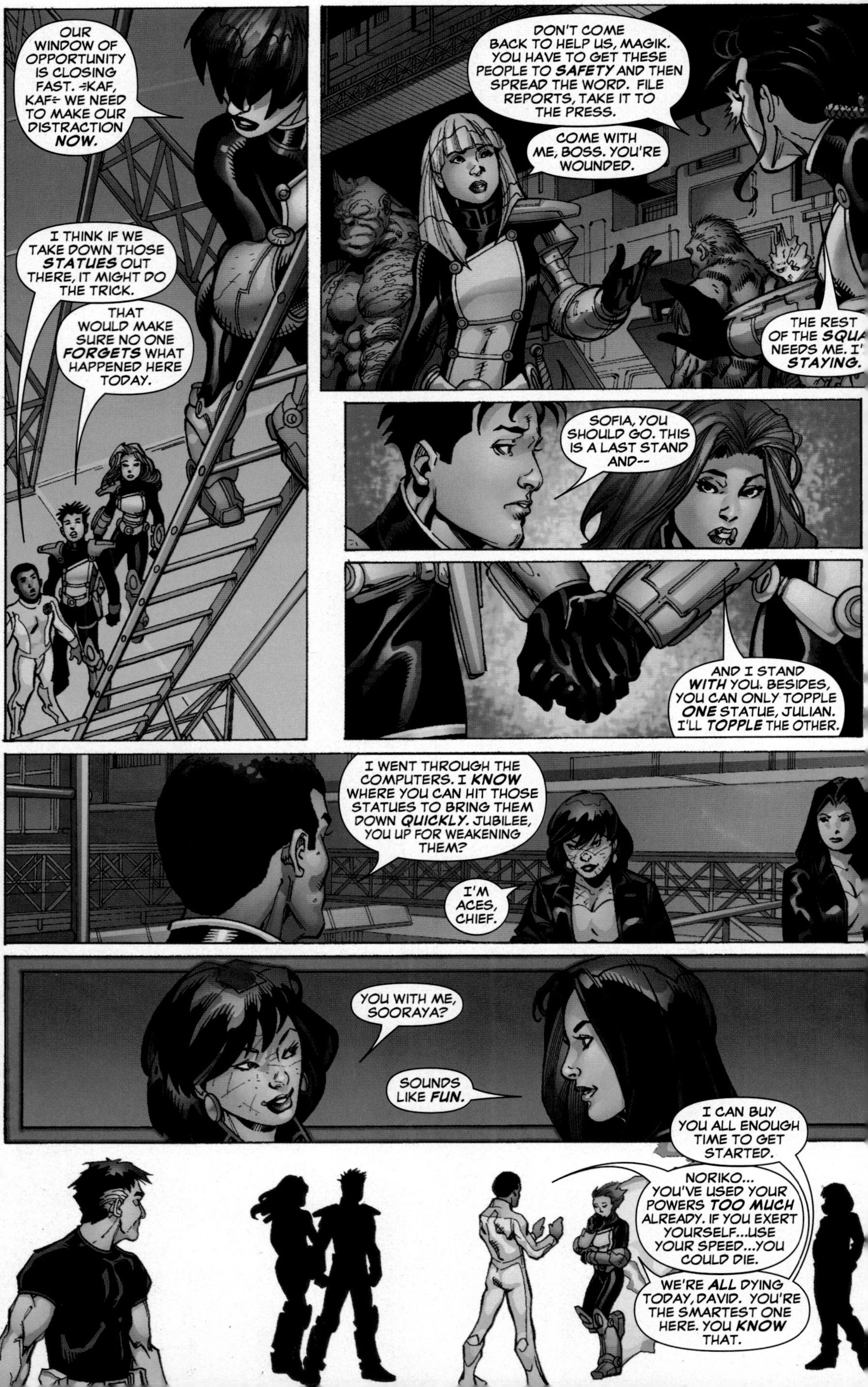
OUR WINDOW OF OPPORTUNITY IS CLOSING FAST. =KAF, KAF= WE NEED TO MAKE OUR DISTRACTION NOW.
I THINK IF WE TAKE DOWN THOSE STATUES OUT THERE, IT MIGHT DO THE TRICK.
THAT WOULD MAKE SURE NO ONE FORGETS WHAT HAPPENED HERE TODAY.
DON'T COME BACK TO HELP US, MAGIK. YOU HAVE TO GET THESE PEOPLE TO SAFETY AND THEN SPREAD THE WORD. FILE REPORTS, TAKE IT TO THE PRESS.
COME WITH ME, BOSS. YOU'RE WOUNDED.
THE REST OF THE SQUA NEEDS ME. I' STAYING.
SOFIA, YOU SHOULD GO. THIS IS A LAST STAND AND--
AND I STAND WITH YOU. BESIDES, YOU CAN ONLY TOPPLE ONE STATUE, JULIAN. I'LL TOPPLE THE OTHER.
I WENT THROUGH THE COMPUTERS. I KNOW WHERE YOU CAN HIT THOSE STATUES TO BRING THEM DOWN QUICKLY. JUBILEE, YOU UP FOR WEAKENING THEM?
I'M ACES, CHIEF.
YOU WITH ME, SOORAYA?
SOUNDS LIKE FUN.
I CAN BUY YOU ALL ENOUGH TIME TO GET STARTED.
NORIKO... YOU'VE USED YOUR POWERS TOO MUCH ALREADY. IF YOU EXERT YOURSELF...USE YOUR SPEED...YOU COULD DIE.
WE'RE ALL DYING TODAY, DAVID. YOU'RE THE SMARTEST ONE HERE. YOU KNOW THAT.

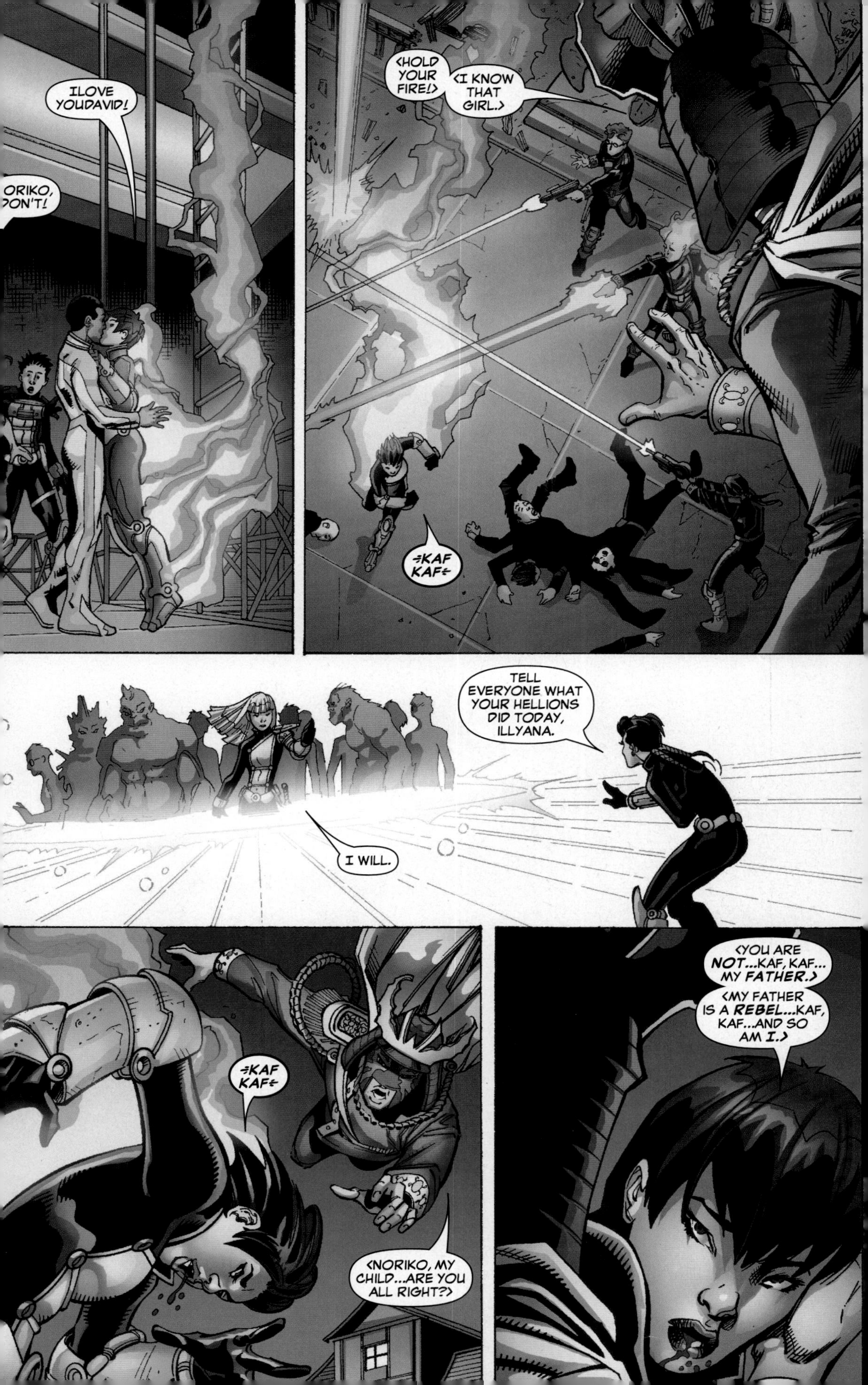
ILOVE YOUDAVID!
ORIKO, DON'T!
<HOLD YOUR FIRE!>
<I KNOW THAT GIRL.>
KAF KAF
TELL EVERYONE WHAT YOUR HELLIONS DID TODAY, ILLYANA.
I WILL.
KAF KAF
<NORIKO, MY CHILD...ARE YOU ALL RIGHT?>
<YOU ARE NOT...KAF, KAF... MY FATHER.>
<MY FATHER IS A REBEL...KAF, KAF...AND SO AM I.>

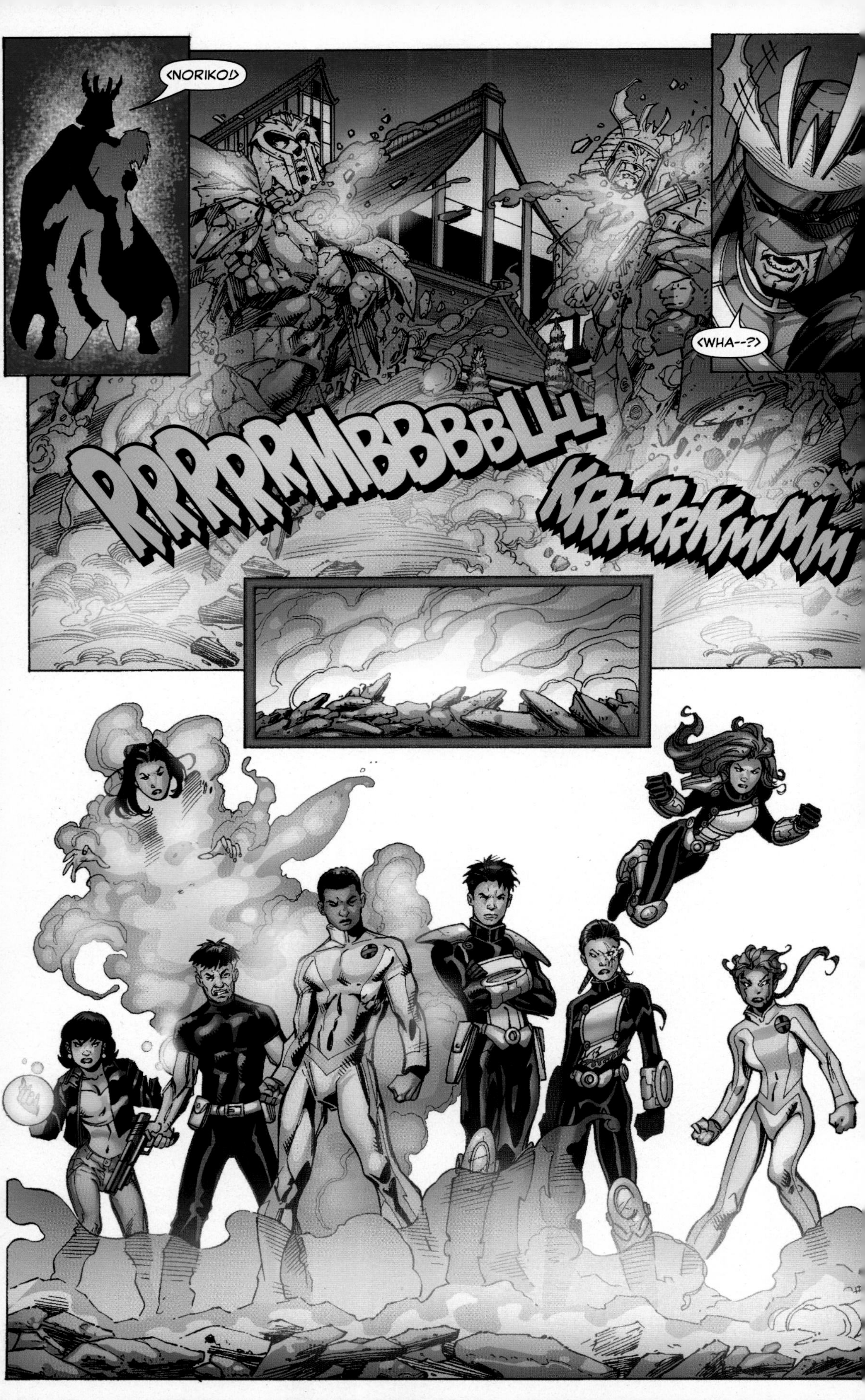
<NORIKO!>
<WHA--?>
RRRRRMBBBBLLL
KRRRRRKMMM

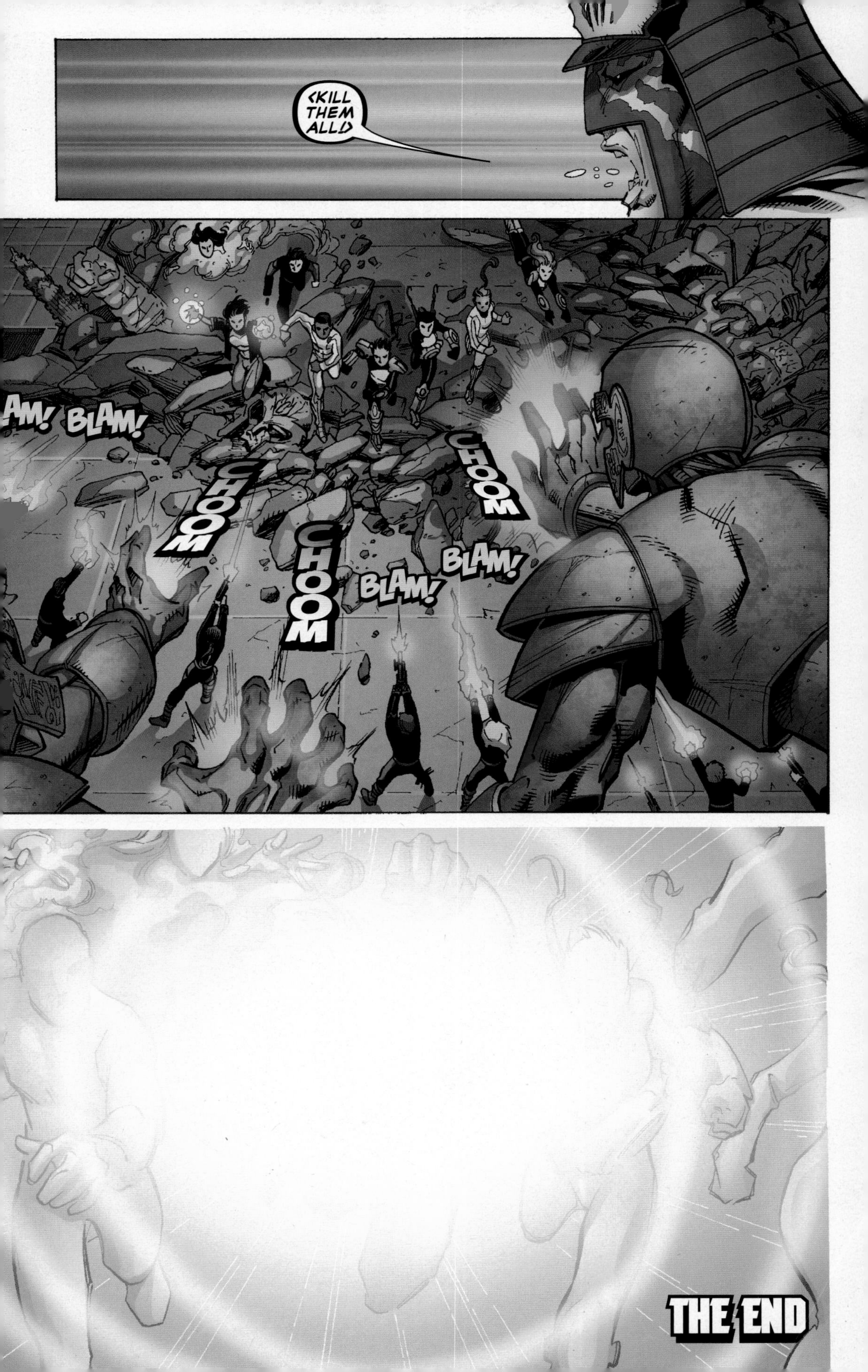
<KILL THEM ALL!>
AM! BLAM!
CHOOM
CHOOM
BLAM!
BLAM!
CHOOM
THE END

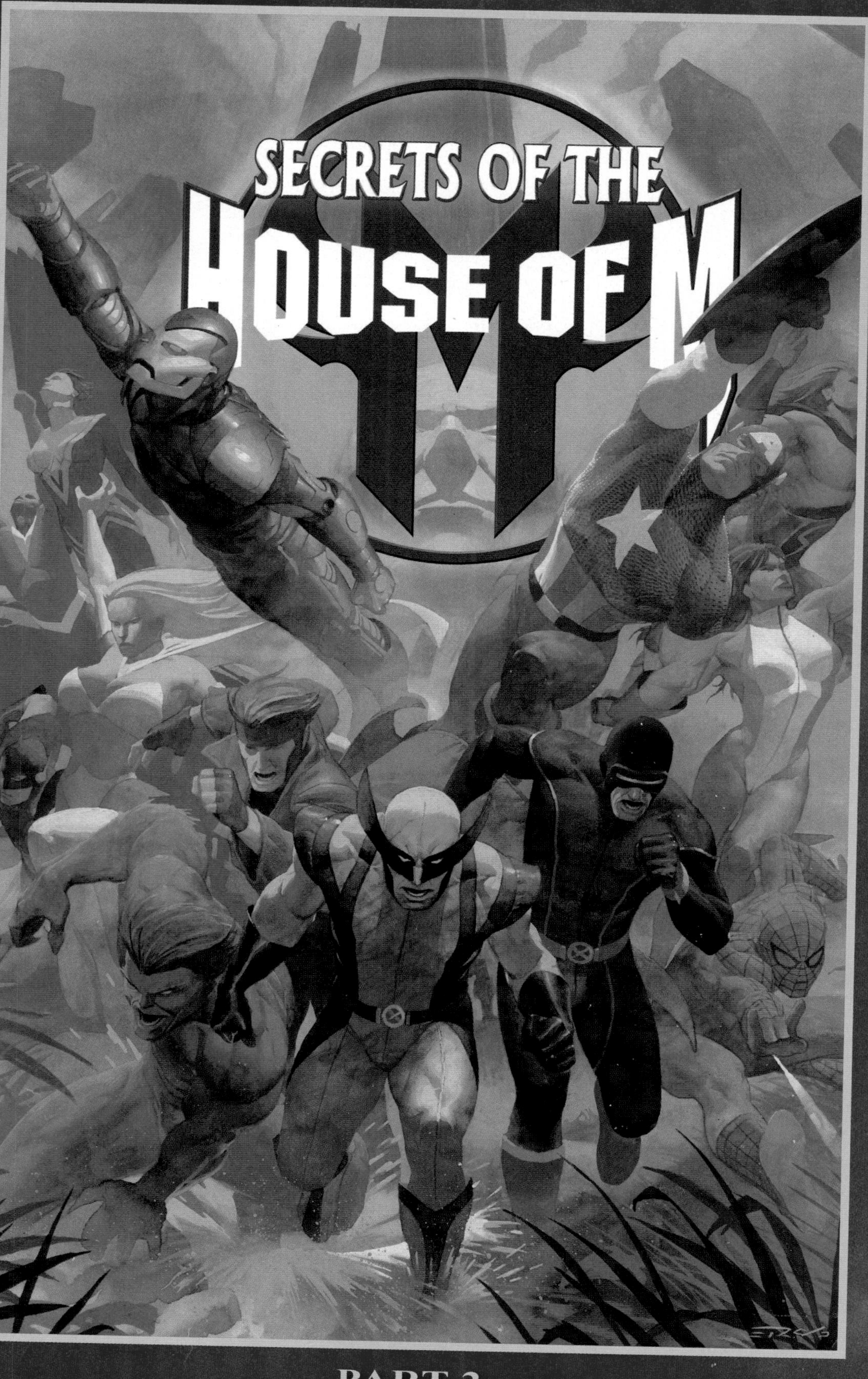
SECRETS OF THE
HOUSE OF M

PART 2

Sapiens

The world has changed. For centuries, the dominant species on the planet was Homo Sapiens, but that is not the case today. Some have evolved. In the mid-twentieth century, humans with amazing powers began to appear in greater numbers. It happened slowly at first, but those with vision could see the writing on the wall. The time of Homo Sapiens was coming to an end, and the time of Homo Superior was dawning.

Following the end of the Mutant-Human War, and the victory of Magneto over the human and Sentinel armies, Sapiens were allowed to go about their lives. Many assumed Magneto would be a vengeful victor, but this was not the case. His vengeance was of a different variety. It was a quiet victory. His species, Homo Superior, would continue on, while the Sapiens would eventually fade away.

Today, normal humans are a minority in the new world order. While they are not a slave race, there is an understanding that this is the end of their time on the planet. Within two to three generations, human beings will be extinct.

Art by Olivier Coipel

Luke Cage

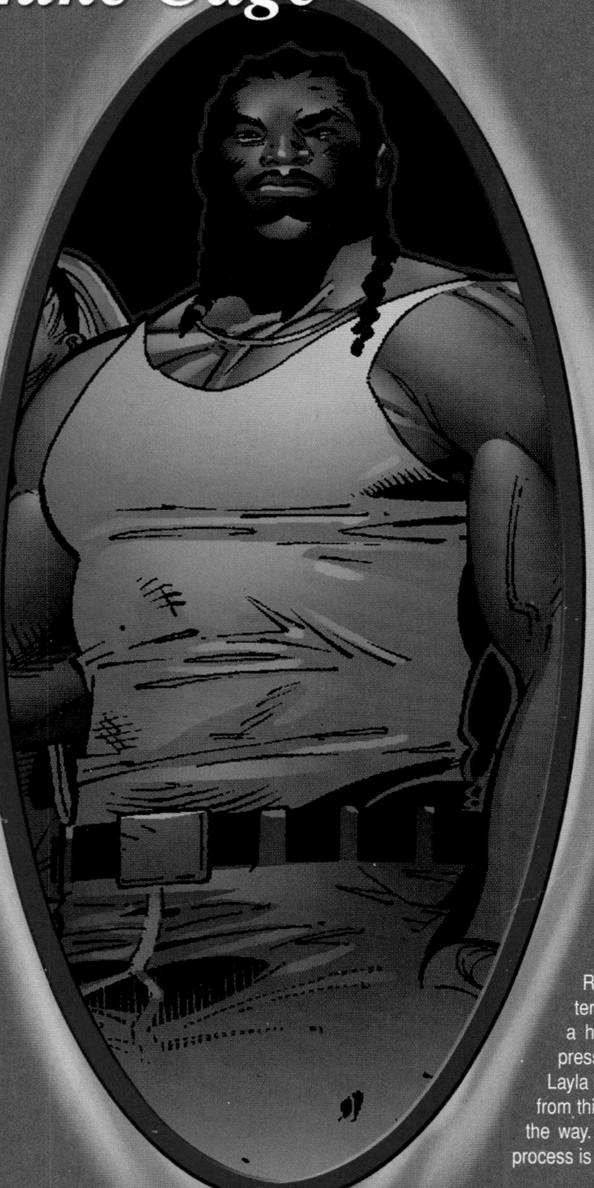

REAL NAME: Carl Lucas
KNOWN ALIASES: None
IDENTITY: Secret, unknown to authorities
OCCUPATION: Leader of an underworld crime group and human terrorist organization
PLACE OF BIRTH: New York City
CITIZENSHIP: U.S.A., wanted for questioning regarding numerous genetic crimes
KNOWN RELATIVES: James Leonard Lucas (father), Esther (mother, deceased), James Jr. (brother)
GROUP AFFILIATION: Luke Cage's underworld organization in Hell's Kitchen, Bloods
EDUCATION: Unfinished high-school education
HEIGHT: 6'6"
WEIGHT: 425 lbs.
EYES: Brown
HAIR: Black

HISTORY: Born and raised in Harlem, Carl Lucas spent his youth in a gang called the Bloods. He was arrested multiple times and sent to prison for a murder he did not commit. He had little chance of parole. During this time, the Mutant-Human War was at its height. With Sentinel armies losing ground against Magneto and his Mutants, the United States government was desperate. In an effort to create their own super-soldiers they began experimenting on inmates at Cage's prison. Luke volunteered for the program and was one of its few success stories. More powerful than his experimenters anticipated, Luke was able to escape. He made his way back to Hell's Kitchen and, in the months following the end of the Mutant-Human War, established himself as a major crime lord.

Recently, Luke and his gang have become the leading crime group in Hell's Kitchen. He gathered other impressive humans and superhumans and was able to destroy the Kingpin's organization, as well as put down the Dragon group.

Realizing it is only a matter of time before mutants move in on his territory, Luke has begun to channel his gang's energy into becoming a human resistance movement. This idea has become even more pressing since Luke was confronted by a young mutant girl named Layla Miller. Layla used her mutant powers to show Luke a world different from this one — one in which Luke is a hero with a girlfriend and child on the way. What consequences this has on Luke and his decision-making process is unknown.

SUPERHUMAN POWERS: Luke Cage is superhumanly strong, able to lift/press approximately 25 tons and punch through barriers as thick as four-inch steel plate. Besides superhuman strength, his skin is steel-hard and his muscles and bone tissue are super-dense. He can also recover from injury or trauma in one-third the time of an ordinary human.

Art by Olivier Coipel

Human Resistance Movement

...ed by Luke Cage, the Human Resistance Movement has only recently made the transition from underworld ...riminal organization to freedom fighters. This group's original goal was to control Hell's Kitchen, and it has ...ucceeded. Now, realizing humankind is fighting over the crumbs of their crumbling world, Cage has created ...new mission for himself and his gang – to strike back against the mutants and reestablish humans in this ...vorld. With Sapiens on the edge of extinction, it appears as if this is going to be an impossible task, but Cage ...nd his Resistance Movement seem equal to it. Whether they can truly make a difference in a world with as ...huch mutant firepower as this one is doubtful.

BLACK CAT
REAL NAME: Felicia Hardy
SUPERHUMAN POWERS: Incredible luck powers

CLOAK
REAL NAME: Tyrone Johnson
SUPERHUMAN POWERS: Darkforce control/
teleportation

HAWKEYE
REAL NAME: Clint Barton
ABILITITES: Expert marksman

IRON FIST
REAL NAME: Danny Rand
SUPERHUMAN POWERS: Martial Arts Expert/
Possessor of the Iron Fist

MERCEDES "MISTY" KNIGHT
ABILITITES: Weapons expert

LAYLA MILLER
SUPERHUMAN POWERS: Untapped psychic abilities

SONS OF THE TIGER
REAL NAMES: Bob Diamond
Abe Brown
Lin Sun
Lotus Shincheko
ABILITITES: Martial Arts experts

WHITE TIGER
REAL NAME: Angela Del Toro
SUPERHUMAN POWERS: Mystically enhanced
martial arts skills

Art by Olivier Coipel

SAPIENS

Doom

REAL NAME: Victor Von Doom
KNOWN ALIASES: None
IDENTITY: Publicly known
OCCUPATION: King of New Latveria
PLACE OF BIRTH: Latveria
CITIZENSHIP: A camp outside Haasenstadt (now Doomstadt), Latveria
KNOWN RELATIVES: Werner (father, deceased), Cynthia (mother), Kristoff (Torch, son), Valeria (Invincible Woman, wife)
GROUP AFFILIATION: Fearsome Four
EDUCATION: College studies in the sciences (expelled before completion of degree); self-educated to doctorate level and beyond in most sciences
HEIGHT: 6'2"
WEIGHT: 225 lbs.; (with Liquid Metal) 300 lbs.
EYES: Brown
HAIR: Brown

HISTORY: With the arrival of mutants into society, Victor Von Doom realized humankind was behind the genetic curve. In order to raise himself above his genes, Victor studied ways to advance himself technologically and mystically. He succeeded in creating a Liquid Metal he could use as a body armor and manipulate into weapons.

Instead of fighting Magneto during the Mutant-Human War, Doom offered to fight by his side. Realizing that mutants were obviously the next step in human evolution, Doom wanted to be on the winning side of the war — and he was. Doom became Magneto's most successful ally. Although neither of them truly trusted each other, each man respected the other's powers and abilities.

After the mutant victory over the humans, Doom took over the nation of New Latveria. He eventually married a woman named Valeria and adopted a child, Kristoff; he transformed them into the superhumans Invincible Woman and the Torch, respectively. They, along with the monstrous It, form the Fearsome Four. The group is used as a strike force by Magneto to keep other superhumans in line. It is a position Doom would prefer not to be in, but with the amount of mutants in the world, and the power Magneto has over them, it would be unwise to lash out in frustration — especially with no concrete plan laid out for victory.

Recently, Doom's frustration at being seen as Magneto's human lapdog has caused him to question his relationship with the House of M. How, and if, he decides to sever that relationship has not been decided.

SUPERHUMAN POWERS: Doom's metallic form gives him superhuman strength which allows him to press/lift close to 10 tons. He can mentally command the liquid metal of his body to morph into a variety of shapes and weapons.

Fearsome Four

The Fearsome Four is Victor Von Doom's superhuman strike force. The team is made up of Doom himself; Valeria, his wife; Kristoff, his son; and the grotesque It. From their castle in New Latveria, Doom and his family control a large section of Europe. They are the most powerful group of super Sapiens on the planet and are considered royalty by human standards.

Used primarily by Victor to keep his country safe and to demonstrate his dominance over his people, the Fearsome Four is also called upon by Magneto as a first strike weapon against other super-humans across the world. Many in the human community question why a man like Von Doom would allow himself to be controlled by Magneto. The reality is that the two of them cannot stand each other, but neither has been able to prevail over the other.

DOOM
REAL NAME: King Victor Von Doom
SUPERHUMAN POWERS: Liquid Metal Body

THE INVINCIBLE WOMAN
REAL NAME: Queen Valeria Von Doom
SUPERHUMAN POWERS: Force Bubbles & Minor Molecular Control
HISTORY: The mother figure of this motley brood, she has no problem transforming from loving mother around Kristoff to sadistic killer when her family is threatened. She controls the actions of the It during battle with a telekinetic leash. It is unknown how she truly feels about Victor, but it is clear she is completely in love with his power.

THE INHUMAN TORCH
REAL NAME: Prince Kristoff Von Doom
SUPERHUMAN POWERS: Flame Control/Flight
HISTORY: As the only son of the world's most powerful human, Kristoff looks at himself as something more than human. He likes to indulge himself with the women of New Latveria and is feared across the land for his vicious temper. He is a spoiled only child and lives his life at the whim of his base instincts. Victor loves his son dearly and is grooming Kristoff to one day succeed him.

THE IT
REAL NAME: Unknown
SUPERHUMAN POWERS: Superstrength/Rocky Hide
HISTORY: The monstrous It is Von Doom's personal bodyguard. By all appearances, this monster is as intelligent as a dog and needs to be controlled by the Invincible Woman during battles. Victor treats him roughly one moment and like an old friend the next.

Art by Scot Eaton

Captain Britain

REAL NAME: Brian Braddock
KNOWN ALIASES: None
IDENTITY: Publicly known
OCCUPATION: Ruler of Britain
PLACE OF BIRTH: United Kingdom
CITIZENSHIP: Braddock Manor, England, UK
KNOWN RELATIVES: Sir James Braddock Sr. (father deceased), Elizabeth (mother, deceased), Meggan (Queen of England, wife), Elizabeth "Betsy" (Psylocke, sister) James "Jamie" Braddock Jr. (brother)
GROUP AFFILIATION: None
EDUCATION: Graduate degree in Physics
HEIGHT: 5'11"
WEIGHT: 180 lbs.
EYES: Blue
HAIR: Blond

HISTORY: Brian Braddock was a brilliant scholar engaged in graduate work in physics at Thames University, London. One summer, shortly after his parents had been killed in an explosion in their laboratory at Braddock Manor, Brian went to work as a student research assistant at the Darkmoor Research Centre, a facility for secret nuclear research.

Braddock was present when the facility was attacked by the psychotic criminal known as the Reaver. Attempting to escape, Braddock ran his motorcycle off a cliff and lay near death. In a vision, the spirits of the god-wizard Merlin and Roma, the Lady of the Northern Skies, appeared to him and bade him choose one of the mystic objects they placed before him: the Amulet of Right or the Sword of Might. Braddock chose the amulet, and was bombarded with mystical energy. The patron spirits decreed that Braddock would be Britain's champion, and gifted him with a mystic star-scepter to enhance his fighting skills. Thus Braddock became Captain Britain.

Keeping his true identity secret, Captain Britain began a career of battling menaces to his country. As the Mutant-Human War escalated in America, Captain Britain made sure his British shores were free of conflict, but Brian had no ill will towards mutants. Both his sister and brother appeared to have mutant abilities, and he was adamant in preaching acceptance of all species of man. The British government had other ideas, however, and entered the war. Captain Britain refused to take part and continued to protect Britain from outside threats.

When the Human-Mutant War calmed down, Britain was left relatively unscathed by outsiders. As the new ruler of the planet, Magneto, looking for a new ruler of the United Kingdom following his defeat of their armies, contacted Brian and asked him to take control of the United Kingdom. Brian accepted, fearing who Magnus would choose if he did not.

As King, Captain Britain ushered in a new age of peace and acceptance across his country. It was a new Avalon: mutants, humans, superhumans, and even some mystical creatures were accepted there. To take the fairy tale even further, Brian eventually married the elemental mutant named Meggan. She now rules by his side as his queen. The United Kingdom is well into a new golden age, all thanks to its new king, Brian Braddock.

SUPERHUMAN POWERS: Captain Britain possesses superhuman strength that allows him to lift approximately 90 tons under optimal conditions. He also possesses superhuman stamina, reflexes, and can fly at a maximum speed of just under the speed of sound (770 miles per hour) for prolonged periods of time.

Art by Alan Davis

Hulk

REAL NAME: Dr. Robert Bruce Banner
KNOWN ALIASES: None
IDENTITY: Secret
OCCUPATION: Currently unemployed; former nuclear physicist
PLACE OF BIRTH: Dayton, Ohio
CITIZENSHIP: U.S.A., with criminal record, previously pardoned
KNOWN RELATIVES: Brian (father, deceased), Rebecca (mother, deceased), Morris Walters (uncle), Elaine Banner Walters (aunt, deceased), Jennifer Walters (cousin), others
GROUP AFFILIATION: Aboriginal tribe in Australia
EDUCATION: Ph.D in nuclear physics
HEIGHT: 5'9" (Banner), 7'6" (Hulk)
WEIGHT: 128 lbs. (Banner), 1,150 lbs. (Hulk)
EYES: Brown (Banner), Green (Hulk)
HAIR: Brown (Banner), Green (Hulk)

HISTORY: Robert Bruce Banner was the son of Dr. Brian Banner, an atomic physicist, and his wife, Rebecca. Brian became convinced that his work in radiation had altered his own genes, resulting in what he saw as a hated mutant offspring. Brian Banner drove himself insane with these fears and murdered Rebecca while trying to kill Bruce. Brian was shot by police before he could harm his son.

Bruce graduated high school and studied nuclear physics in Navapo, New Mexico, at Desert State University. With mutants exploding onto the worldwide scene, and the belief that radiation might be the cause of this epidemic, Bruce was invited to work for the United States Defense Department at the nuclear research facility at Desert Base, New Mexico. Bruce's main goal was to create a way for the United States to manufacture its own super-army. Banner went to work immediately, but met with little success.

With General "Thunderbolt" Ross constantly breathing down his neck for results, Bruce took some shortcuts in his research. These shortcuts ended with disastrous consequences. During the preparation for one of his new Gamma Radiation tests, Bruce was dosed with a lethal amount of Gamma rays. These rays, however, did not kill him. Instead, Bruce was transformed into a huge monster. He rampaged across Desert Base and destroyed it completely.

Believing the attack to be mutant in nature, Ross ignored his superiors' orders and pursued the monster that would become known as the Hulk with the remaining men of Desert Base for close to a month. As the Hulk, Bruce eventually destroyed Ross' army in San Diego, CA. Following the battle, the Hulk fled into the ocean.

Bruce awoke days later in Australia in the care of Aboriginal people who had taken him in. Bruce vaguely remembered his time as the Hulk. At one point, Magneto himself, assuming the Hulk to be a mutant, visited Banner and offered him a chance to join him in his fight against the humans. Banner declined and asked to be left alone. Magneto reluctantly agreed. Banner is happy to remain out of the public eye and fears what would happen if the Hulk was ever released onto the world again.

SUPERHUMAN POWERS: The Hulk possesses the capacity for superhuman strength ranging beyond the limits of virtually any other known humanoid being. His strength increases in direct proportion to his anger. The gamma radiation that mutated the Hulk's body fortified his cellular structure and added, from some as yet unknown (presumably extradimensional) source, several hundred pounds of bone, muscle, and other tissue to his body. As Banner, he possesses the normal human strength of a man of his age, height, and slight build who engages in no regular exercise.

Art by Andy Brase

Iron Man

REAL NAME: Anthony Edward "Tony" Stark
KNOWN ALIASES: None
IDENTITY: Secret
OCCUPATION: CEO of Stark Industries
PLACE OF BIRTH: Long Island, New York
CITIZENSHIP: U.S.A.
KNOWN RELATIVES: Howard (father), Maria (mother)
GROUP AFFILIATION: Stark Industries
EDUCATION: Advanced degree in electrical engineering
HEIGHT: 6'1"
WEIGHT: 225 lbs.
EYES: Blue
HAIR: Black

HISTORY: Born to Howard and Maria Stark, the heads of th
powerful business conglomerate Stark Industries, Tony Sta
grew to be an imaginative and brilliant inventor. He worke
side by side with his father from an early age, and surpasse
his father's technical brilliance by the age of 16. After som
poor business decisions, Tony's father retired from th
business and left Tony in charge to do as he saw fit.

With Tony's brilliant tech ideas becoming the principal produ
of Stark Industries, the business boomed. Stark became th
key supplier of hi-tech weaponry used to fight mutants acros
the planet. While the tech was not always successful, Sta
was on the cutting edge of science. Stark was on the verg
of a technological breakthrough when the Mutant-Human Wa
came to an end. Stark had designed an armor suit that coul
possibly counter the strongest mutants on the planet. In th
years since, those suits have been powered down to becom
part of a game called Sapien Death Match — a televisio
sport with giant robots fighting each other. Tony and his fathe
are avid competitors and are two of the best in the sport.

Recently, Stark Industries scored its biggest victory when
secured the Sentinel production contracts, pushing his majo
competitor, Jason Wyngarde, out of business. This contrac
was the largest in the world and will ensure the existence o
Stark Industries for years to come. Magnus and Sebastian Shav
awarded Tony the contract under the condition that he hire Dr. Henr
McCoy and Forge as observers. Tony agreed, and McCoy has been
key contributor along with Dr. Pym on The Vision Project.

Tony has been secretly working on a special project beneath Star
Industries — a brand new suit of hi-tech armor he plans to use as his nev
Sapien Death Match suit.

SUPERHUMAN POWERS: The Sapien Death Match armor provides superhuman strength and physical protection for Tony Stark, jetboot
that allow him to fly, and a variety of weapons including repulsor rays, pulse beams, missile launchers, lasers, tasers, and flamethrowers. The
unibeam in the center of his chest can emit various types of light energy, and the helmet contains communication devices (including FM radio)
scanning equipment, and recording devices.

Art by Pat Lee

Spider-Man

REAL NAME: Peter Benjamin Parker
KNOWN ALIASES: None
IDENTITY: World famous celebrity; the general public believes Peter Parker is a mutant
OCCUPATION: Actor, professional wrestler, owner of Spider-Man, Inc.
PLACE OF BIRTH: New York City, New York
CITIZENSHIP: U.S.A.
KNOWN RELATIVES: Richard (father, deceased), Mary (mother, deceased), Benjamin (uncle), May (aunt), Gwen (wife), Richard (son), George Stacy (father-in-law)
GROUP AFFILIATION: Spider-Man, Inc.
EDUCATION: Ph.D in biochemistry
HEIGHT: 5'10"
WEIGHT: 165 lbs.
EYES: Hazel
HAIR: Brown

HISTORY: Peter Parker was orphaned at the age of six and left in the care of his elderly uncle and aunt, Ben and May Parker. Peter was academically gifted, displaying an uncanny affinity for science that was nothing short of genius. As a student at Midtown High School, Peter attended a public evening exhibition where a spider, accidentally irradiated by a particle beam, fell onto Peter's hand and bit him. Peter left the exhibition in a daze and walked into the path of an oncoming car. Without thinking, Peter jumped onto the side of a wall to which he stuck with his bare hands. Stunned, he realized he had acquired superhuman powers similar to those of a spider: enhanced strength and agility, and the ability to cling to almost any surface.

To test his new powers, Peter donned a mask and took part in an all-comers wrestling match against Crusher Hogan, winning with ease. Spotted by a talent scout who promised to arrange a TV appearance, Peter hurried home and created a more elaborate costume. Thus Spider-Man was born. With his new powers and sudden fame, Peter promised himself he would take care of Uncle Ben and Aunt May. Following his first appearance on television Peter ended up making the decision that would change his life. Peter tackled a burglar escaping past him, saving the owner of the wrestling arena thousands of dollars. The wrestling arena owner thanked Peter by promising Spider-Man a prominent role in his brand new wrestling league.

The wrestling league was a huge success and Spider-Man became its star. As the money rolled in, he decided to reveal to his aunt and uncle the powers he had acquired from the spider bite. Initially, his aunt was frightened by these powers, but Uncle Ben was ecstatic. He was happy for his nephew and could see these amazing powers gave Peter a self-confidence and a belief in himself he did not have before.

At this time the Mutant-Human War went into full swing. Peter, as the mysterious Spider-Man, was accused of being a mutant by the local press. Peter wanted to deny it, but Uncle Ben advised him to stay quiet. Ben could see that Peter was the idol of mutants everywhere. Finally, one of them was not afraid to be seen in public. Ben believed if Peter could give hope to those children who were born different than normal humans, then he should. Uncle Ben's wisdom paid off in the end when the Mutant-Human War ended with mutants victorious. The most public and popular of mutants, Peter revealed his true identity and became an international superstar as a wrestler and an actor. He even starred in a movie with Mary Jane Watson, a controversial move since normal humans rarely scored major lead actor roles. The movie ended up launching Mary Jane's career and established Peter as a "can't miss" star.

Shortly thereafter, Peter took a break from public life. He married his college sweetheart, Gwen Stacy, and the two of them attended college

SAPIENS

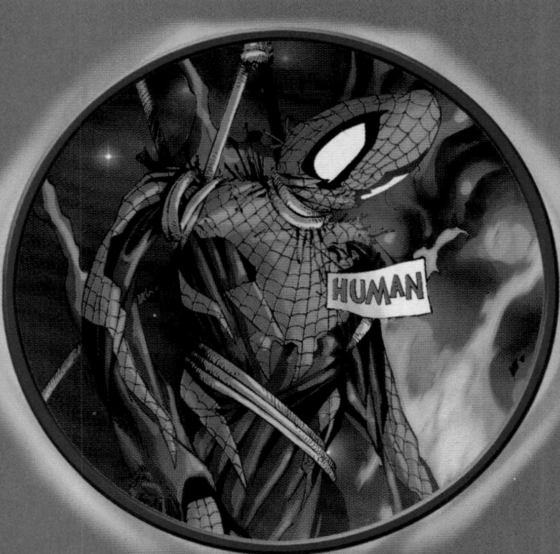
HUMAN

together, earning doctorates. Peter returned to public life a he and his Uncle Ben set up Spider-Man, Inc., spreading c into many areas including science and charity work.

Today, surrounded by his family, including his young s Richard, and close friends, Peter Parker is the envy of t world and its most popular mutant; but lately, Peter has f like something is wrong in his world. And he has beg to worry about his secret. What would happen if the wo discovered he was not truly a mutant?

SUPERHUMAN POWERS: Spider-Man possess superhuman strength, reflexes, and equilibrium; the abil to cause parts of his body to stick with great tenac to most surfaces; and a subconscious premonition "danger" sense.

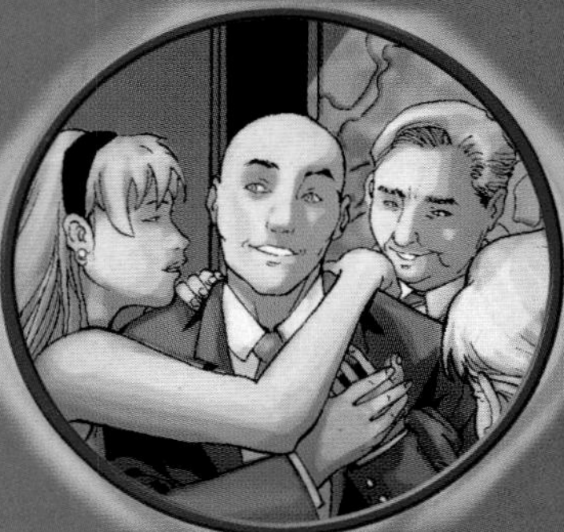

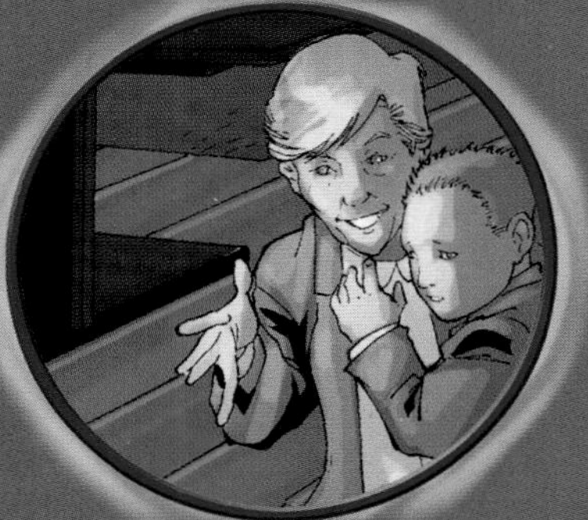

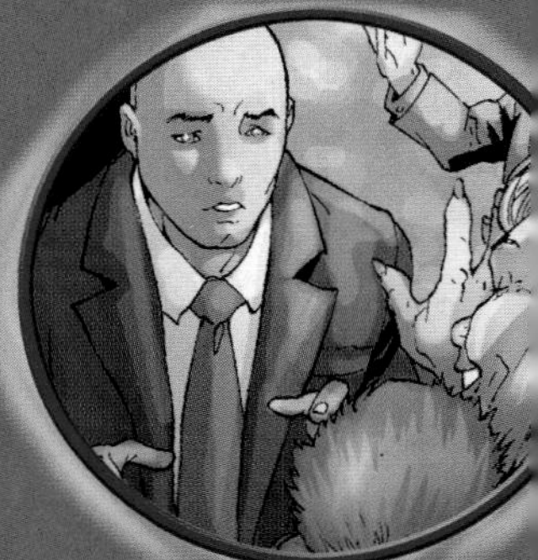

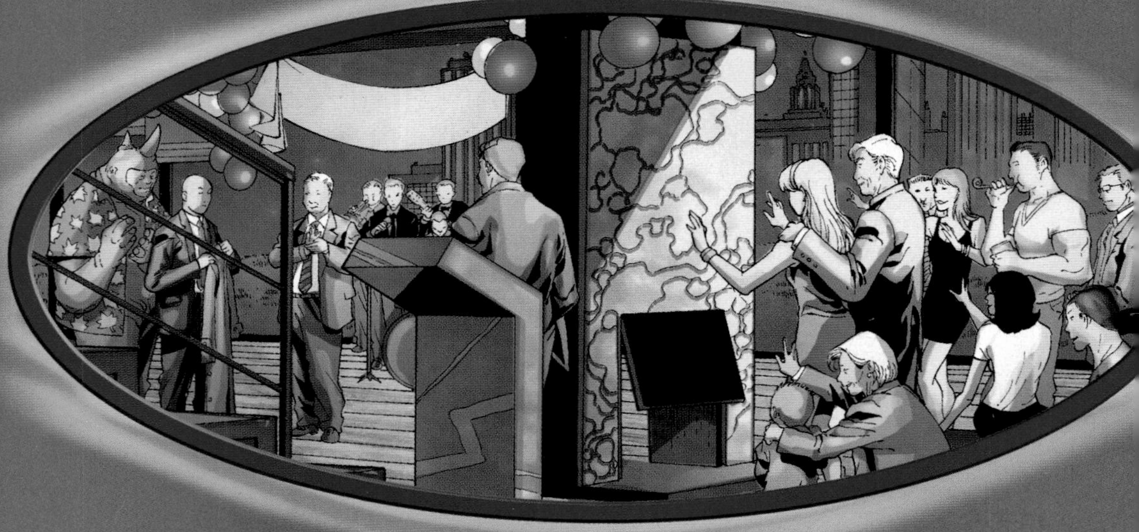

Art by Salvador Larroca

EAL NAME: T'Challa
NOWN ALIASES: None
)ENTITY: Publicly known
CCUPATION: Monarch of Wakanda
LACE OF BIRTH: Wakanda
ITIZENSHIP: Wakanda

KNOWN RELATIVES: T'Chaka (father, deceased), N'Yami (mother, deceased)
GROUP AFFILIATION: None
EDUCATION: Ph.D in physics
HEIGHT: 6' WEIGHT: 200 lbs.
EYES: Brown HAIR: Black

Black Panther

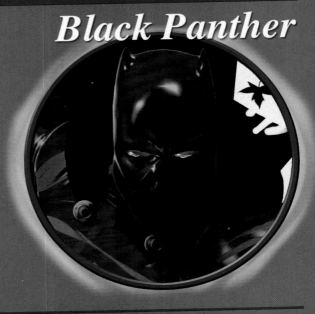

TORY: T'Challa is heir to the centuries-old ruling dynasty of the :an kingdom Wakanda and ritual leader of its Panther Clan. During early days of the Mutant-Human War, Wakanda did its best to remain tral; however, due to Wakanda's congenial relations with the United es, some mutants took it upon themselves to make a statement by cking the Wakandan Royal Family. During one such attempt, T'Challa saved by a mutant girl named Ororo. The two fell in love and T'Challa ed for her hand in marriage, but she declined.

ime, the Mutant-Human War ended and Magneto was victorious. halla, now king of Wakanda, was taught by his father to think two steps ad of enemies and three steps ahead of friends. Seeing the world's tant population as a potential threat to Wakanda, T'Challa invited gnus to his country. They established a treaty, but it is one neither man y believes in. T'Challa is currently drumming up support for a possible p attempt with other world leaders against Magneto. He knows it is a matter of if, but rather when Magneto attacks him and his beloved intry, Wakanda.

PERHUMAN POWERS: T'Challa's senses and physical attributes ve been enhanced to near-superhuman levels by the heart-aped herb.

REAL NAME: Steve Rogers
KNOWN ALIASES: None
IDENTITY: Publicly known
OCCUPATION: Retired
PLACE OF BIRTH: New York City, New York
CITIZENSHIP: U.S.A.

KNOWN RELATIVES: Joseph (father, deceased), Sarah (mother, deceased), Peggy (ex-wife)
GROUP AFFILIATION: The Invaders
EDUCATION: High School
HEIGHT: 6'1" WEIGHT: 180 lbs.
EYES: Blue HAIR: White

Captain America

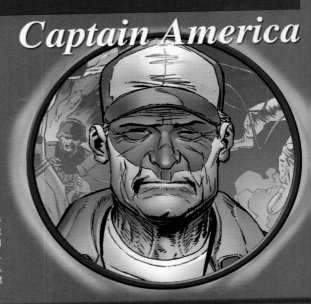

STORY: Steve Rogers has seen many things in his 89 years. He was e first and most successful recipient of the Super-Soldier Serum and ught alongside the Invaders during World War II, personally capturing dolf Hitler and ending the war in Germany. Following the end of the ar, Steve joined NASA, and was the first man to set foot on the moon 1955.

s time has passed, Steve has withdrawn from the public eye, even iough most people remember him and know who he is. Many mutants elieve he was never truly given a serum and that he was in fact, one of ie first mutants. With most of his friends and family dead and gone, Steve pends his time quietly, alone in his apartment in Brooklyn. For him, there vill be no more wars. He has officially retired.

SUPERHUMAN POWERS: Steve Rogers is 89 years old and the effects f the Super-Soldier serum have begun to fade, although they have kept im more fit than an average 89-year-old. He now possesses the normal strength of a man half his age who engages in intensive regular exercise. During his prime as Captain America, he possessed phenomenal agility, speed, strength, and endurance. He was also a master of many different orms of combat and possessed a virtually indestructible alloy shield.

Black Panther Art by Kaare Andrews

Captain America Art by Lee Weeks

REAL NAME: Carol Danvers
KNOWN ALIASES: None
IDENTITY: Publicly Known
OCCUPATION: Super hero
PLACE OF BIRTH: Boston, Massachusetts
CITIZENSHIP: U.S.A.

KNOWN RELATIVES: Joseph (father), Marie (mother), Steve (brother, deceased), Joseph Jr. (brother)
GROUP AFFILIATION: Formerly S.H.I.E.L.D.
EDUCATION: B.A., extensive training in espionage
HEIGHT: 5'11" WEIGHT: 124 lbs.
EYES: Blue HAIR: Blonde

Captain Marvel

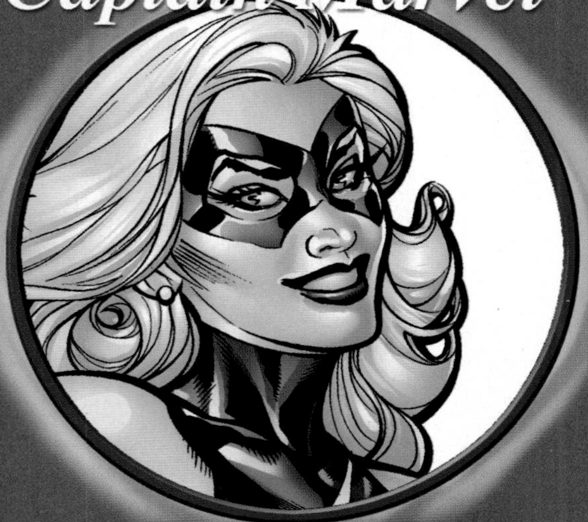

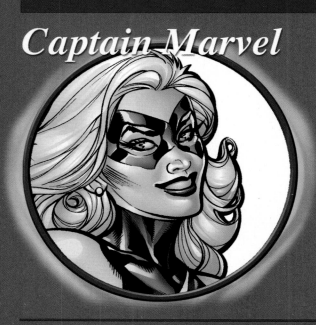

HISTORY: Carol Danvers was a top S.H.I.E.L.D. Agent for years, h her superhuman powers from the world. During the Mutant-Human Carol fought alongside her S.H.I.E.L.D. comrades but did not revea powers for fear of their reaction to her. This prejudice led her to becor spy for Magneto during the darkest days of the war. Following Magn victory, Carol was granted an "honorary" status as a mutant Magneto even named her Captain Marvel — the champion of Mu and humans around the world.

Currently, Captain Marvel is perceived as the most popular super he the world despite her lack of mutant genes. Some perceive this as a v rooting for the underdog while others in the mutant community view it warning sign. The human race may see Carol's abilities as a sign of for themselves, a chance to become something more. Regardless, C is reveling in her status as the world's greatest hero — mutant or no

SUPERHUMAN POWERS: Carol Danvers possesses superhu strength, enabling her to lift/press 50 tons under optimal condition addition, Captain Marvel has superhuman durability, the ability to fly, can absorb and channel energy.

REAL NAME: Tyrone Johnson
KNOWN ALIASES: None
IDENTITY: Secret
OCCUPATION: Criminal
PLACE OF BIRTH: South Boston, MA
CITIZENSHIP: U.S.A., wanted for questioning in regards to numerous genetic crimes

KNOWN RELATIVES: Unnamed parents, Otis (brother), Anna (twi sister)
GROUP AFFILIATION: Luke Cage's underworld organization in Hell' Kitchen
EDUCATION: Unfinished high-school education
HEIGHT: 5'9" WEIGHT: 155 lbs.
EYES: Brown HAIR: Black

Cloak

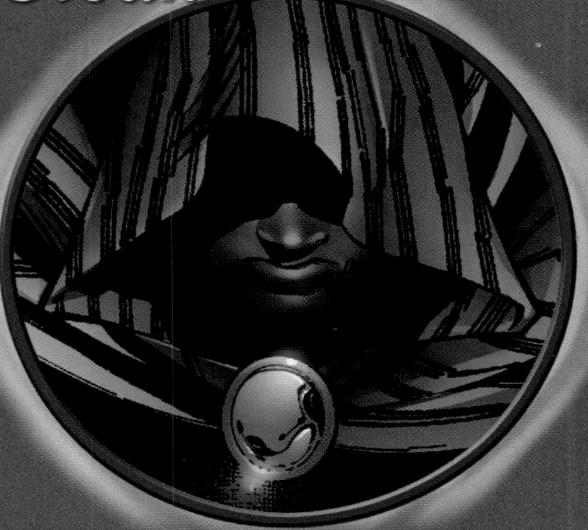

HISTORY: When Tyrone Johnson was 17, he ran away to New York When he arrived, Tyrone was offered a place to stay by a man na Marshall. Tyrone accepted. Marshall, an agent of a criminal organiza called the Maggia, used Tyrone as a guinea pig for his new synth "mutant" drug which supposedly supplied the user with superhu powers. The drug usually delivered mixed results, mostly ending in subject's death.

Luke Cage, who was on his way to becoming underworld overlord in H Kitchen, led an assault on the complex in search of Maggia agents. Du the battle, Tyrone's body exploded with Darkforce energy, inadverte saving Luke Cage's life. Tyrone collapsed to the floor, but it was obv the drug was a success. Luke took the sick boy under his wing and pleasantly surprised by Tyrone's new teleportation powers, talents would prove quite helpful in Cage's rise to overlord. Luke event became a father figure to the boy who would become Cloak.

SUPERHUMAN POWERS: Cloak's body is a portal to the "Darkf Dimension," a world of strange ebony energy. He can teleport himself others by entering the Darkforce dimension and also uses the Darkf itself as a weapon of darkness.

Captain Marvel Art by Terry Dodson Cloak Art by Olivier Coipel

EAL NAME: Nicholas Joseph Fury
NOWN ALIASES: Various used while undercover
ENTITY: Publicly known
CCUPATION: Former S.H.I.E.L.D. director; current leader of Human esistance
ACE OF BIRTH: New York City, New York
TIZENSHIP: U.S.A., wanted for questioning regarding genetic crimes
NOWN RELATIVES: Jack (father, deceased), Katherine (mother, presumed deceased), Jacob (Scorpio, brother), Dawn (sister), Mikel (Scorpio, son)
GROUP AFFILIATION: S.H.I.E.L.D. (pre-mutant incarnation), Human Resistance
EDUCATION: High school, possibly unfinished; extensive military and intelligence training
HEIGHT: 6'1" WEIGHT: 221 lbs.
EYES: Brown HAIR: Brown, white at temples

Nick Fury

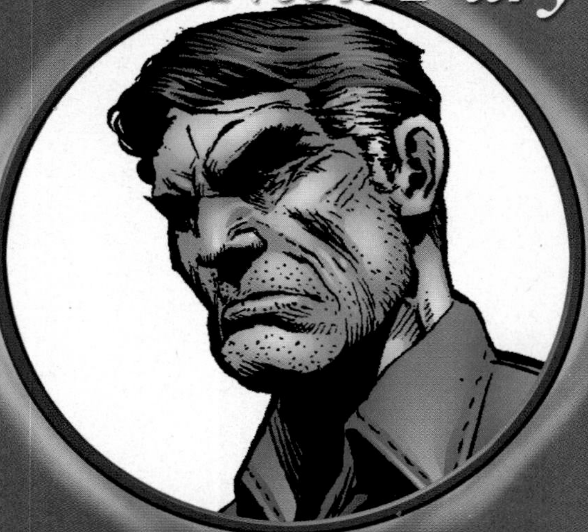

ORY: Nick Fury was a soldier during World War II. During his time mbat, he was gravely injured. Treated by French doctor Professor old Sternberg, Fury was not only treated for his injuries but also was ed with the "Infinity Formula," a formula intended to slow human . It was a success.

returned to America a war hero. He was invited to join S.H.I.E.L.D. and ually ascended to the position of Director. During his tenure as Director, eto rose to power and the Mutant-Human War began. Fury, forced to d humankind against Magneto and his mutant army, failed. Wanted for s against mutantkind, Fury went into hiding. After years of training, Fury ble to easily avoid the genetically superior mutants chasing him.

ntly, there have been rumors of Fury's return as the leader of the an Resistance. This makes many leaders in the mutant community mely nervous.

ERHUMAN POWERS: Nick Fury ages very slowly, retaining the arance and vitality of a man less than half his age. He possesses the al strength of a man of his physical age, height and build who engages in ive regular exercise.

TIES: Nick Fury is a superb athlete, hand-to-hand combatant, marksman, actician.

EAL NAME: Clinton Francis Barton
NOWN ALIASES: None
ENTITY: Secret
CCUPATION: Criminal
ACE OF BIRTH: Waverly, Iowa
TIZENSHIP: U.S.A., wanted for questioning in numerous genetic crimes
KNOWN RELATIVES: Harold (father, deceased), Edith (mother, deceased), Bernard "Barney" (brother, deceased)
GROUP AFFILIATION: Luke Cage's underworld organization in Hell's Kitchen
EDUCATION: High school dropout
HEIGHT: 6'3" WEIGHT: 230 lbs.
EYES: Blue HAIR: Blond

Hawkeye

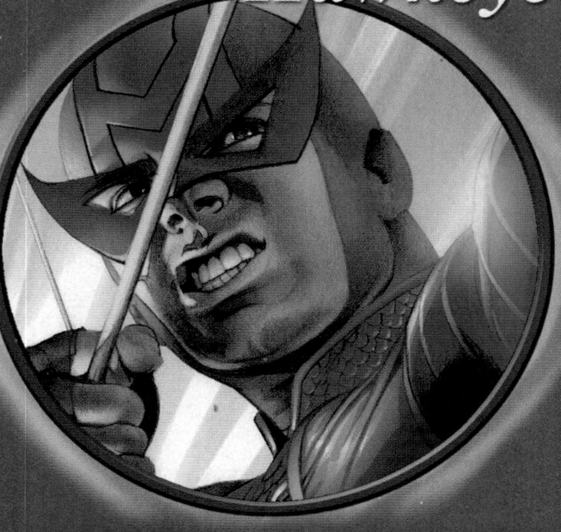

ORY: Clint Barton and his brother Bernard ran away from home young age and joined a circus. While there, Clint trained with a and arrow under the tutelage of Trickshot, the carnival marksman. g this time, Bernard left Clint behind and ended up becoming an t of S.H.I.E.L.D. Taking the stage name Hawkeye, Clint stayed with arnival until it shut down during the initial stages of the Mutant-an Wars.

no place else to turn, Clint searched for his brother. When he vered Bernard had been killed during a mutant battle, Clint became ed. He decided to stand up to his mutant oppressors. His travels him to New York City, where he was recruited by Luke Cage as a part underworld organization.

ntly, Clint has been experiencing unexplained blackouts. Their cause nown.

SONAL WEAPONRY: Hawkeye is a master archer, and is trained use of regular bows, longbows, compound bows, and crossbows. as designed a variety of "trick arrows" including sonic, explosive-tip, e-bomb, flare, tear-gas, acid, suction-tip, cable, putty, bola, electro, ocket and boomerang.

Nick Fury Art by Javier Saltares

Hawkeye Art by Mike Mayhew

SAPIENS

REAL NAME: Otto Octavius
KNOWN ALIASES: None
IDENTITY: No dual identity
OCCUPATION: Atomic research consultant
PLACE OF BIRTH: Schenectady, New York
CITIZENSHIP: U.S.A.

KNOWN RELATIVES: Torbert (father, deceased), Mary (mother deceased)
GROUP AFFILIATION: President's Council on Nu-Bioethics
EDUCATION: Doctorates in nuclear physics, honorary doctorate ir biochemistry
HEIGHT: 5'9" WEIGHT: 245 lbs.
EYES: Brown HAIR: Brown

Otto Octavius

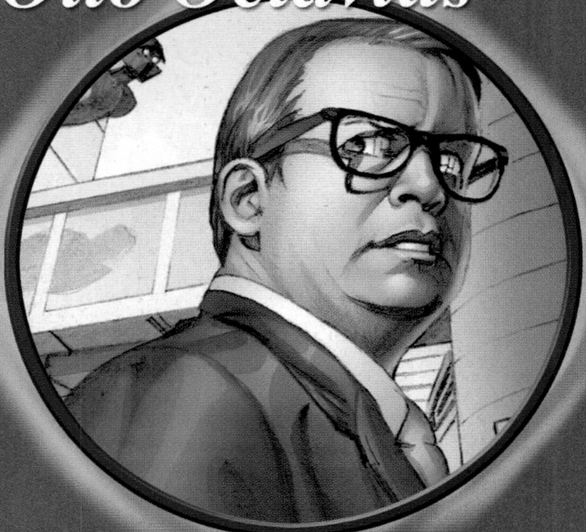

HISTORY: The son of an overbearing mother and a bullying fathe Octavius grew up to become a reclusive but brilliant atomic rese It was this area of expertise that first brought him to the attention United States government. He was originally brought in to help find for the mutant threat because many believed mutations were cau radiation and not actual evolution.

Otto could find no basis for this theory, but during his many experi he discovered mutants were immune to many diseases and illness struck down humans. He began to research the possibility that h could greatly benefit from mutant stem cells. Since there is curr ban on research conducted on real mutant embryos for fear that h might discover a way to reverse the mutant process, Otto has mad life's work to create a synthetic equivalent to the mutant gene in o further his research.

REAL NAME: Henry J. Pym
KNOWN ALIASES: None
IDENTITY: No dual identity
OCCUPATION: Scientist/biochemist
CITIZENSHIP: U.S.A.
PLACE OF BIRTH: Elmsford, New York

KNOWN RELATIVES: Maria (wife, deceased)
GROUP AFFILIATION: Stark Industries
EDUCATION: Ph.D. in Biochemistry
HEIGHT: 6' WEIGHT: 185 lbs.
EYES: Blue HAIR: Blond

Henry Pym

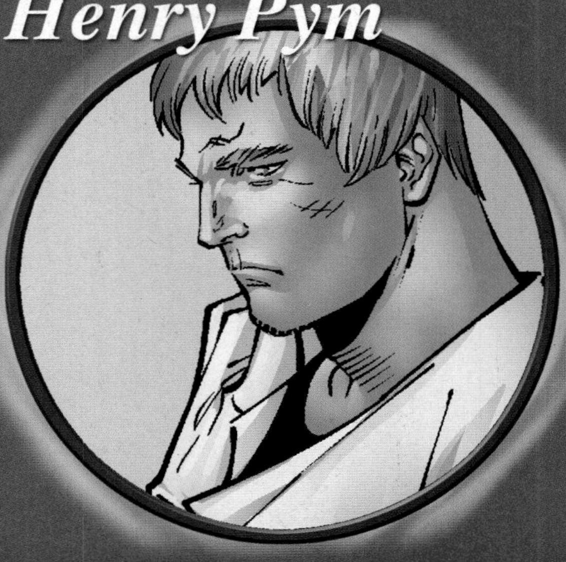

HISTORY: Henry Pym's wife, Maria, was killed during the early c the Mutant-Human War when a Sentinel slammed into the plane to take her home to Hungary for a visit. Pym mourned in solitu months until he was contacted by Tony Stark, an old colleague a owner of Stark Industries. With no place else to turn, Pym ac his job offer.

Pym is currently working on the Vision Project for Stark unc watchful eye of mutant researcher, Dr. Hank McCoy. Lately, Py become more and more obsessed with the mutant gene and how it from that of normal humans. He has even begun to conduct exper in secret in an attempt to isolate the mutant gene. These exper are considered illegal because of the danger their discoveries ma to all of mutantkind. With the ability to find the cause of mutation believe there may be a way to reverse its effects. Pym's mood and eagerness to discuss illegal experiments have caused to be concerned, including Stark, McCoy and even Otto Octa representative of the U.S. government.

REAL NAME: Robert Reynolds
KNOWN ALIASES: None
IDENTITY: No dual identity
OCCUPATION: Unemployed
CITIZENSHIP: U.S.A
PLACE OF BIRTH: Unknown
KNOWN RELATIVES: Lindy (wife), unnamed son
GROUP AFFILIATION: None
EDUCATION: College
HEIGHT: 6' WEIGHT: 194 lbs.
EYES: Blue HAIR: Blond

Robert Reynolds

HISTORY: Robert Reynolds' life wasn't perfect, but he was content; however, as Mutants rose to power, things changed. Now Robert believes he is going insane. He remembers being able to fly and having amazing superpowers, but this is clearly a symptom of the "Dead-End Syndrome" that is currently making its way around humankind — a feeling of inadequacy following the rise of Magneto and mutantkind across the world. Unable to hold onto his job, he has also developed agoraphobia — the fear of the outside world.

Recently, at the insistence of his wife, Robert has been visiting renowned psychologist, Dr. Stephen Strange. The two have been discussing his psychosis, but have not been able to make any significant breakthroughs. Currently, Robert believes blackness is following him wherever he goes. Whether or not Dr. Strange can cure him of this belief remains to be seen.

SUPERHUMAN POWERS: Robert Reynolds believes he possessed superhuman powers. These powers included flight and superhuman strength, durability, and intelligence.

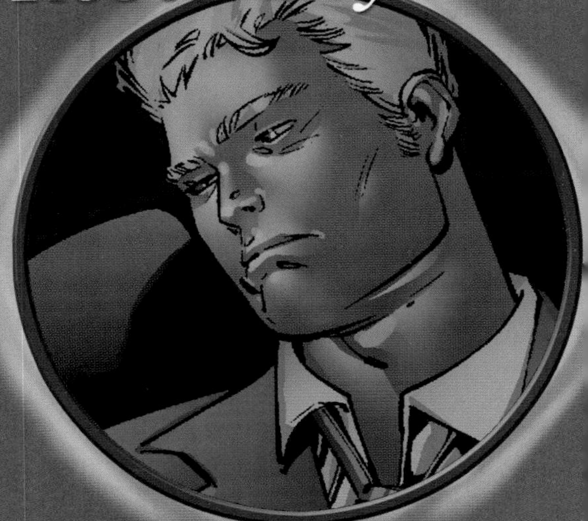

REAL NAME: Marc Spector
KNOWN ALIASES: None
IDENTITY: Secret
OCCUPATION: Criminal, former U.S. Marine, C.I.A. operative, and heavyweight boxer
PLACE OF BIRTH: Chicago, Illinois
CITIZENSHIP: U.S.A., wanted for questioning in regards to numerous genetic crimes
KNOWN RELATIVES: Elias (father, deceased), Mrs. Spector (mother, deceased), Randall (brother, deceased)
GROUP AFFILIATION: Luke Cage's underworld organization in Hell's Kitchen, formerly U.S. Marines, C.I.A.
EDUCATION: High-school graduate
HEIGHT: 6'2" WEIGHT: 225 lbs.

Marc Spector

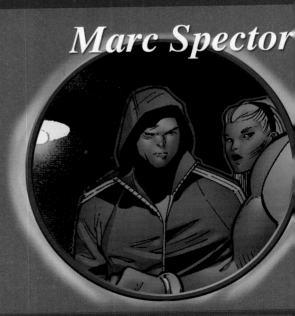

HISTORY: Marc Spector was a successful heavyweight boxer when the Mutant-Human War broke out and all sporting events were cancelled indefinitely. With no direction, Marc joined the Marines. He was subsequently invited to join a small C.I.A. Black Ops unit created to disrupt mutant operations. During a mission to hinder Apocalypse's forces in Egypt, Marc was injured and left for dead in an abandoned temple. When he awoke, he found he had strange new powers.

Eventually, Marc made his way back to the United States and decided to return to boxing full-time. Unfortunately, the only place human fights were taking place was in secret in Hell's Kitchen. During his first fight it was obvious he was a superhuman, and Spector beat his opponent severely. Spector fled, afraid for his life, but was tracked down by Luke Cage, who invited him to join his underworld organization. Spector has been by Cage's side ever since.

SUPERHUMAN POWERS: Mark Spector gains enhanced strength during the night, and sometimes has prophetic visions.

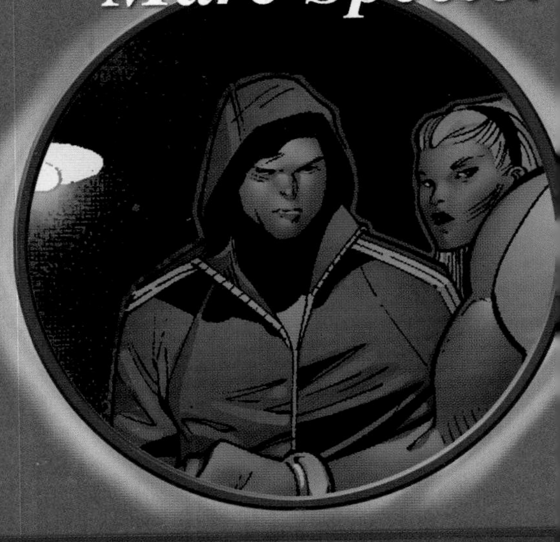

Art by Olivier Coipel

SAPIENS

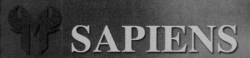

REAL NAME: Stephen Vincent Strange
KNOWN ALIASES: None
IDENTITY: No dual identity
OCCUPATION: Psychologist
PLACE OF BIRTH: Philadelphia, Pennsylvania
CITIZENSHIP: U.S.A.

KNOWN RELATIVES: Eugene (father, deceased), Beverly (mother, deceased), Donna (sister, deceased), Victor (brother, deceased)
GROUP AFFILIATION: None
EDUCATION: Medical doctorate; Ph.D in Psychology
HEIGHT: 6'2 1/2" WEIGHT: 180 lbs.
EYES: Gray HAIR: Black, white at temples

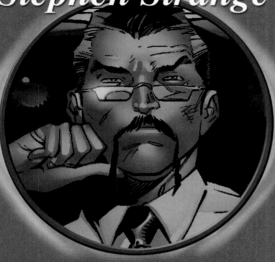

Stephen Strange

HISTORY: Dr. Stephen Strange is the most successful psychologis New York City. He is an expert in most psychological disorders, but dealt almost exclusively in a new human distress condition comm known as "Dead-End Syndrome." The syndrome became promi following the rise of mutantkind. It was an extremely profitable field, one he excelled at. He seemed to be able to relate completely to th who are overwhelmed by their "average" human standing in this world order.

Recently he has trimmed back his patient load, feeling a little stres by the enormous number of patients with similar problems. Currently is treating Robert Reynolds, a man who claims he is being followe blackness and believes he may have had superpowers at one time. W this is not that different from some of Strange's other patients, he f differently about Robert Reynolds, as if Reynolds' psychosis may b sign of something bigger.

REAL NAME: Janet Van Dyne
KNOWN ALIASES: None
IDENTITY: No dual identity
OCCUPATION: Fashion designer
PLACE OF BIRTH: Cresskill, New Jersey
CITIZENSHIP: Citizen of the United States of America with no criminal record

KNOWN RELATIVES: Vernon (father, deceased)
GROUP AFFILIATION: None
EDUCATION: Degree in Fashion
HEIGHT: 5'4" WEIGHT: 110 lbs.
EYES: Blue HAIR: Auburn

Janet Van Dyne

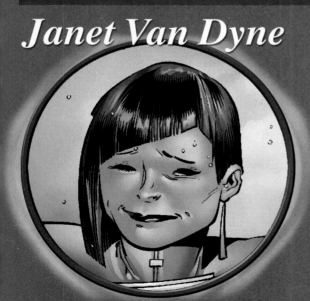

HISTORY: Janet Van Dyne was the daughter of a renowned scier Dr. Vernon Van Dyne, who was working on a way to detect signal intelligent life on other planets using gamma radiation. Comple obsessed, Van Dyne unknowingly neglected his daughter. Bored lonely in her father's huge lab, Janet spent her time fantasizing a living a different life — one with glamorous parties and friends she didn't really have. She began to design clothing for the imagir parties, drawings her father found lying around the lab. Without knowledge, he sent the designs off to a friend who happened to h contacts in the Paris fashion scene. Impressed with her design se he invited Janet to enroll in a top fashion institute in Paris, France.

Today, Janet is one of the world's top fashion designers and owr fashion design firm in Paris. She is most famous for designing Cap Marvel's uniform and is the first person most respectable mutants to for their hero uniform or party wear.

Art by Olivier Coipel

REAL NAME: Mary Jane Watson
KNOWN ALIASES: None
IDENTITY: No dual identity
OCCUPATION: Actress
PLACE OF BIRTH: New York City
CITIZENSHIP: U.S.A.

KNOWN RELATIVES: Anna May Watson (aunt), Philip (father), Madeline (mother, deceased), Gayle Watson-Byrnes (sister)
GROUP AFFILIATION: None
EDUCATION: College Degree
HEIGHT: 5'8"   **WEIGHT:** 120 lbs.
EYES: Green   **HAIR:** Red

Mary Jane Watson

HISTORY: Born into an abusive family in the Bronx, Mary Jane Watson always wanted to escape her life. She longed to be an actress. But as the world changed around her and mutants became the stars of stage and screen, it looked as if Mary Jane would be left behind, forced to perform in off Broadway human sideshows.

That all changed when former college friend, and world famous performer, Peter Parker asked her to play his love interest in his newest movie. The role made her America's sweetheart. Now, with the release of *Funny Valentine*, Mary Jane is one of the only human movie stars in the business able to launch her own solo vehicles.

But will mutant and human backlash for a true human movie star be too much for her to be able to succeed? She has made it this far — much further than most of her mutant peers would have considered possible a few short years ago.

REAL NAME: Simon Williams
KNOWN ALIASES: None
IDENTITY: Publicly known
OCCUPATION: Actor
PLACE OF BIRTH: Paterson, New Jersey
CITIZENSHIP: U.S.A.
KNOWN RELATIVES: Sanford (father, deceased),

Martha (mother), Eric (brother)
GROUP AFFILIATION: Actors Guild
EDUCATION: Advanced degree in Electrical Engineering
HEIGHT: 6'2"   **WEIGHT:** 380 lbs.
EYES: Red (permeated with shifting spots of ionic energy, no visible irises)
HAIR: Gray

Wonder Man

HISTORY: Simon Williams claims he gained his powers during an industrial accident, but not even he truly remembers how he became Wonder Man. Although he is not an official mutant, he has been embraced by the mutant community as one of their own. He is currently working on a television series, *Me and Mine*.

While his exploits as a superhuman have been less than impressive, Simon is known more for his romantic exploits. It has been rumored that he even dated Magneto's human daughter, Wanda. Simon has consistently denied this and claims he was just in Genosha on a charity trip. Currently he is dating the world's most famous superhuman, Captain Marvel. As usual, Williams is remaining coy about this relationship. Regardless, Simon is one of the tabloids' favorite television stars.

SUPERHUMAN POWERS: Wonder Man possesses greatly enhanced physical strength, durability, and stamina. When utilizing his powers, his physical form becomes charged with ionic energy.

Art by Olivier Coipel

Mutant Week

with Trish Tilby

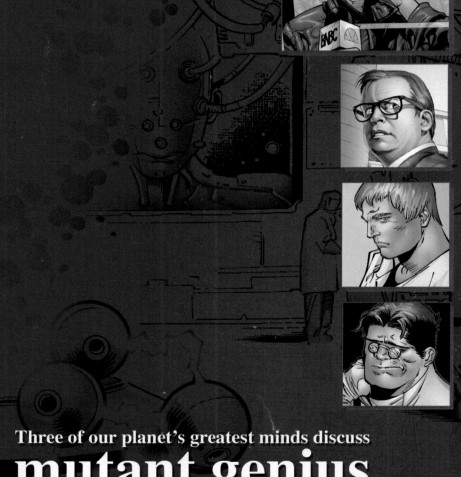

Three of our planet's greatest minds discuss
mutant genius,
"Dead-End Syndrome,"
and what scares them the most about the direction of our society today...

Three geniuses. One mutant. Two humans. All working together to improve our ever changing society.

...ough only one of them is truly a ...ant, it has been suggested recently that ...nius" could be considered a mutant ...ity. Is expanded brainpower something ...y mutants possess? Is there a way for ...rage human beings to be more than ...inary? We will get their opinions on ...se and other questions today.

...SH TILBY: First off, welcome; it's an ...nor to have you all here in Chicago ... Stark Industries. To have three of the ...eatest minds of this generation in one ...om is amazing and we thank you for your ...e. Let's start off with the obvious one. Is ...enius" a mutant gift?

...R. HENRY MCCOY: First off, it's great to see ...u again, Trish. Secondly, intelligence can be ... mutant trait, but it is not the sign of mutation. ...y esteemed colleagues here are most certainly ...man, like yourself, but nowhere near as beautiful. ...s a shame your television career was cut short.

...LBY: Yes. Well, times have changed, haven't ...ey?

...CCOY: They have. They have. But a beautiful ...oman is still a beautiful woman regardless of ...enes... or as some would say, because of them. ...ur readers are certainly missing out by not seeing ...ou in person. Your picture at the top of the page ...oes not do you justice.

...ILBY: Are you flirting with me, Doctor?

...MCCOY: (*Laughing*) If that's one of your questions, ...ll answer it—but otherwise I will have to decline ...omment.

...But seriously, the capacity for expanded thought is ...not limited to those with the mutant gene. Surely, ...men like Einstein were intelligent well before ...mutants appeared. Although, in his case, who ...knows...

...will say that the men next to me are two of the ...smartest human beings left on the planet. Men ...like Tony Stark... our missing colleague Bruce

Banner... and even, as unpopular as it is to admit, Victor Von Doom... these men are a credit to their race. Can they stand up to a mutant with extreme mental capabilities? Probably not. But through their struggle to find answers to questions that some mutants don't even consider is where they bring the most to our society. Humankind may be on the verge of extinction but these are not dinosaurs. They will leave their mark on society as a whole.

TILBY: Interesting... Dr. Pym? Your thoughts?

DR. HENRY PYM: While my answer won't be as entertaining as my department head's, I would have to say I agree with him. The capacity for expanded human brain function has been exhibited for centuries. Man has long been able to think for himself. He didn't need mutants to do that for him.

As far as extinction is concerned, an animal backed into a corner is often the most dangerous of all.

TILBY: What do you mean by that, Dr. Pym?

PYM: Just that a species does not disappear overnight. Even Magneto himself is said to have a human offspring. Nature has a way of correcting itself either through natural means or—

MCCOY: Dr. Pym is always overstating things. He spends more time in Stark's doghouse than in the actual lab. What say you, Otto?

Not that I want to take over your interview, Ms. Tilby...

DR. OTTO OCTAVIUS: I don't want to take anything away from your genius and mutanity, Dr. McCoy, but as usual you are as subtle as a brick. Yours and Dr. Pym's attitudes may be the exact reason why you and your employer are continually being monitored by the President and Magnus. It is thinking like that which brings humans in conflict with mutants.

But the question was originally on whether or not genius was a mutation, correct? I say no. The brain is a powerful weapon, Ms. Tilby... one that humankind has long used to its advantage.

Recent scandals involving Warren Worthington III have left Worthington Industries out in the cold on many contracts.

(Photo by Sean Phillips)

Bankruptcy forced Jason Wyngarde out of Sentinel Tech race.

(Photo by John Byrne)

Trish Tilby
Mutant Week Editor-In-Chief

Doctor Henry McCoy
Head of Research and Development for Stark Industries, Ph.D in biochemistry

Doctor Henry Pym
Synthetics and Biological Development for Stark Industries, Ph.D in biochemistry

Doctor Otto Octavius
Representative of the President's Council on Nu-Bioethics, Ph.D. in nuclear physics, honorary Ph.D. in biochemistry

Pym, McCoy Photos by Olivier Coipel   Octavius Photo by Mike Mayhew   Trish Tilby Photo by Leinel Francis Yu

Only recently have we established that mutants are the next step in evolution on a genetic scale. Perhaps there will come a time when the human brain will evolve, but for right now we are all — mutants and humans alike — dealing with the same brain capacity. It's what portion of the brain we use that makes us geniuses.

And to be blunt, I'm more concerned about my legacy in the scientific world than the legacy of humankind. Things change. Life evolves. But if I can contribute to mutant theories, I am more than willing to be the last rung on the ladder of humanity. Who wouldn't want to be a mutant?

TILBY: True. I've always wondered what it would be like to fly.

Something you said interested me, Dr. Octavius — about Stark Industries and their relationship with the President. Is there a need to monitor the actions of a company like Stark Industries as closely as you obviously are?

OCTAVIUS: I think any country that takes itself seriously is going to monitor its most successful companies. I wouldn't be here in Chicago if not for the need to monitor the advancements of Stark Industries. They provide our country with a great deal of security. With the bankruptcy of Jason Wyngarde's company and the scandal surrounding Worthington, Stark has moved up to become our number one tech supplier. And they have always been the major supplier of the technology used for our Sentinel program. That alone guarantees the involvement of the President, S.H.I.E.L.D., and even Magneto himself. And two of the greatest minds on our planet reside in their labs important to make sure those minds are not wandering, although I que what Dr. Pym is truly doing there.

MCCOY: As always, we appreciate your interest, Otto; and, believe me resident human rights advocate is focusing on the job at hand.

OCTAVIUS: I'm sure he is.

TILBY: Before we get too excited let's move on to the next issue...

As you all know, the so-called "Dead-End Syndrome" is a phenome rapidly affecting humans across the globe. A feeling of hopelessness... a normal person cannot possibly compete with mutantkind's amazing g There has come a cry from human diplomats for something to be done. already have super-powered humans like Captain Marvel flying through skies. Humankind even had Captain America in World War II, although s claim he, like Namor, was one of our earlier mutants. What I'm asking abo experimenting on humans. Many have suggested using mutant embryos genetics to enhance humans. To give all people gifts so we're on an e playing field. To help open the possibilities for the "Dead-End" humans h theoretically become.

OCTAVIUS: As you know, Trish, the President and Magnus himself h discouraged this type of talk. I have always believed research on mu embryos could lead us... no, it would lead us down a dangerous path. T President's Council on Nu-Biothics to which I belong has studied this and know the temptation to mess with the genetic strain is there. But to actua experiment on real mutant embryos would be a terrible mistake.

Instead our committee proposes a synthetic equivalent. Not to deal with t so-called "Dead-End Syndrome," which is affecting beings to make them f genetically equal, but to help us heal the truly sick. To use genetics to crea homo-superior embryonic stem cells to find cures for diseases and vaccin for illnesses that some mutants are fundamentally immune to. Using th process to "advance humans" is absurd and dangerous.

TILBY: Dr. McCoy? Dr. Pym?

MCCOY: Stark Industries leaves policy to those who are in charge. We a not interested in dealing with mutant embryos or synthetic whatchamacallit Our experiments concentrate on advancing the Sentinel program and oth tech ventures.

TILBY: Dr. Pym?

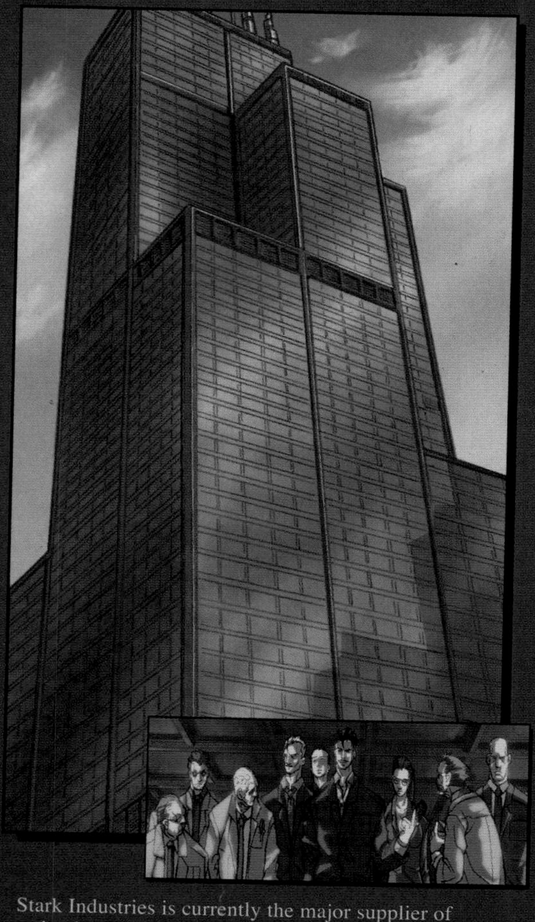

(Photo by Pat Lee)

Stark Industries is currently the major supplier of technology for the restructured Sentinel program.

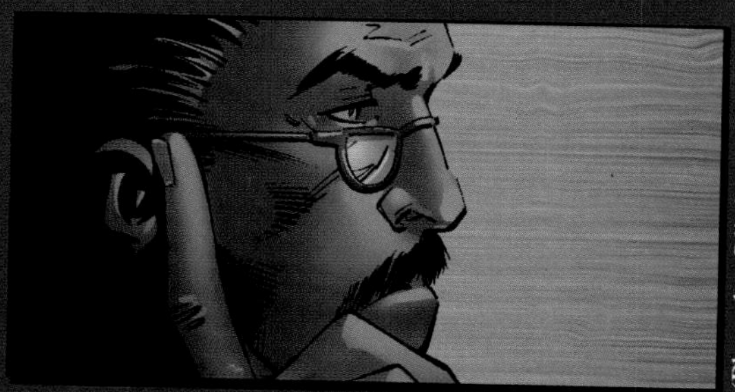

(Photo by Olivier Coipel)

Dr. Stephen Strange is the foremost expert on the new phenomenon called "Dead-End Syndrome."

COY: I believe Dr. Pym shares that feeling as well.

3Y: Really?

COY: Yes. I do.

BY: Well, maybe he could address the idea of a "Dead-End Syndrome"? ʾym?

COY: That really isn't what we do at—

M: I'll take the question, Hank.

s syndrome is an obvious problem for all of us. Does it exist? I don't really w. I know a colleague of ours, a psychologist in New York City, Dr. Stephen ange, believes it is out there. To be honest, Trish, I know at times I feel dequate. That I want more. Who wouldn't, looking at the amazing things tants can do? But there are downsides. People don't talk about it much, but all mutations are good.

CCOY: Dr. Pym... Let's keep this to science fact and not science fiction. ase. Not just for the sake of the readers but for your position at Stark.

M: I'm just answering the question, Hank. What if there was a way to isolate mutant gene? To actually figure out the destiny of a mutant before they re born? Or to fiddle with the human gene in order to match what happens th the mutant gene? This "Dead-End Syndrome"? It's something we all have deal with. At least three of us here do. The rise of mutantkind could be gnaling the end of humankind. Otto seems content to be a footnote but I'm t so eager.

ckily, it appears as though Magnus has much kinder ends in mind for my ecies than many of our former government leaders had for our genetically perior friends. Instead of hunting us down he is going to be content to just let us fade away. But that doesn't prevent us from wondering why some people mutate and others don't. Surely people have to see that it's the nature of science to question. What if there's a way to isolate the mutant gene and find out more about it? "What if" is the basic foundation of all great scientific discovery, isn't it?

MCCOY: It's not what we do, Henry. At Stark we build little robots, we don't break down the human body.

Besides, the idea of one mutant gene making the difference is absurd. It's not one strand of DNA, it's millions strung together. It's a combination so complex that it will not be figured out in our lifetime, regardless of the eventual mutant genii appearing around the planet. We've discussed this time and again and still you ask the same questions. It's truly futile.

PYM: The interesting thing to me is that no one seems to consider that they, too, will eventually become obsolete. Humans thought they were the top of the evolutionary ladder, but they were wrong. If history is any indicator, mutants are far from the end of the line.

TILBY: Response, Dr. McCoy?

MCCOY: Trish, my dear, any response I have will only inspire more foolishness from my colleague, I'm afraid. And in an attempt to keep him on the staff at Stark Industries I think we will end the interview here.

TILBY: Of course. No problem. I thank you for coming. Any final thoughts, Dr. Octavius?

OCTAVIUS: None. But I ask you... is it any wonder the President and Magnus asked me to inspect the Stark labs?

—Trish Tilby

(Photo by Aaron Lopresti)

A group of young Mutants trains at the New Mutant Leadership Institute. What will the next step on the genetic ladder deliver?

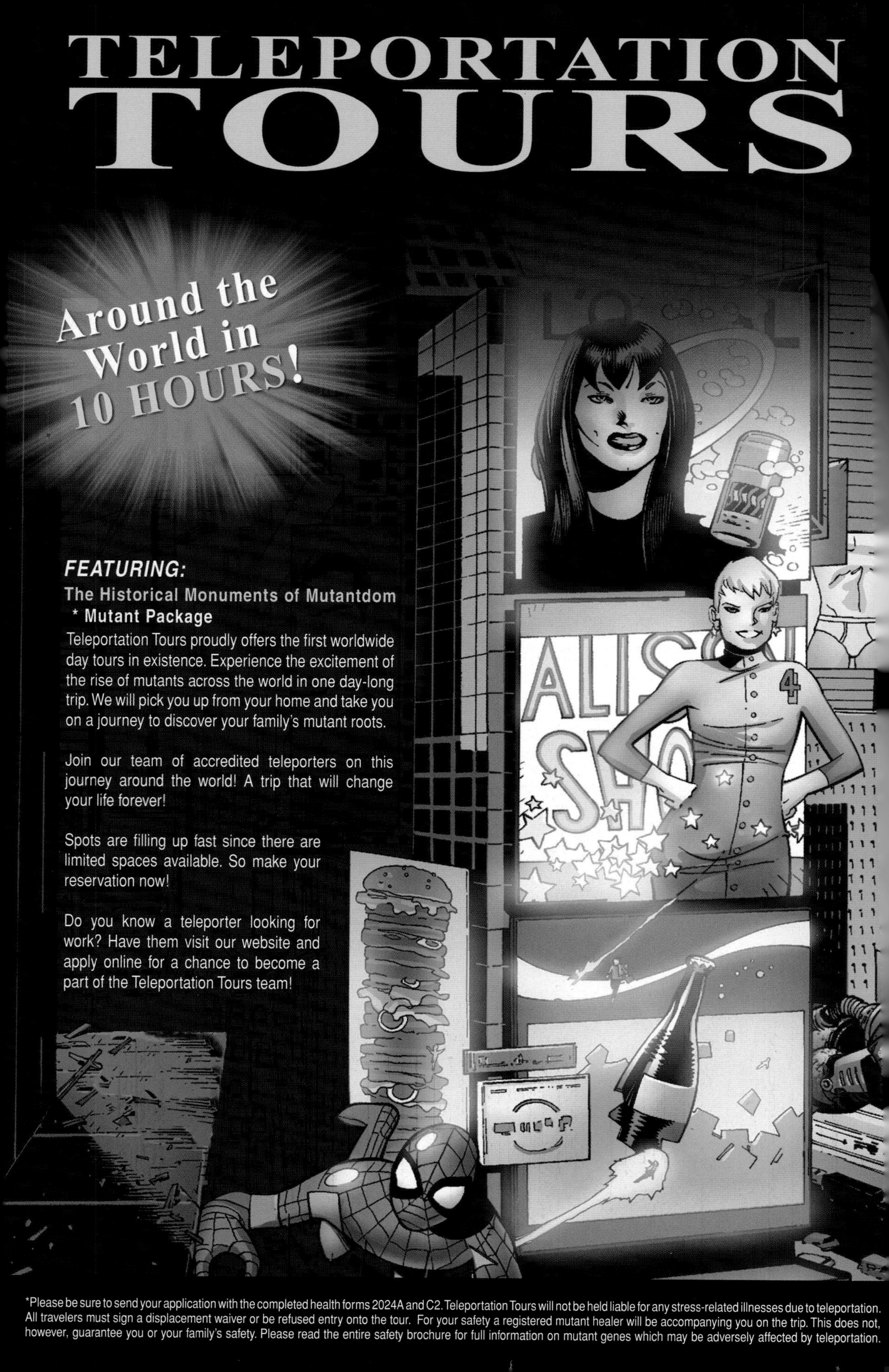
TELEPORTATION TOURS
Around the World in 10 HOURS!
FEATURING:
The Historical Monuments of Mutantdom
* Mutant Package
Teleportation Tours proudly offers the first worldwide day tours in existence. Experience the excitement of the rise of mutants across the world in one day-long trip. We will pick you up from your home and take you on a journey to discover your family's mutant roots.
Join our team of accredited teleporters on this journey around the world! A trip that will change your life forever!
Spots are filling up fast since there are limited spaces available. So make your reservation now!
Do you know a teleporter looking for work? Have them visit our website and apply online for a chance to become a part of the Teleportation Tours team!
*Please be sure to send your application with the completed health forms 2024A and C2. Teleportation Tours will not be held liable for any stress-related illnesses due to teleportation. All travelers must sign a displacement waiver or be refused entry onto the tour. For your safety a registered mutant healer will be accompanying you on the trip. This does not, however, guarantee you or your family's safety. Please read the entire safety brochure for full information on mutant genes which may be adversely affected by teleportation.

he First Mutant Memorial and Museum of Mutant History

Our first mutant hero...

he people of the Hamptons welcome you to e Museum of Mutant History for a beautiful unrise look at the only monument to history's rst mutant hero.

(Photo by Alex Ross)

egin your journey on the coast of Long Island ith a sunrise in the Hamptons. Reported to e the site of the first appearance of Namor, he Hamptons claim to be the birthplace of nutants. Whether or not that's true will be lebated for years, but the statue of Namor listening in the sunrise is a sight to behold. ocated off the coast of Southampton, this 0-foot-tall statue stands as a testament to he first recorded mutant hero in history —the Mutant King of the Seas, Namor!

You will also have a chance to visit the Museum of Mutant History! Decide for yourself whether or not he first photographic evidence of Namor in the sea is actually a mutant being... or a school of fish as some historians claim. This disputed photograph documents the first recorded appearance of Namor. The Hamptonites claim they have the only photographic proof from pre-World War II of Namor's existence and you'll be able to look at the evidence firsthand. The Museum of Mutant History also holds hundreds of pieces of memorabilia from mutant history including Quicksilver's original battle uniform, Sebastian Shaw's first signed document as the head of S.H.I.E.L.D., a microphone used by Alison Blaire on her TV show *Alison*, and Magneto's helmet from the Battle for Mutant Justice in New York City.

New Mutant Leadership Institute

"Our leaders will be better. They will be trained to make the hard choices. And they will always serve in the best interest of mutantkind." – *Magnus*

Our morning continues in the place where our future is seeded. See the inspirational campus where mutant leaders of tomorrow learn their craft.

(Photo by Aaron Lopresti)

Established less than ten years ago, the New Mutant Leadership Institute was built by Magneto himself to train exceptional mutants in the field of diplomacy. This beautiful site is built on the same ground that once housed the United Nations Headquarters. It is a state-of-the-art facility and an inspiration, especially to those with young children! The Institute will be forever known as the birthplace of our future leaders.

You and your family will have more than enough time to wander the grounds and possibly mingle with the students. Please let us know if your child will be attending the Institute and we will guarantee a meeting with Professor Manh or one of the other fine faculty professors

Magnus Tribute Memorial

"The mutant blood lost here was the last that will ever be lost in war." – *Magnus*

Visit the remnants of the ultimate battle for mutant justice.

Walk on the hallowed ground that is regarded as the turning point in mutant history. You and your family will visit the site of the actual battle. You will see actual footage of the battle and the moment of Magneto's greatest triumph. You will also hear his mutant V-Day speech in all of its glory as a telepath who witnessed the speech takes you back in time and allows you to hear and feel the day as it actually happened. Feel the sunshine on your face... the excitement in the crowd... even

smell the smoldering metal of the destroyed Sentinels! It's a once-in-a-lifetime experience that will leave you feeling prouder to be a mutant than you ever have!

You can also visit the Magnetic Pull concession stand for the most recent memoir of that battle, By His Side, by decorated S.H.I.E.L.D. Agent Mortimer Toynbee, also known as The Toad.

We will also serve a picnic lunch in Central Park in the shadow of the monument. Please make sure you check out the lunch options which include sandwiches and barbeque.

Mutopia and The Temple of Mutopia

"Who doesn't want to visit Mutopia?" – *Alison Blaire*

In a short teleportation across town we will take you to the beautiful city of Mutopia, the ideal mutant community. Look out for celebrities like Alison Blaire and pop star Jazz as they travel the streets of Mutopia living their everyday lives. Shop in the most glorious mutant stores on the planet. Live like a star!

The tour will also provide you with a beautiful view of the controversial Temple of Mutopia located on the edge of Human Town.

*Warning: This trip takes you close to the Temple of Mutopia which lies on the very edge of Human Town. Because of the Temple's location, we cannot stop you from inspecting the building, but this part of the tour is open only as long as conditions are safe for travel. Those who wish to travel inside the Temple and see the Tree of Transformation will most likely be turned away. We will be spending a total of 2 hours in Mutopia. Remember this is not meant to be a visit for Sapien Transcendence and those who attempt to stay behind will forfeit their Teleportation Deposit. Teleportation Tours cannot be held responsible for anything that happens while near or inside the Temple of Mutopia.

Visit the palace of Queen Ororo on Mt. Kilimanjaro

"The symbolic Queen of Mutantkind... and the savior of a continent." – *Magnus*

We end our tour with a sunset on the slopes of Mt. Kilimanjaro. You will see the beauty that is Africa, as well as the Crystal Cathedral that is the home of the elemental goddess, Queen Ororo of Kenya. You will sip champagne in the shadow of royalty as the sun sets in the beautiful African nation of Kenya. And if you are very lucky you may see the Queen herself as she flies high above her thriving nation on the winds.

At the completion of the sunset you will be teleported directly to your homes wearing your complimentary Teleportation Tours T-Shirt and Hat.

(Photo by Trevor Hairsine)

We thank you for your patronage and hope you join us soon. Please see our website to keep track of your Telepoints which could earn you a free teleportation to anywhere in the world.

Warning: Although we have not been officially asked to cease and desist bringing the tour this close to her home, Queen Ororo has from time to time made it known that she would prefer we did not. Travelers will be provided with raincoats on the off chance Queen Ororo is in one of her moods. For those mutants who are allergic to rain it is suggested you skip this part of the tour. Teleportation Tours cannot be held responsible for the weather, created or otherwise, which may affect the patrons.

Coming soon...

The Royal Genoshan Gardens

It is our hope that we will eventually obtain the exclusive rights to enter the Royal Genoshan Gardens with the permission of Lord Magnus himself. Only those screened by our telepaths will be allowed on this journey into the inner sanctum of our mutant leader's home. Also, you will be afforded a glimpse at the rarely visited monument Magneto built to his own fallen hero.

A waiting list has already begun. With a small donation to the New Mutant Leadership Institute you can add your name to the list as well!

(Photo by Olivier Coipel)

Lila Cheney's Star Tours

Interstellar Teleporter Lila Cheney has offered you this once-in-a-lifetime chance to see the stars. More information as this tour develops. One thing is for sure — it will be out of this world!

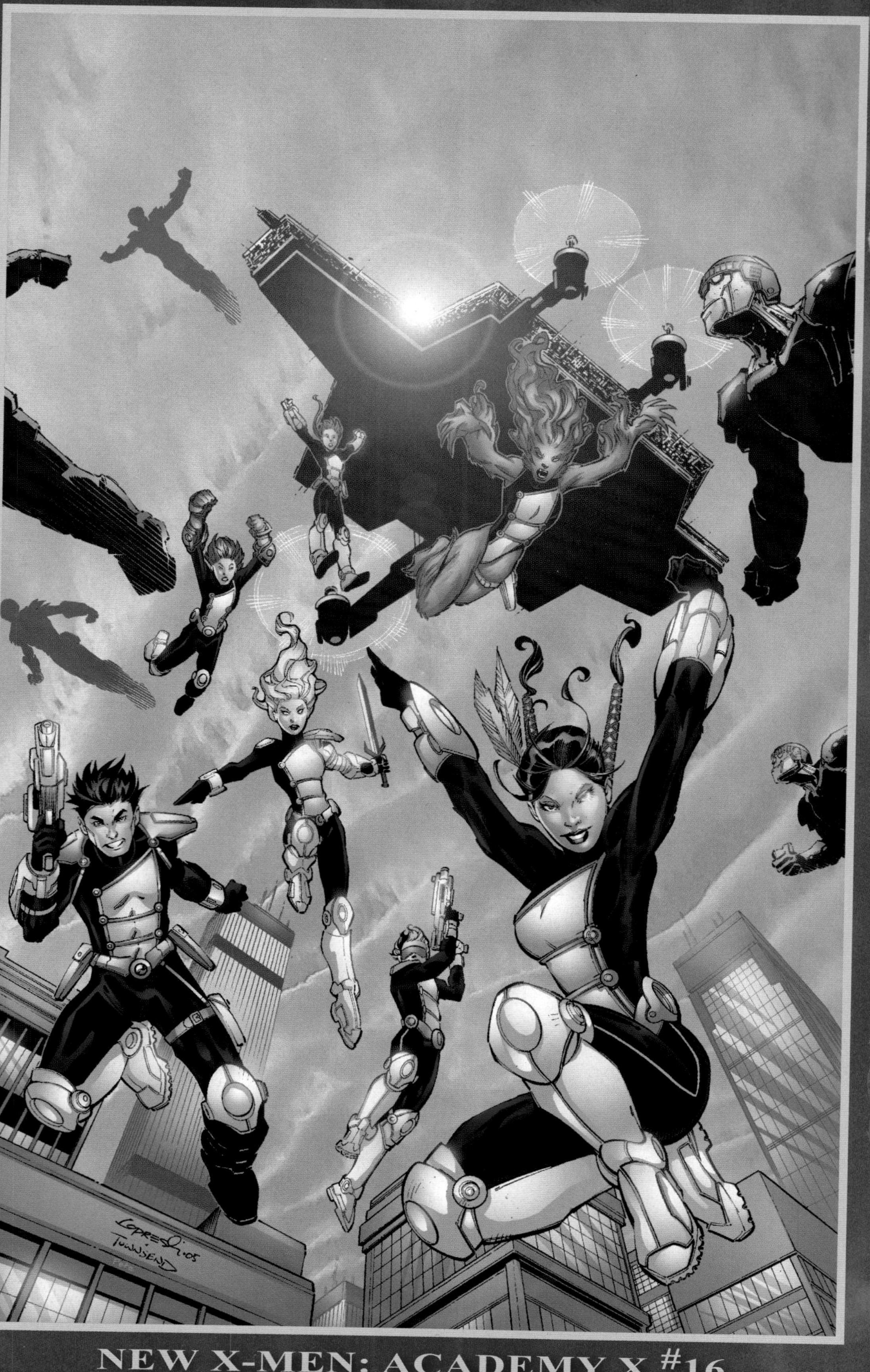

NEW X-MEN: ACADEMY X #16

Variant cover

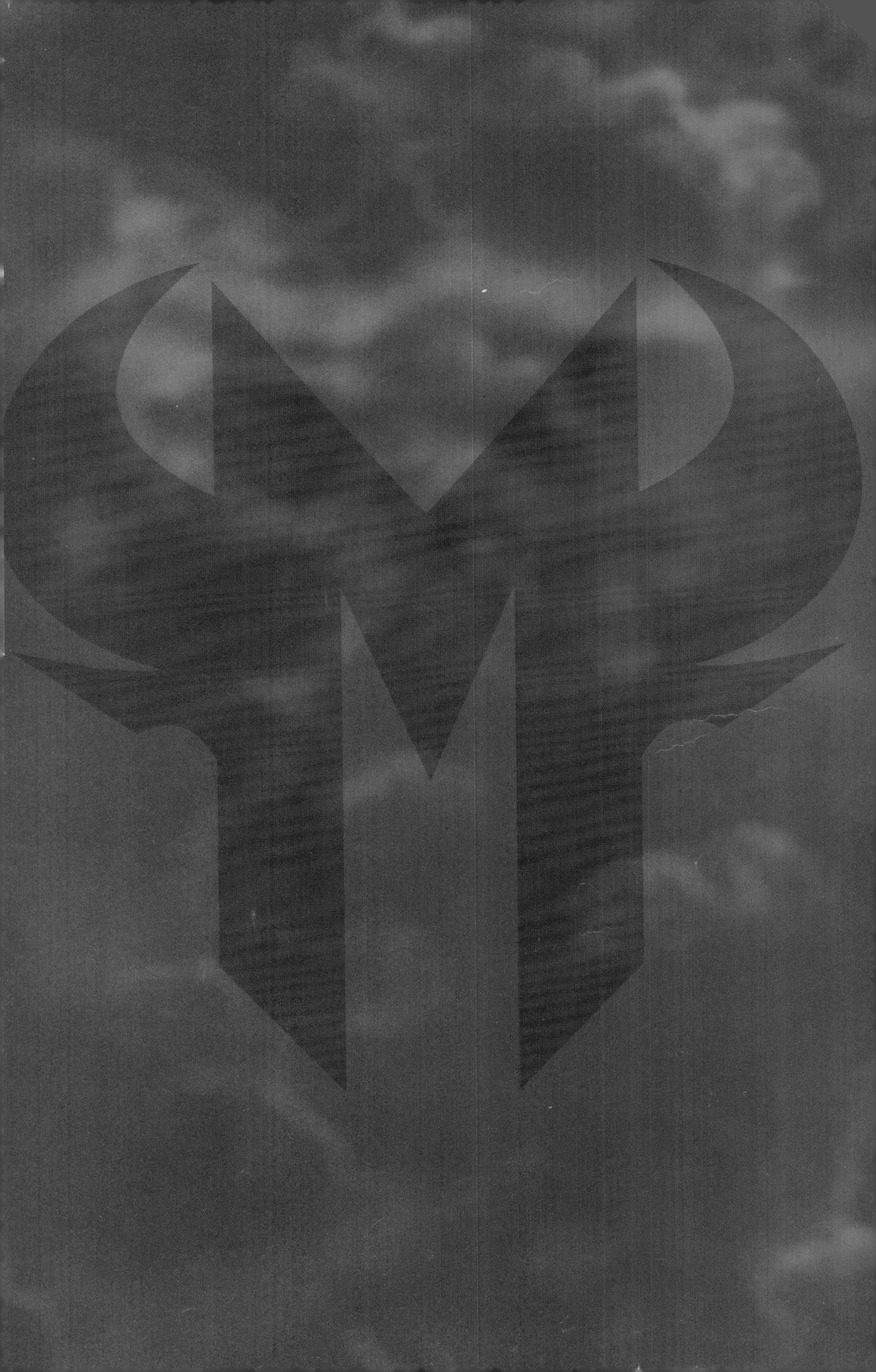

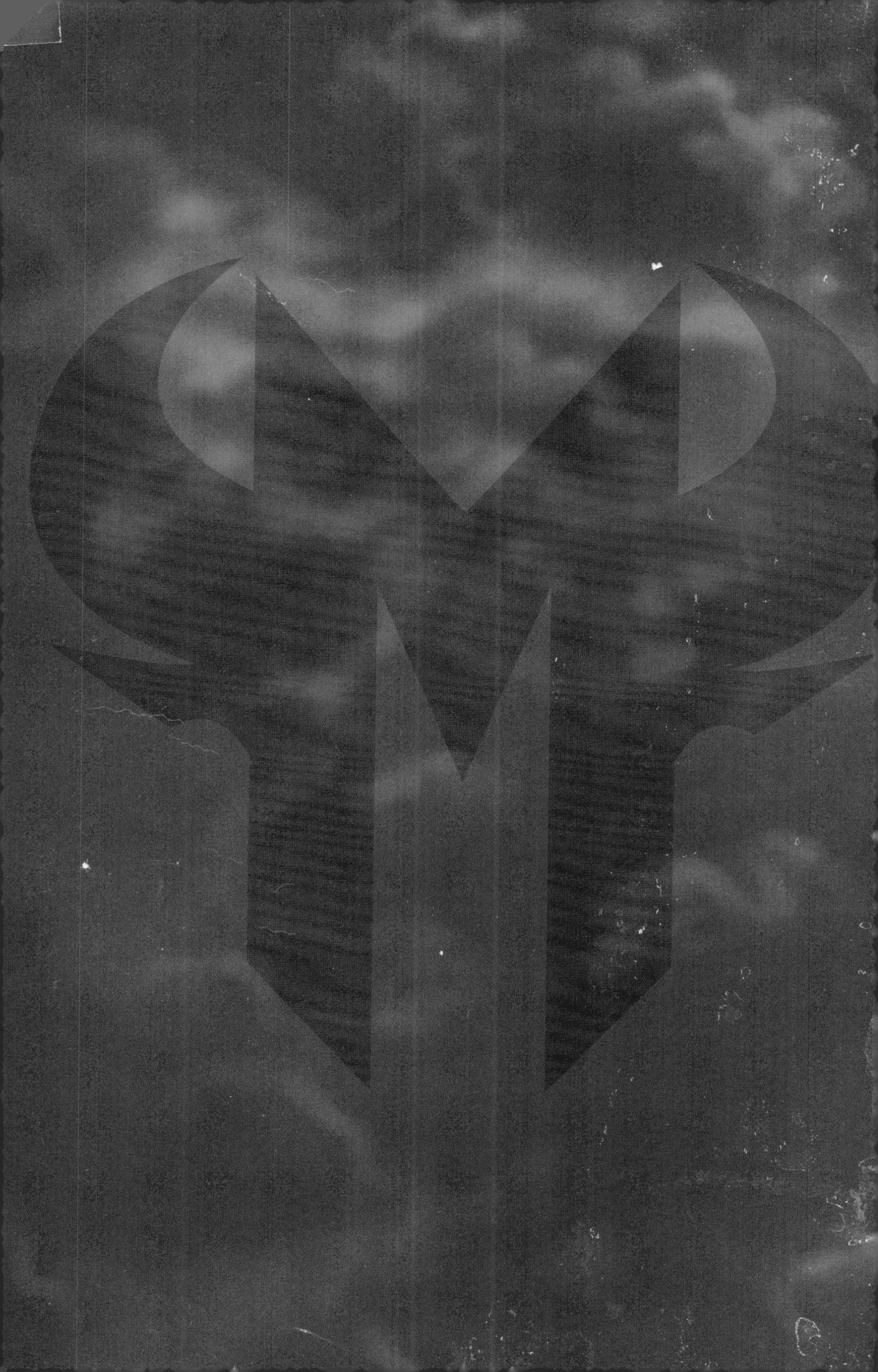